HOW HOCKEY EXPLAINS CANADA

The Sport That Defines a Country

Paul Henderson and Jim Prime
Foreword by Prime Minister Stephen Harper

TRIUMPH
BOOKS

Triumph Books and colophon are registered trademarks of Random House, Inc.

Library of Congress Cataloging-in-Publication Data

Henderson, Paul, 1943-
  How hockey explains Canada : the sport that defines a country / Paul Henderson and Jim Prime.
     p. cm.
  ISBN 978-1-60078-575-7
  1. Hockey—Canada 2. Hockey—Social aspects—Canada. 3. Canada—Civilization. 4. Canada—History. I. Prime, Jim. II. Title.
  GV848.4.C2H46 2011
  796.9620971—dc23

                    2011018191

This book is available in quantity at special discounts for your group or organization. For further information, contact:

Triumph Books
542 South Dearborn Street
Suite 750
Chicago, Illinois 60605
(312) 939-3330
Fax (312) 663-3557
www.triumphbooks.com

Printed in U.S.A.
ISBN: 978-1-60078-575-7

Design by James Slate

To my wife, Eleanor, who lives life better than anyone I know as a wife, mother, and grandmother. She is my hero.

To our three daughters (Heather, Jennifer, and Jill) and their husbands (Alex, Mike, and Bryan). They have given us our grandchildren: Josh, Jacob, Brandon, Zachary, Charlotte, Alton, Brynley, and Logan. All are in my heart, thoughts, and prayers daily. —P.H.

To our beautiful daughter-in-law, Jung-Hyun Park Prime. Since arriving in Canada from Korea just over a year ago, she has soaked up our culture and language at an alarming rate. One of her first rites of passage to Canadian citizenship was embracing the game of hockey. We watched the 2010 World Junior Championships together on TV and despite lacking any previous knowledge of the game, she was immediately hooked.

To my grandson Finley Canton, a two-year-old with the irresistible charm of Jean Beliveau and the endless energy of Alexander Ovechkin. He wears his Toronto Maple Leafs jersey with pride and already knows how to shout "Goal" whenever he picks up his little plastic hockey stick. With his wonderful parents Catherine and David, and his loyal sidekick Frankie, he is destined for greatness in whatever field he chooses.   —J.P.

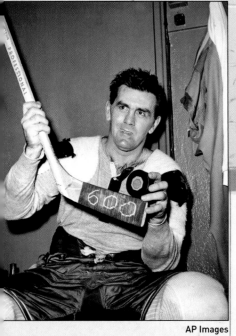

AP Images

AP Images

AP Images

Bruce Bennett Studios/Getty Images

Melchior DiGiacomo/Getty Images

FOREWORD

by Prime Minister Stephen Harper

I HAVE TO ADMIT that my memory of when I first got interested in hockey is misty. I was born in 1959, and when I was very small my parents followed the Toronto Maple Leafs very closely. I know that more from later stories than from much actual memory of the time. Living in New Brunswick, my mother—and in particular my father—grew up rooting for the Maple Leafs. That was their team.

My father's first cousin was married to Leafs defenceman Carl Brewer, so my parents knew most of the Toronto players of the great 1960s teams. They obviously didn't know them well, but they had met them. They followed those teams very closely, but when you're following a championship team and suddenly they're no longer a championship team, you lose interest. That's really what happened to my parents after Brewer's first retirement and after the Leafs stopped winning the Stanley Cup. Even though I knew they'd been big fans, they never really introduced me to the game. I vaguely remember when the Leafs won the '67 Cup, but I wasn't following it that closely at that point. I actually started following it the next year, in 1968 with a schoolmate. We'd watch the games on TV. That's how I really got into following it. I was about 9 or 10 years old at the time.

I didn't play ice hockey until I was 10, and I still can't skate well. I did play for three years, but I was pretty marginal. I played a bit of pond hockey but not nearly as much as road hockey. I played a lot of road hockey! We played from the time school was out on Friday afternoon until we were back Monday morning. All we did was play road hockey. A while back some ex–school chums threw a little reunion for me and they reminded me of a game we used to play in the schoolyard. It was invented by me and a friend named George Cribb. We called it "foot hockey." According to my friends this game had extremely elaborate rules, but I don't remember it as being all that elaborate. We played with relatively small nets—the size of a real hockey net—using a tennis ball. You just played with your feet, like in soccer. That's what we played at recess and before and after school for years. That was my contribution to Canada's game, "foot hockey."

The rest of the time we played road hockey. We played from the time I was about 9 until I had almost graduated high school when I was 17 or 18. I've played it quite a few times since. In fact when I was Leader of the Opposition, we used to play every weekend with the local kids at Stornaway. We haven't played much at 24 Sussex—we just haven't had time for it. Frankly, the kids are a bit older now and I can't keep up with them, but when I used to play a lot I was actually a pretty decent road hockey player.

We had a pretty well-understood rule among those of us who played regularly and that was "no contact." But we went even further; not only were you not allowed to play the man, you were not allowed to play the stick either. You had to play the ball, so you couldn't lift sticks or hack at the stick, and the reason was simple—because with no gloves the guys got their hands injured. Basically, you had to play the ball at all times and for playing the stick the penalty was essentially that you were kicked out of the game for a while. Still, even though you could not play the stick, somehow we managed to have brawls every so often, I don't know why.

When a vehicle came down the road we'd yell, "car!" and there was always one old lady who didn't like us going across her lawn. But you always have to navigate those things. It was good practice for politics. Those incidents are the exceptions. The fact is that kids are often very inconsiderate but with a little bit of consideration you can place the net to avoid the lawn that wants to be avoided.

As a kid my favourite player was Dave Keon, who I later had a chance to meet. It was a great thrill when he came back to the Leafs reunion in 2007, a very special moment. I loved all those guys but he was my favourite player. When I was a teenager it became Borje Salming, who I also got to meet a couple of years ago at an International Ice Hockey Federation event. Salming is also a very nice man and a very tough guy! You sometimes hear the knock on Europeans that they're not tough or they don't play in the clutch. Salming was one of the toughest players in the NHL. He was not necessarily the best fighter but he certainly could take a punch and he wasn't afraid to block shots.

Prime Minister Stephen Harper and his son, Benjamin, watch the Ottawa Senators host the New Jersey Devils during Game 3 of the 2007 Eastern Conference semifinals.

AP Images

Later on, I actually was a big fan of the Oilers Cup teams and I loved Jari Kurri. Jari Kurri scored more clutch goals than any player I can remember. Look back at some of those Oilers victories when they were down and they came back and scored a last-minute goal and see how many times it was Jari Kurri. Interestingly, he was successful not because he was a player who played with great passion, it was actually the opposite. He was so cool that even in the most high-pressure situations he never seemed flustered. The stereotype about Europeans is like all generalizations. There may be a small element of truth in it, but if you look at it closely it is as flawed as any other generalization.

I consider my area of hockey expertise, if you can call it that, to extend from 1875—which is founding of the modern sport—up to 1926 when the NHL consolidated its control. My real focus within that span is the 1900–1910 period—the early professional era. The birthplace of hockey is a hotly debated topic, especially in those communities that have legitimate claims to the title. Windsor and Halifax-Dartmouth, Nova Scotia; as well as Kingston, Ontario; Montreal; and Deline in the Northwest Territories all have made persuasive cases. I am a member of the Society for International Hockey Research and the Society's view is that the modern sport was founded in Montreal. What distinguishes any modern sport from its "folk pastime" status is the formal codification of rules by James Creighton, the fixing of dimensions, the fixing of numbers of participants, and time frames. And that was clearly done in Montreal in 1875. It's also possible that it might have been done in other places as well but it's clear that the sport we know today evolved from that 1875 event.

There are some who turn this notion on its head and argue that Montreal in 1875 was then Canada's most important commercial centre. It was because of its importance that the game was founded there. In other words, what they are saying is that because Montreal was the country's most important city—and most important sports centre at the time—it was almost inevitable that that would be the place that determined the rules, just by sheer weight of influence. There were certainly distinctive rules in Halifax. Creighton, the father of hockey, was after all a Haligonian, but there's no doubt that eventually the Montreal rules, the so-called McGill rules, came out on top of the Halifax rules and to a large extent this is because Montreal is a

much more powerful centre. I'm currently exploring this theory in greater depth.

If you could look back prior to 1875, I think you would find the immediate antecedents of hockey being engaged in by various different cultures—meaning guys on skates playing with hooked sticks and batting around a ball. Nevertheless there seems to be no doubt that prior to the 1850s and earlier in the 1800s that English-speaking people were definitely doing that. In all parts of the country where there were English settlers or British troops, there is some evidence that this game was being played. Obviously we know about Windsor and Halifax. It's also true in the Kingston area; it's also true in the Northwest Territories. That's not to say that aboriginals and French Canadians and other European immigrants didn't have ancestral games similar to hockey, but my own read of the evidence is that the precursors of the modern sport were played in virtually all parts of the country where there were English-speaking people. There were clearly some Englishmen in most settled parts of the country, and in the case of unsettled parts like the Northwest Territories, there were British soldiers.

Hockey is one of our greatest exports, and it's played by Canadians in all parts of the world. I've delivered a speech at the hockey rink in Kandahar, Afghanistan. I've also been to the rink in the United Arab Emirates—although I've never seen anybody doing anything on it, understandably because every time I've been there it's been 50 degrees. What I would say is this: anytime people are relaxing and having fun in any society, sports and cultural entertainment play an important role. All societies do that in their own way. One of the things that makes us unique as Canadians—and it's true whether you are aboriginal, English, French, or multi-cultural—is that we play hockey. So when you go to a foreign country and you see the game being played there it *means something*, and it's not just soldiers in war zones who play. I've seen Canadian hockey teams in Hong Kong and other unlikely locales. When Canadians go to a foreign country and they're relaxing by playing hockey, they aren't just having fun. They are also experiencing being Canadian. That is a deeper need when you're away from home. The pastime is deeply engrained in the Canadian psychology, and it is one of the things that transcends all regions, all classes, and all ethnicities within the country.

Hockey is a unifying activity that defines the country. At the same time, it has historically helped to add to our pride of place within Canada. In the past there certainly used to be distinctive styles of play in each region of the country. I can remember 20, 30 years ago Quebec was known for offense, Ontario for balanced traditional hockey, and western Canada for a tougher style—even for the goon side. You see some differences even today. You still see the disproportionate number of goaltenders from Quebec, which is a funny consequence of a more wide-open style. I should not pretend to be an expert because I'm really more of an historian, but my casual observation is that as the game internationalizes, as players move around, less and less do players even at the junior level come from the locale or even the region. They are often foreigners, or they've moved long distances. And as the feeder system for the professional sport they become more and more disciplined and kind of heavily structured. My own feeling is that those differences are narrowing in the game.

The Summit Series in 1972 was where it started. If you look at the style of hockey played in the NHL today, even by the most disciplined teams, no one plays a straight up-and-down style anymore. At the same time, no European team plays the pure Ice Capades style that you once saw in countries like Sweden. I think there has been a tremendous narrowing of these differences. That's also consistent with the planet itself.

When newcomers arrive in Canada they not only embrace the game, but for many immigrants, the participation in hockey and in community hockey very quickly becomes a strong sense of their belonging in the community. NHL owners in Canadian cities have told me that when immigrant families become ticket buyers, they actually become more passionate. In a way I guess what's partly at play is the support of a convert.

I'm not as sure about the participatory levels in the game. In terms of following it and being enthusiastic supporters, that's all there. Although the game is followed by as many people—if not more—than ever before, the number of participants among young people and children, specifically in percentage terms, has been falling dramatically. When I was a boy, I'd say 75 percent of the young kids in grade school played organized hockey. Today in my son's experience it would be no more than 10 or 20 percent playing organized hockey, and the fact of the matter is that some groups—like many Asian groups where people tend to be smaller—are not very well represented at the elite level, so I just don't know whether they have the same kind of participation levels that you used to see amongst the more established ethnic groups. I think that's something to watch. It doesn't diminish their interest in the game or their support for it, but whether they are actually playing or participating in the same numbers, I'm not sure.

Even within the National Hockey League, there's a big difference between the support for Canadian franchises and those in the northern states compared to farther southern US. We have reason to suspect that a disproportionate number of fans in a lot of southern NHL buildings are actually displaced Canadians.

Obviously that's not universally true but certainly very few of the Americans who are there have any direct contact with the game.

Hockey in Canada today is everyone's game, regardless of race, creed, or gender. I'm a big fan of elite level women's hockey and really enjoy watching it. I think in terms of calibre of play, the women's game has come a long way. It still probably has a ways to go, but there are some great female players at the top level. As a historian my observation is that there's a bit of a myth that women's hockey was taboo or repressed for decades and then gradually came into its own with feminism. That story doesn't actually hold up. If you look at the history, women's hockey has had periods where it has flourished and periods where, inexplicably, it has all but disappeared. It's been a cyclical thing. In the early decades of western Canada, the sport was quite common on the frontier and then for whatever reason it died out. If you look at the period I'm studying—late 1800s, early 1900s in eastern Canada—there was very little women's hockey. It became much bigger around the First World War and for some time after and then interest seemed to wane again after the Second World War. There is no doubt today that women's hockey is played more and at a much higher level than any time in history.

Canada is known throughout the world as the hockey nation. I meet with many world leaders and representatives of foreign governments and invariably the subject comes up. Many have observed to me that we Canadians are seen as generally a pretty modest, quiet, unassuming-type people—but they notice with Canadians that when the subject of hockey comes up we get very loud and start waving our arms around. It's a bit of a standing joke. Everybody notices this!

I've met a number of leaders who are familiar with hockey. The president of Slovakia, for instance, follows it closely. President Obama and I have never talked at length about it. He's certainly familiar with the sport but it's not in his top one or two. President Dmitry Medvedev of Russia is extremely knowledgeable, follows it, knows the players, and has strong opinions on the game. He is a passionate fan, and I recently got a Russian national team jersey signed by all the Olympic participants, which was a great gesture.

When people ask me about Canada's greatest moments in international play, I have to answer carefully because to some extent it's a generational thing. I don't want to take anything away from the Sidney Crosby goal or the 2010 Olympics victory. It had a huge significance, especially for any Canadian that was much younger than I am. This was the moment of their lives in hockey. It also happened to coincide with Canada reaching a record number of 14 gold medals that day. That was a pretty special thing for the country, and the hockey win was the centrepiece. But I think so many of us that are from that older generation would argue that the 1972 Summit Series was different in two ways.

Of course what were similar were these big Canadian victories in significant international encounters with a massive percentage of Canadians captivated by them. Those two occasions—that 1972 Game 8 final and the 2010 gold-medal game—were watched by virtually everyone. They shut down the entire country. In those two ways they were similar, both huge moments, both exciting, and both thrilling victories. The differences are at the bigger level. The first is that in terms of hockey, the game between Canada and the United States was a game between two teams of players that, while all the passion and competition was there, compete with each other in the National Hockey League and essentially play the same style of hockey. The game in '72 was between two hockey *worlds*, featuring athletes who did not know each other and didn't approach the game in remotely the same way or play the same style.

It was a different experience and maybe one that could never be repeated. I've tried to explain the bigger context of that series to my kids and other people who were not alive then. As the series progressed, the intensity rose. In particular the experience of Canadian fans with the police in Moscow became a kind of symbol of the Cold War. It actually became a confrontation of systems, a confrontation of values. It became a microcosm of the fact that Canada was allied with the West against Communism and the East in the Cold War.

My memory of that period is particularly sharp about things that were happening in the stands, things like the mugging of Alan Eagleson. It really became a proxy for war and that puts it on a completely different level. The Cold War has been over for 20 years now and no one who was not alive in 1972, and certainly no one who was not alive during the Cold War, could know the feeling that existed between the two different ways of life in the world at the time. It was as if the freedom of Canadians versus the repression of the Soviet system was being showcased in the individualism of the Canadian players as opposed to the regimentation of the Soviet players. It was there for everyone to see.

In fairness to them, there was some significant artistry to what they were doing and in criticism of us, although there was a lot of individualism, there was in fact a lot of pretty unimaginative play. But that said, even the way they wore their hair showed the individualism of the Canadian players as opposed to the cog-in-the-machine approach of the Soviets. For everyone alive at the time, it became more than just a game. It wasn't really about whether we were going to win at hockey. What it came down to was whether the system of a free people was going to triumph over the system of one that had no respect for individuals. Now, if you weren't alive then, that sounds almost bizarre. I was 13 years old at the time and obviously wasn't anywhere near as political in those days as I am now, but I was of that time. For someone who was right of centre, it was an event that reminded Canadians of why we were in the Cold War. It was a pretty important moment in history.

You didn't need a classroom to learn this history lesson. You could see it happening right before your eyes, the whole concept that because fans were too boisterous at a game they could be arrested for cheering too loud. We had our apologists trying to say that we weren't really that different—and then you see that.

I used to be a hockey dad. My son retired from hockey the year before last. He played for eight years, but now he's gotten into other sports and competitive volleyball is now his thing. I miss it, but it was always his decision to play. I never pushed him into it. I enjoyed watching his games—he was the player I wanted to be but never could be. He was just a better athlete and a better hockey player. I was an energetic fan, but generally speaking, even at my most boisterous, I'm more restrained than most people. I'm not a yeller.

There's probably a lot I'd change about today's game, but probably most fundamentally, if I had my perfect world, I would make the ice surface somewhere between the NHL and the international dimensions. I think it needs to be expanded. I think the international ice is too large but we could use a bit of alteration—that's probably the most fundamental.

There are many other things. I guess the thing on my mind these days continues to be this problem with the equipment and head shots. This Sidney Crosby thing really has me just furious. I saw the hit in the Washington game and I couldn't believe it—no penalty, no suspension, no complaint from the Penguins. I find this amazing and as someone who followed the Oilers Cup teams, I couldn't imagine someone doing that to Gretzky, I just can't. I'm mystified by it, but I hope the powers that be wake up. I'm concerned that Sidney Crosby is not back. This is the best player in the game today, and if this is as serious as it's starting to look, then I think the game has to really look at itself. You cannot allow this kind of thing to happen!

I've been asked if I have ever considered using the floor between the Government and Opposition benches for a floor hockey game to decide some of the issues of the day. I think it would be great fun. It would be more fun for me to have a floor hockey game than a real hockey game. Of course I also realize that whether I'm good or not, if I got in that kind of environment, I'd be Gretzky—I'd be a marked man. Actually there is a Conservative Party of Canada hockey team, and no they are not all right wingers, not on the ice anyway. We play a handful of games every year, mostly for charitable causes. Occasionally I "coach" them. The truth is that when I'm available I stand behind the bench with a clipboard. I am *not* a good hockey coach. It's one of the toughest jobs anywhere, so hard that I can't imagine doing it for a living.

Until recently we used to get together every year to play the Liberal Party of Canada. We played for something that we called the Hec Clouthier Memorial Trophy. Hector Clouthier is a fedora-wearing former Liberal Member of Parliament. I don't know why we called it "memorial," because Hec Clouthier is still alive and well. I guess because he's no longer a Member of Parliament. The games were fun and while there was competition it was a good exchange. It's a bit of a myth of Parliament—I think that people think that

because the politicians are always going at it on issues that there is a lot of personal animosity. The truth is that there are *some* personal animosities but not anywhere near what people would think. These are political disagreements. A lot of times on committees and other situations these people have to work together. What finally happened was that every year the Liberals kept dressing more and more ringers. It was supposed to be Members of Parliament. In fairness they never dressed Liberal MP and former Montreal Canadiens goaltender Ken Dryden or Senator and former NHL winger Frank Mahovlich so that was good for us, but they started dressing more and more sons who were Triple A midget players, so we haven't done that in the last couple of years.

Hockey is a game of memories and milestones for many Canadians. When people found out that I'm a big hockey fan and historian they started sending me all kinds of stuff, in particular books. As a result, I've now got a veritable library of history books, including some short-run first editions.

In the Harper household, we've got the so-called hockey room upstairs where we keep various souvenirs—national club jerseys, things like that. I've got a lot of special stuff up there. Vladislav Tretiak gave me one of his hockey sweaters, which he autographed for me. Bobby Orr gave me a Bruins baseball cap, also autographed. I could go through the list, but I think the most special was in 2007 when I got the 1967 Stanley Cup team. All the living members gave me an autographed jersey from that Maple Leafs team.

It doesn't get much better than that.

—Prime Minister Stephen Harper

PREFACE

by Paul Henderson

I HAD A PASSION for hockey that surprised me, even though I didn't get a pair of skates until I was nine. We just couldn't afford them. It all started with road and floor hockey. That's when I had my first taste of what the game's all about. In Lucknow, Ontario, where I grew up, we didn't have artificial ice. We played hockey out on the street, and I used to go to Cub Scouts and Boy Scouts mainly to play floor hockey. I couldn't wait to get a hold of the stick and play. It was just such a wonderful sport. I was fast, I was good, I was strong, and I could dominate.

When I started to play on ice I had trouble sleeping the night before a game. And then I'd go to school and have trouble concentrating on the classes. I was always thinking, *Oh, we're going to play hockey tonight!*

Little did I know back then that I would be involved in one of the most famous hockey series in Canadian history, let alone score three winning goals. It's been almost 40 years, and I'm still asked about it frequently. There have been countless media interviews, retellings, and retrospectives. I'm approached all the time by fans on the street and in restaurants. Pretty much everywhere I go. They want to thank me, shake my hand, and let me know what an important moment it was in their lives. Even people who weren't alive at the time want to ask me about it.

Just the other day I had a conversation with an Asian gentleman. He told me that although his family didn't immigrate to Canada until 1975, he got into hockey and became entranced with the '72 Summit Series. He went on and on, just bubbling about the role I played, and this guy never crazy with joy and felt an immediate kinship with his adopted country. That goal, he said, helped to transform him from a transplanted Brit to a proud Canadian. It's humbling to think that I played a part in something so profound.

I was talking with this guy recently who told me that his high school chemistry teacher wouldn't allow his class to go down to the gym to watch the final game, even though the government of Ontario had encouraged every school to do this. Talk about someone with no foresight whatsoever. The teacher couldn't stand hockey, hated the game. As he was telling me about it, the veins in this guy's neck started sticking out and his face got redder and redder. Finally he said, "I've hated that teacher ever since. I missed one of the greatest sports moments in Canadian history because of this SOB!" I mean this guy was still very angry all these years later.

People want to know everything about the series. They want to know why I called Pete Mahovlich off the ice so I could get out there in the dying seconds of the final game. People ask me that all the time. I feel embarrassed that I can't really answer the question properly. It was so totally spontaneous

Paul Henderson wears his original 1972 Canada jersey from the Summit Series in a Mississauga, Ontario, office in June 2010. Henderson authenticated the jersey, which he had not seen in more than 38 years, before it was auctioned off. The winning bid for the jersey was more than $1 million. AP Images

saw me play until he watched the tapes of the series.

A man from Cape Breton recently told me he immigrated to Canada from England in 1965. At first he felt like a Brit living in Canada. There was no connection to his new country. But when I scored the goal, he said that he went

that it even surprised me. I never, ever, did it before in my life, and I never did it again. Professionals just don't do that. It's the only time that I stood and started yelling at a teammate to come off the ice. It still amazes me. Wow! Wow! Wow! I must have felt that I had to get on the ice. I just started yelling at

Peter Mahovlich. "PETER!" Thank goodness Pete thought it was the coach yelling at him!

I do know that the goal had a huge impact on me and on the country I love. I do know that it changed my own life. I know that I didn't deserve as much credit as I got, and I know that fame alone can't fulfill you or make you happy. I know that I grew close to an amazing group of men in a very short period of time and that we were all altered by the experience, as were countless other Canadians.

When people praise me for scoring the goals, including the Game 8 winner, I know it's not me that they want to honour. It's hockey. It's Canada. Sometimes the two things seem interchangeable because hockey is Canada and Canada is hockey. The sport has that kind of impact in this country. It's our point of pride. It's within our Canadian psyche. It's in our DNA.

We as a country can be so divided—by politics, by language, even by geography. There is so much potential for division in a country as broad and culturally diverse as ours. We really have five distinct countries within the one nation. Even when it comes to hockey, if Toronto is playing Montreal, it is more than just a game. It's as if it's one country battling another. That's just the way it is. But with Team Canada '72, there was none of that. Suddenly, we were all Canadians. That was the commonality. It was the first time and maybe the only time—except in war—when we all got together and all the other contentious issues were cast aside. We were Team Canada and all of Canada was united behind us.

I think if you look across the whole spectrum of the country—from Newfoundland and Labrador to British Columbia and into the northern communities—there are many more people who follow and relate to hockey more than any other aspect of our culture. Hockey is the one thing that a majority of Canadians

embrace. Is everyone into it? No, they're not. That's the wonderful thing about our Canadian society. People grow up in certain situations, and that's where their interests lie. There are a lot of people who just aren't sports-minded, but when Canada plays hockey in the Olympics, even they become fans.

Music and art and dance are all parts of the fabric that make a country great, and we rightly celebrate these things. You need a cultural identity that recognizes accomplishments in the arts. Music, art, and dance are all expressions of us as Canadians. They are a proud part of our culture and our national fabric. But they can never unite us. God bless their souls but ballerinas are never going to bring our country together. That's the difference. It is likely that more people can name seven stars in the lineup of the 1967 Leafs than name each of the artists in the Group of Seven.

Recently, people have asked me how my goal compares with Sidney Crosby's overtime goal at the 2010 Vancouver Olympics. Whether his is bigger than mine or mine is bigger than his is the wrong question. In terms of the impact of the goals . . . both were certainly felt across the country. Crosby's goal is an identifying marker for this generation. For my generation it was the same thing. People sometimes say, "Don't worry, Paul, your goal is still *the goal.*" In my mind, which goal was bigger is incidental. They are two goals that need to be celebrated and remembered. Hockey defines us. When we win on the ice most Canadians feel *they've* won.

International hockey aside, look at the annual battles for the Stanley Cup. Even when no Canadian team is involved, people are still totally engrossed. But if you ever get two Canadian teams in the finals—man, oh man, oh man! Everyone's talking about it— and it doesn't matter where you are—in every little village and town, people are into it.

As great as Canadian hockey fans are from coast-to-coast, I've come to believe that some of the most knowledgeable hockey people I've ever met are those from Newfoundland, a place without an NHL franchise. I don't know why it is. I've gone down there so many times and they will tell me things about my hockey career that I don't even know. You talk about passionate people! "Do you remember this…? Do you remember when…?" I find them just great, and loyal to a fault. Maybe they're so used to adversity that they hang tough in their support of the Leafs!

Like all aspects of our country, Canada's hockey culture changes and evolves. A lot of people go to Tim Hortons and don't know that he was once a hockey great. Aside from being a man with an entrepreneurial spirit, he played the game the way it was meant to be played, with passion. He was one of the strongest men in hockey but, thank goodness, without a mean streak. It's amazing how fleeting the fame can be. You better learn to laugh at yourself. Laughter is therapeutic and fame is fleeting. After I first retired, someone would look at me and ask, "Are you Paul Henderson?" And I'd jokingly say, "No, I'm Gordie Howe," and it always got a laugh with, "No, you're not." Well there's a point when it made no sense saying Gordie Howe anymore so then I said, "No, I'm Darryl Sittler." Then that got to be passé and I was Wayne Gretzky. Now Wayne Gretzky is out of the spotlight so it's, "Are you Paul Henderson?" "No, I'm Sidney Crosby." And obviously I say that tongue in cheek but I do that all the time. Can you imagine the prayers that would be answered for the people of Ontario if Crosby were ever traded to Toronto? The point is you have to pick a current star because players move on quickly.

What remains is the respect that Canadians have for their hockey heritage. We have so many hockey icons in this country. That's one thing about Canadians—people recognize and celebrate hockey greatness. The Hockey Hall of Fame recognizes them as members, but even if it didn't exist, Canadians have a place for these guys in their hearts.

If you want to talk about players who represent the sport well, I would start with one man—Jean Beliveau. Beliveau carried a stature that is unequalled. If you asked the players from my era who they admired and respected, I'm confident that Beliveau would win by a country mile. The way he conducted himself on and off the ice was exemplary. To me, Beliveau was one of the great heroes of the game and would be high on my list of heroes—period. As a former Leaf, I get a lot of flack for saying that, but it is my bias because I had so much respect for him as a person. He'd have made a wonderful Governor General because he represents the best of Canada.

The wonderful thing about hockey is that you can lose and get booed off the ice and all you need to do is come back and win the next game and score a couple of goals and you're the toast of the town again. Life is somewhat more complicated.

Your life is a journey. As a youngster I made several decisions about what I wanted to do with my life, things I wanted to accomplish. First, I hated being poor, which we were. The lack of money caused great stress for my whole family. I vowed I was not going to live like that as an adult. I wanted to be financially secure and even independent. I wanted to have a career that I was passionate about. I wanted to look forward to going to work each day. My ultimate dream was to be an NHL hockey player. I also wanted to find a great wife and build a family that would enjoy "the good life" as I imagined it. I felt that if I had these three things, life would be almost perfect. I know how fortunate and blessed I am today. I had an 18-year hockey career, married the greatest woman in the world, and now have children and grandchildren who we enjoy immensely.

When I was selected to play for Team Canada in 1972, I never for a moment thought about scoring winning goals, let alone "The Goal of the Century." I was a good hockey player but that one goal put me in the ozone layer in the minds of Canadian hockey fans. The fame came so quickly and, as I look back, I was ill-prepared to handle it properly.

I had no spiritual dimension to my life in '72. As a result, I started to become someone I was not very happy or pleased with. When you start to believe you are somehow special, it opens the door to arrogance and pride. These are downright ugly elements in a person's life. I knew there was an emptiness inside me. I was frustrated and unsatisfied, with many questions and no answers.

It was at this point that Mel Stevens, who ran Teen Ranch near Orangeville, Ontario, introduced himself to me. He encouraged me to examine the spiritual side of life. I was very skeptical at the beginning, as I was not into religion. I thought it was only for the weak people who couldn't make it in the world, that they were the ones who needed God. From my perspective, religion caused more problems than it solved. But because I was restless and knew I needed something, I started meeting with Mel weekly. I became a student of the Bible, spending hours reading it and other Christian books. It was only after two years of intense investigation that I decided to become a follower of Jesus—a Christian.

I have had some wonderful mentors along the way who have deeply impacted and shaped my life. One mentor encouraged me to write a purpose statement for myself that would define the man I wanted to become and what I wanted to do with my life. It took almost a year to fine-tune it, but today when I wake up, I know what I want to do with my life and the type of man I want to be.

I was diagnosed with lymphocytic lymphoma chronic leukemia in November 2009. Although there is no known cure, today I live each day expectantly without any angst or fear. This is because of my faith.

Recently, I've travelled across Canada with the jersey I wore as a member of Team Canada in '72. People of all ages and backgrounds come out to meet me and see the jersey. I know that the sweater has come to symbolize something much larger than just a hockey series. It is as if it is another Canadian flag, one that instills pride in our country but also pride in our country's game. These people had really come to see a piece of their history and their heritage. They were coming to remember a time when Canada stood on the world stage and staked her claim as The Hockey Nation. I will always be proud that I was a member of that wonderful team. I am even prouder to have played the game that I love, the game that has helped to explain Canada to the world and to ourselves.

—Paul Henderson, April 2011

Acknowledgements

I couldn't have written this book without the help of a large number of generous people. Despite a personal schedule that would rival the NHL's, Paul Henderson was always available to discuss hockey and provide thoughtful insights and cheerful encouragement. It would be difficult to overstate the respect I have for this man and the way he has decided to live his life. He is the Canadian hero who doesn't want to be treated like one.

I'd also like to especially thank Ted Foreman of Winnipeg who, through a stroke of luck, I met just as I was in the early organizational stages of writing this book. Ted provided me with an amazing list of NHL contacts and opened the door for me to interview some of the giants of the game. Thanks also to my friend Bruce Alexander for introducing us.

Thanks also to the dozens of hockey personalities who were willing to share their thoughtful comments on the subject of *How Hockey Explains Canada*. They include: Ron Ellis, Tiger Williams, Ron MacLean, Bob Clarke, Terry Clancy, Marc Cloutier, Ken Dryden, Jean Beliveau, Serge Savard, Dick Irvin Jr., Fred Sgambati Jr., Paul MacLean, Howie Meeker, Chris Thurber, Bob Sirois, Johnny Bower, Bobby Baun, Harry Sinden, Brian Conacher, Jim McKenny, Terry Clancy, Dennis Vial, Ralph Mellanby, Alan Eagleson, Connie MacNeil, Darryl Sittler, Jim McKenny, Chris Besse, Geoff Molson, Jeff Hutt, and Morris Mott.

Thanks also to Olivier Bauer for describing his fascinating theology course, my sometime writing partner Bill "Spaceman" Lee for giving his always refreshing views, and Richard Johnson for his insight from south of the border. Thanks to Joel Tichinoff and Amrit Ahluwalia. Thanks to my son Jeff Prime, brother-in-law Mark Hoare, and neighbour Bill Wilder for their computer expertise, Tom Keddy for his helpful suggestions, and Richard Galpin and Rob MacGregor for their evil senses of humour.

I would like to thank Prime Minister Stephen Harper for being so gracious as to speak with me at some length about his favourite sport. Regardless of partisan politics, I think it's wonderful that our national leader is so engaged with the game that helps define us as a nation. Thanks Andrew MacDougall for stating my case so convincingly with the PM.

A special thanks to Noah Amstadter, Tom Bast, Don Gulbrandsen, and the rest of the team at Triumph Books. You gave me free reign to take my own approach to the book and I appreciate the faith that you placed in me. Noah, thanks for helping to so judiciously trim a 600-page book to a 200-page book!

Lastly, I would like to thank my family for their steadfast love and encouragement. Thank you Glenna, Sophie, Margaret and Ray, Catherine and Dave and Finley, Jeff and Jung and Gatsby, and Marcia and Gerald.

—Jim Prime

Thanks to Jim Prime, who carried the burden of organizing and writing this book. The many hours of conversation were stimulating and memorable. He is a thoughtful and dedicated man.

To my teammates, fellow NHLers, and friends who freely gave us their time and thoughts to legitimize this book. Jim has named each of them.

Lastly, I am so thankful and grateful for the people who have encouraged, exhorted, and stimulated me to live a spiritual life that is full, abundant, and joyful. I can't think of anyone more fortunate than myself.

—Paul Henderson

INTRODUCTION

by Jim Prime

Hockey and Canada have grown up together. In their infancy they stumbled along with little guidance or sense of direction and when the growth spurts came they were painful. Moving from callow youth through awkward adolescence, they arrived at midlife only to face a variety of crises. In the intervening years and seasons, Canada has revised its laws and hockey has refined its rules. As they have matured, both have become more tolerant and inclusive. Through it all they have remained inseparable.

In 2004, CBC TV sought to attract viewers by having Canadians engage in an exercise to select the greatest Canadian of all time. The show was based on a BBC model known as *Great Britons*. From an initial pool of 40 nominees, a top-10 list was eventually established. The distinguished group included eventual winner Tommy Douglas, the father of Canadian Medicare, followed by Terry Fox, the valiant young cancer victim who inspired the nation with his heroic attempt to run across Canada on one leg. Pierre Trudeau, the Prime Minister whose social and language policies profoundly changed the country, finished third, and Sir Frederick Banting, co-discoverer of insulin, was fourth, ahead of crusading environmentalist David Suzuki.

The seventh-place finisher, wedged firmly in place below Nobel Peace Prize–winning Prime Minister Lester Pearson and just above Sir John A. MacDonald, Canada's first Prime Minister, was Don Cherry. Cherry also finished in front of Alexander Graham Bell and, interestingly, Wayne Gretzky.

How did this happen? How did a high school graduate and career minor league hockey player, whose between-period commentaries and rants are only slightly less loud and obnoxious than his suits, come to be on a list of noted scientists, humanitarians, and statesmen? What kind of national delirium could explain such a result? How does it come to pass that a man who unabashedly advocates mayhem; questions the courage of Swedes, Russians, and Quebecers; and profits from hockey brawls via a series of videos called *Don Cherry's Rock 'em, Sock 'em Hockey (*currently in its 22nd edition*)* could even be considered for such an exclusive list?

What does this say about Don Cherry? What does this say about hockey? What does this say about Canada? It says that Don Cherry has succeeded in tapping into the very heart, soul, and psyche of the country.

In the United States there can be a reasonable argument about what sport best reflects the national character: football with its combination of committee meetings, strategic manoeuvres, and controlled violence; baseball with its tradition, social history, and apple pie sensibility; or basketball, which reflects the nation's confident, streetwise, in-your-face individuality.

The worldwide popularity of soccer (better known as football to all but North Americans) cannot be denied. The passions that it engenders—occasionally displayed in the form of rioting and other aberrant shows of national pride—make "the beautiful game" the world's game, hands down. Each soccer nation has developed a slightly different approach to the sport, often mirroring the country's personality. When they congregate at the World Cup every four years, the world is treated to what basically happens at the United Nations every day, without the vuvuzelas; i.e., participants more or less stick to their positions, there is little action, hands-on activity is frowned upon, and only occasionally do they use their heads to score a point.

Whereas Americans venerate—some would say worship—their Constitution, few Canadians could quote from their Charter of Rights. The American anthem is sacrosanct; we change the words to ours as often as we change our shoes. Some people interpret these things as a lack of patriotism on our part.

In Canada there is only one sport. Others come and go, are humoured—even embraced during their seasons of play—and quickly forgotten after the season ends. Baseball holds our attention when we have a winner; basketball has a coolness factor that appeals to a certain youthful, largely urban demographic; soccer has a strong ethnic and Old World base in our larger cities. Canadian football has a parochial appeal with elements of national pride and tradition mixed in. We are pleased to point out to our American friends how different and therefore superior our passing game is to their grind-it-out four-down version. But ultimately we know that the NFL product is superior in athleticism and sex appeal. It might be argued that curling is also Canadian in spirit, if not in origin. Certainly we have taken the game to new heights of competition and popularity. But unless body-checking is instituted and the occasional high-brooming penalty is assessed, the roaring game will remain the boring game compared to the other ice sport.

There are few aspects of life in the Great White North that do not have a hockey connection. Every season is hockey season in Canada. From live theatre to movies to television to music, art, and literature we celebrate the game. Hockey is with us always, in every hamlet, village, and city from coast to coast to coast.

It permeates virtually every aspect of our lives and impacts even those on the sideline of the game. Viewers of the popular British soap opera *Coronation Street* used to complain

loudly and vociferously about their show being preempted by playoff hockey coverage. Those complaints have pretty much died out of late because nonhockey people (yes, there are some) realize that *everything* is preempted by hockey—entire *lives* are preempted by hockey. Even democracy suffers. During the 2010 Vancouver Olympics our government was prorogued and frontbenchers and backbenchers were benched to make way for faceoffs of a more physical, and no doubt more civil, nature. Our Prime Minister, a huge hockey fan, was unapologetic even as legislation ground to a halt. Aside from the opposition parties and political pundits, few seemed to notice—possibly because they were too busy watching hockey. New citizens quickly learn that resistance is futile. Like it or not, they can expect a total immersion in this part of our culture.

What does all of this say about us as Canadians? How do Canadians explain this obsession—because it is nothing less— with this unique but simple game? Perhaps more importantly, how does hockey explain Canada? What is there about us that led us to create this game, establish its unique structure and set of rules, periodically refine that

A Canadian hockey fan carries a sign as he celebrates Canada's victory over the United States in the gold-medal game at the Vancouver 2010 Olympics.

AP Images

structure and those rules, and all but deify the players who excel at the sport?

Canada is a young country and hockey is still a young game. Even as the Fathers of Confederation were busy creating a country in 1867, young men were playing hockey on Lake Banook in Dartmouth, Nova Scotia. Truth be told, the boys at King's College School in nearby Windsor, Nova Scotia, had been playing it even earlier, using a disc of wood as a puck and a tree limb with a crook as stick. James Creighton from Halifax then introduced the sport to Montreal where the first organized game was played in 1875. From there it spread to Ontario and by the 1890s it was being played across Canada.

The game has been with us ever since, in wartime and peacetime, on foreign soil and at home. For many Canadians it remains a constant companion throughout their lives.

Canada is a gangly, sprawling, unwieldy country that skeptics once predicted would be ungovernable. Surely the land mass was too large to foster any sense of unity or commonality. What could St. John's, Newfoundland, possibly have in common with Vancouver, British Columbia? And what could either have in common with Toronto and Winnipeg? As for Montreal and Quebec City, how could English Canada possibly have anything in common with Quebecers? Well, there is hockey. Hockey has brought Canadians closer together than 100 federal-provincial conferences and 50 federal elections. It is the glue that bonds the East to the West and the Arctic to southern Ontario.

The hockey rink represents our common ground and our level playing field. Canada's men and women both captured gold at the 2010 Olympics. The men won with a roster that included players from 7 of the 10 provinces. The large cities were well represented but so were communities like Warburg, Alberta—whose population of 621 includes coach Lindy Ruff—and Aneroid, Saskatchewan, where the entire town of 45 cheered on hometown hero Patrick Marleau. The team was a microcosm of Canada. The women's team was similarly diverse.

Prime Minister Stephen Harper is much more than a casual hockey fan, he's a serious student of the game. "I strongly believe that our 'Canadian' game is a unifying force within this country and an intrinsic part of our national identity," he said. He sees hockey as "deeply reflective of the character of the nation" and has described its power to topple social barriers as "culturally cross-cutting." The Prime Minister also sees it as a rite of passage for new Canadians. "You see immigrants start to belong to Canadian society when their kids start to come to the hockey rink. Then the parents integrate with the other parents. It crosses social and class lines. So it's a great common denominator."

When pressed by Michael Farber of *Sports Illustrated* on whether he'd rather be Prime Minister or play in the NHL, Harper put all political correctness aside: "It's probably terrible to say, but any Canadian boy, if he could play in the NHL, would play in the NHL."

Little wonder then that when Sidney Crosby, from Cole Harbour, Nova Scotia, (population 25,934) scored the winning goal to give Canada the gold medal, it was a single cheer that went up across the country. Canadians of all ages simultaneously sprang from their living room chairs and chesterfields. Couch potatoes sprouted legs and danced around living rooms. Thousands of these viewers secretly believed that it was their own incantations, prayers, or the sheer power of their willing it to happen that had propelled the puck into the American net.

The reaction was downright un-Canadian in its fierceness. After all, Canadians have a well-deserved reputation for being mild-mannered, reserved, and self-deprecating. We have an aw-shucks attitude that has earned us many friends and disarmed and deflected many enemies. We do not show our emotions readily, and almost never openly. Except when hockey is involved. Like peeling onions, heavy drinking, wedding receptions, and *Old Yeller*, hockey gives us an excuse to become emotional.

When Wayne Gretzky left Edmonton for Los Angeles, there was a press conference that had the solemnity usually associated with state funerals. Overcome with emotion, Gretzky cried on national television. Fair enough, the Alberta capital had been his home for his entire professional life, the scene of his greatest triumphs. He led the Oilers to four Stanley Cups and had become a rich man in the process. He was leaving friends and teammates. But try to explain why the whole country had a tear in its eye? The nation mourned as if a Father of Confederation had died. Our boy, The Great One, Captain Canada, had left us for the glitz and glamour of Hollywood. It was as if Anne had left Green Gables to work the streets of Halifax.

The fact is that the game of hockey and the Canadians who play it at the highest level are our identity—and no one wants to lose part of their identity. Certainly not to the United States of America. Sure we all knew that Gretzky would become an ambassador and raise the profile of the game in the most important (read: most profitable) US market. But this was a rational argument and rationality doesn't really enter into it where hockey is concerned. At the emotional level, in the Canadian gut, it felt like a betrayal, yet another great natural resource gone south. We were not only hewers of wood and drawers of water, we were also cultivators of hockey stars for export. As for our American friends, they still don't quite get it. They are, after all, the ones who introduced to television coverage the highlighted puck so that fans could follow it more easily. To which a Canadian countered, "Hell, I can see it on the *radio.*" And we all knew exactly what he meant.

Every Canadian over a certain age knows where he or she was when President John F. Kennedy was assassinated. They also know where they were when Neil Armstrong walked on the moon, when Lady Diana died, and when the Twin Towers fell. And they definitely recall where they were when Paul Henderson scored The Goal. In my case I was driving an American colleague to the Halifax International Airport where he was catching a return flight home to Minnesota. I resented having to drive him because I was unable to watch Game 8 of the Summit Series between Canada and Russia. But I was able to listen to it on the radio and the more I listened the more nervous I became.

As I was approaching the airport, Paul Henderson scored the winning goal. Not only did I have trouble controlling the car, but also I immediately got a nosebleed. There I was, one hand on the steering wheel and one pushing Kleenex into my nose. My American colleague gave me a puzzled, slightly bemused look. "It's a Canadian thing," I said proudly.

—Jim Prime, April 2011

HOW HOCKEY EXPLAINS CONFEDERATION AND EVOLUTION

A 17-year-old Sidney Crosby follows through on a pass while playing for Rimouski Oceanique of the Quebec Major Junior Hockey League in November 1994. Crosby, considered by many the best player in the NHL, was born in Cole Harbour, Nova Scotia, about 100 miles from Windsor.

Andre Ringuette/ Getty Images

AFTER A LONG and harrowing Atlantic crossing, Antoine Beliveau arrived in Port Royal in 1642 with a shipload of other settlers. Now known as Annapolis Royal, the town is located at the western end of the fertile Annapolis Valley of Nova Scotia. The site for the town was discovered by explorer Samuel de Champlain and Port Royal was settled by the French in 1605, making it the first permanent settlement in North America. From this strategic base, the French spread across what are now the Maritime Provinces to create a North American stronghold known as Acadia.

The subsequent arrival of the British brought traditional hostilities between England and France to the shores of the New World. Countless attacks, treaties, counterattacks, more treaties, skirmishes, attacks, and still more treaties followed. In all, Port Royal was attacked 13 times. Finally, by 1763 the British had assumed complete control of the region. During this period of unrest, the peaceful, hardworking, innovative Acadian farmers, including the Beliveau family of Port Royal, continued to work the rich land and fish the bountiful waters of the Bay of Fundy. The military and political ambitions of their faraway ancestors were not a part of their daily lives.

In 1755, their idyllic world was torn asunder with a royal proclamation from the British government that demanded that the Acadians swear an oath of allegiance to the British crown. They were no threat to the British and were resigned to live under their rule, but loyalty to their French culture caused them to refuse. The shameful result was that thousands of innocent people were declared noncitizens, uprooted, and deported, an event known as the Expulsion of the Acadians. Their houses, farms, and barns were then torched, and soon the place called Acadia was no more.

The Beliveaus, along with thousands of other families, were gathered together at Grand Pre to hear the decree. From there they were taken aboard ships and transported to points south of the border where they dispersed like seeds in the wind. Most never returned, opting instead to begin anew in places like Louisiana, where the name Acadian was soon shortened to Cajun. They put down new roots and added greatly to the rich culture of the state.

Some, like the Beliveaus, made their new home in Boston, where they remained for several decades before migrating back to Canada in the mid-nineteenth century. One branch of the family continued on to western Canada while others were tempted by a generous offer from the government of Quebec. Good, farmable land was being made available on the south shore of the St. Lawrence River near present-day Trois-Riviere. These Beliveaus pursued the offer and obtained a grant of land in the Saint-Gregoire region.

On August 31, 1931, some 175 years after this uniquely Canadian odyssey began, Arthur and Laurette Beliveau—direct descendants of Antoine Beliveau of Port Royal—celebrated the birth of a son. He was christened Jean Arthur Beliveau, and he went on to become one of the greatest players in NHL history. After his retirement he was so respected by all Canadians that the Prime Minister offered him the position of Governor General of Canada.

Not only was the Expulsion of the Acadians one of the most shameful episodes in Canadian history, but it also deprived the East Coast of a rich cultural resource, not to mention some of the best farmers on the continent. It may also have deprived Nova Scotia of its first hockey

superstar, the Sidney Crosby of his time. On such whims of fate are the history of Canada and the history of hockey written.

Some 250 years after the expulsion, Jean Beliveau returned to the Land of Evangeline to receive an honorary degree from Acadia University, located just three miles down the road from the site of the deportation. After Beliveau and the other distinguished honorees received their doctorates, they were seated in a row of chairs near the dais as the graduating Acadia students filed across the stage to get their degrees. The procession of students continued for some time as each faculty's list of graduates was called upon alphabetically. They received their sheepskins from the university's chancellor, shook his hand, and returned to their seats.

Amid the extended pomp and circumstance, one student received his degree and shook the proffered hand like all his classmates had done before. Instead of following the others back to his place, however, this rebellious lad veered to his right, strode purposefully to where Jean Beliveau was sitting, pulled a pen from the folds of his robes, and extended the degree for him to sign. The distinguished white-haired gentleman obliged with a broad smile and applause from the audience. It was the perfect, triumphant return to Acadia from an unjust exile for the famille Beliveau.

The fact is that Canada and hockey both began in the Maritimes. No Canadian would dare dispute the fact that Charlottetown, Prince Edward Island, is the "Cradle of Confederation" and the "Birthplace of Canada." It is an honour that all other provinces and territories are willing to concede to the nation's smallest province despite the fact that PEI didn't actually join Confederation until 1873, six years after Nova Scotia, New Brunswick, Ontario, and Quebec. It is significant, then, that at least five Canadian

Jean Beliveau poses with the NHL Lifetime Achievement Award following the 2009 NHL Awards. More than 250 years earlier, the Hall of Famer's French ancestors were deported from Canada during the Expulsion of the Acadians.

Photo by Harry How/ Getty Images

communities stake vehement claim to being the birthplace of Canada's birthright, hockey. Those vying for the distinction include Windsor, Nova Scotia; Halifax-Dartmouth, Nova Scotia; Montreal, Quebec; Kingston, Ontario; and Deline, Northwest Territories.

Hockey's Birthplace?

The signs leading into Windsor, Nova Scotia, proudly proclaim it to be "The Birthplace of Hockey." Strong evidence suggests that, at the very least, the sport was conceived there some cold winter's day in the early 1800s. Located just 40 miles from Halifax, the historic town of 3,778 was settled around 1684 by Acadian farmers. It later became the site of a British garrison known as Fort Edward. Windsor is the eastern gateway to the beautiful, bountiful Annapolis Valley.

Windsor is a twin community of Cooperstown, New York—the home of the National Baseball Hall of Fame and Museum. In 1995 the town created a museum of its own, the Windsor Hockey Heritage Centre, a small but impressive walk-up museum devoted to the local origins of the game of hockey. For decades, Dr. Garth Vaughn has been a tireless advocate for Windsor's compelling case. His well-researched 1996 book, *The Puck Starts Here,* presents Windsor's argument in great detail and with enough evidence to convince any dispassionate observer. Unfortunately, observers of hockey are nothing if not passionate.

The students of Windsor's King's College, Canada's first college (founded in 1788), were the first to play the British game of hurley on the frozen surface of Long Pond, near the school. From this humble beginning the evolution of ice hockey was underway. Once within the Windsor town limits, a modest sign directs visitors to Long Pond, "The Cradle of Hockey." Located on the Dill Farm, this is reputedly the site of the first hockey game ever played. Even within the confines of Windsor there is conflicting opinion on the exact location of the original Long Pond, showing just how difficult this birthing business can be.

References to hockey first appear in the writings of another notable Windsorite, Thomas Chandler Haliburton (1796–1865), Canada's first internationally best-selling author. Sam Slick, the fictional hero of his stories, was a Yankee clock peddler who uses his rough-hewn wit to point out the foibles of human nature. Among the phrases that Haliburton added to the lexicon are "It's raining cats and dogs," "The early bird gets the worm," "Don't take any wooden nickels," "A stitch in time saves nine," "Quick as a wink," "Don't look a gift horse in the mouth," "Truth is stranger than fiction," and "Seeing is believing." The last expression is significant since Haliburton writes about having seen hurley being played on Long Pond around and about the year 1800.

In *The Attache* or *Sam Slick in England,* Haliburton reminisces about his Windsor boyhood through the voice of Sam: "the school room, and the noisy, larkin', happy holidays, and you boys let out racin', yelpin', hollerin', and whoopin' like mad with pleasure, and the playground, and the game at bass in the fields, or hurley in the Long Pond on the ice..."

Despite the compelling evidence for Windsor, there are pretenders to the title of birthplace of hockey. Let's first deal with Kingston's claim. It is largely based on the cheerleading of two formidable Kingstonians, one from the past and one omnipresent. Former World War I Army officer Captain James T. Sutherland was a travelling shoe salesman with a genuine love of the game and his adopted hometown. The *Canadian Hockey Year Book,* published in 1924, included an article by Sutherland in which he asserted: "I think it is generally admitted and has been substantially proven on many occasions that the actual birthplace of organized hockey is the City of Kingston in 1888 [Note: it was actually 1886]." He described a game played at a rink between Queen's University and the Royal Military College, with players using "a set of sticks which had been borrowed from an eastern firm." While it seems that Sutherland's supporting documentation for the Kingston claim was all but nonexistent, his persistent campaigning convinced the Canadian Amateur Hockey Association to give its official thumbs-up in 1943.

This ignored the fact that there was a fundamental inconsistency in Sutherland's case. The "eastern firm" referred to was in Nova Scotia, and if they had provided the hockey sticks for Kingston to play their first games of hockey, it begged the question: What were these Nova Scotians using them for? Clubbing seals? Common sense dictates that they must have been using them to play hockey, the game for which they had been designed. The sticks in question were returned to Halifax after the game and some Maritimers maintain that Ontario has been sticking it to them ever since.

To his credit, Sutherland eventually acknowledged the flaw in his logic, withdrew Kingston's claim, and conceded the provenance that the hockey sticks gave to Nova Scotia as creators of the sport. "Otherwise," he admitted, "why send to Halifax for sticks?" In fairness, there is no doubt that Kingston was a hockey hotbed early on and certainly served as an incubator for the newborn game. Many Kingstonians refer to their city as "the hub of hockey," a designation that seems accurate and holds no shame. Of course Don Cherry, the other formidable Kingstonian cheerleader, remains a stubborn member of the Kingston hockey revisionists. "Make no mistake," Grapes has said, "Kingston is the cradle of hockey and I'm proud to be a Kingstonian." Perhaps due to such high-profile support, even today disciples of Sutherland have dubbed him "the father of hockey" despite the fact that a simple paternity test would prove otherwise.

"I think that Kingston has the weakest case," said Paul Henderson. "I don't think that they are in the running. For Cherry, where else *would* it be? Everything comes out of Kingston! According to him the best hockey players who ever played in the NHL were Kirk [Muller] and Dougie [Gilmour]!"

Montreal has also presented its credentials as hockey's hometown, and there is no question that the city was instrumental in the sport's development, refinement, and promotion. The first organized game was at the city's Victoria Skating Rink and featured students from McGill University. In 2002, the International Ice Hockey Federation (IIHF) threw its considerable support behind this historic rink and this city as the birthplace of organized hockey.

In a May 2008 ceremony in Montreal, it became official when two plaques were unveiled at the Bell Centre, home of the Montreal Canadiens. The Bell Centre is located less than three NHL rink-lengths—two blocks—from the Victoria Skating Rink. In attendance at the event were Prime Minister Stephen Harper—a hockey historian of some note—and IIHF President Rene Fasel, as well as Montreal Mayor Gerald Tremblay. It was the 100th anniversary of the IIHF, and Fasel said that he was honoured to unveil the plaques in Montreal "where the game was born."

The first plaque recognized the Victoria Skating Rink as the "birthplace of organized hockey" even though as Dr. Vaughn so rightly pointed out in his book, "it wasn't exactly in total disarray in Nova Scotia before that time." The second plaque was dedicated to James Creighton (1850–1930), the "father of organized hockey." Creighton was appropriately

Al MacInnis fires a shot. MacInnis, who starred for the Calgary Flames in the 1980s and early '90s, is the only Nova Scotia–born Hall of Famer.

Bruce Bennett Studios/Getty Images

lauded as the man believed to have codi-fied the game's rules, the base on which the organized sport was built. He was also cred-ited with organizing the first indoor game at the Victoria Skating Rink on March 3, 1875. The game was played between two sides of nine players, and among other innovations, Creighton replaced the usual ball with a puck. Two years later, in 1877, Creighton introduced the so-called "Montreal Rules." That same year he served as captain of the first organized hockey club, the McGill University squad.

"It's doubly appropriate that we're hon-ouring him here in Montreal," said the Prime Minister, "because this is where he organized the first indoor hockey game. Creighton is the closest thing hockey has to a founding father."

Speaking for the international body, Fasel was even more effusive in his sup-port of Montreal as hockey's ground zero: "For the preservation of the heritage of our game, for hockey fans all over the world, and for the world governing body of ice hockey, it is important to finally and officially recognize the site where the Victoria Skating Rink once stood and James Creighton as the person of

Nova Scotia Sidney

If, as our Prime Minister has suggested, hockey was the product of evolution rather than a single "Eureka!" moment, Nova Scotia has indeed contributed much to that evolution. Nova Scotians were there at the beginning and are very prominent 211 years later.

From the primordial swamp of Long Pond where the rudiments of the game emerged, hockey has evolved rapidly and continuously. It was in Nova Scotia that the game grew appendages such as hockey skates, hockey sticks, and pucks. Goalie pads borrowed from the King's College cricket pitch morphed into hockey pads. The fitting result of all this evolution and intelligent design is the most highly evolved player of our era, one Sidney Crosby, born in Cole Harbour, Nova Scotia, about 100 miles from Windsor. As Sam Slick would say, "Seein' is believing."

Before Crosby there were other great NHL players from Nova Scotia, some 65 in all, including eight current players. Not bad for a province with less than a million people. Among the best known are Glen Murray, Al MacNeil, Lowell MacDonald, Parker MacDonald, Bobby Smith, and Al MacInnis. MacInnis, who played 23 seasons for Calgary and St. Louis, is the only Hall of Famer. The former defenceman with the blazing slap shot has little doubt that Crosby will one day surpass him as Nova Scotia's preeminent hockey export. In 2009 he joked that it has already happened, telling NHL.com staff writer Rocky Bonanno of a conversation with Crosby at an NHL awards ceremony. "I worked 23 years to get that [top position]," MacInnis claims to have told Crosby, "and it ended after four months of Sidney Crosby being in the NHL. We got a good chuckle out of it."

Nova Scotia–raised Paul MacLean is effusive in his praise for, and pride in, fellow Bluenose Sidney Crosby. "When I was playing in Nova Scotia I never would have thought about the greatest player in the world coming from Nova Scotia," MacLean admitted. "But why not? When you look at some of the best players, Bobby Orr was from Parry Sound, an obscure town. Gordie Howe was from a small town in Saskatchewan [Floral]. So it's not surprising that a player could come from what is deemed as nowhere and end up being the best player in the world. It's a freak of genetics, I guess, more than anything—that and desire.

"What makes Sidney so good is his tenacity. He sticks to it like all Nova Scotia players. That's what they're all about, and I think he's the best symbol of it. He sticks to it and he stays with it until he succeeds in what he wants to do. We battled the Pittsburgh Penguins to two Stanley Cup Finals and [Detroit] won one and they won one, but I'm here to tell you that Paul MacLean is a huge Sidney Crosby fan. I think it's great that as a Nova Scotian we can say that the best player in the world is from Cole Harbour, Nova Scotia. I think that's a pretty good calling card."

hockey historic significance. Not many sports can, as hockey, precisely identify the origins of its game. This is of great historical value to us."

Not every sport can be so precise—or so self-serving. The full force of governments—city, province, country, and international—stood behind the gala event. The Government of Canada's expert advisory body on historical matters in Canada helped to organize it, as did Parks Canada, the IIHF, Hockey Canada, the City of Montreal, the Historic Sites and Monuments Board of Canada, and the Montreal Canadiens. The only official groups that failed to sanction it appear to be the Vatican and the Nova Scotia Chamber of Commerce, although as our Prime Minister wisely indicated: "The evolution of hockey, like any sport, [is] an incremental process. Creighton deserves recognition because he formalized the game, bringing it indoors."

Tiny Windsor, Nova Scotia, on the other hand, had been formally left out in the cold.

Even evolution has to start somewhere, and for hockey that place was Windsor's Long Pond. It is much more than the genesis of the sport, it provided the perfect environment for it to thrive and grow. Windsor had ample ponds and lakes. It also had a surplus of young, healthy men from the garrison at Fort Edward and King's College, not to mention the "townies"—and it had a climate that allowed for outdoor skating. Of course it may be the white man's extreme hubris that suggests that the game had not been played by first nations people in Windsor and environs years earlier. Certainly the Mi'kmaq presence in the area was significant and the natives provided the first carved sticks and wooden pucks.

As for the name of this new ice game, whether it was called hurley, ricket, bandy, or finally hockey, the bottom line is—to paraphrase—"If it looks like a puck and acts like a puck . . . it is probably a hockey puck."

To add to the historical intrigue, the surname Hockey is a common one in the Annapolis Valley, and a plausible, albeit unproven, theory is that a man named John Hockey was a colonel serving at Windsor's Fort Edward where he used the game to keep his troops in shape during long winters. Vaughn's research confirms that in the middle of the nineteenth century a John Hockey does appear on the British Army list kept at the Legislative Assembly in Halifax. "Truth is stranger than fiction," as Sam Slick so rightly observed.

One thing that we can all agree on: James Creighton was the Johnny Appleseed of hockey and he spread the seed of the game far and wide. Eventually he would become the sport's Martin Luther, nailing his hockey theses to the door of the Victoria Skating Rink. Creighton was born and raised in Halifax, attending Halifax Grammar School before entering Dalhousie University. Like his father before him, young James was an enthusiastic figure skater of great repute. He worked as a construction engineer in Nova Scotia for a time before his move to Montreal.

The "Montreal Rules" that are often cited as the codification of hockey were essentially the "Halifax Hockey Club Rules" that Creighton took with him when he left Nova Scotia in 1873 to further his engineering career. As an athlete, he gravitated to other sports-minded young men and soon became a member of the Montreal Football Club. He was responsible for indoctrinating this gridiron group in the game of hockey and its fundamental rules. They are the same rules, with some innovations added, that were employed in the initial game in Montreal. The fact that Creighton succeeded in having them published in Montreal gave them an official status that had been lacking up to that point. There were some changes. Forward passes, for example, were legal in Halifax but outlawed under the Montreal Rules. These changes were evolutionary rather than revolutionary. Also imported from Nova Scotia were the Mi'kmaq hockey sticks used in that historic game.

There is yet another claim, this one from the Far North in Deline, a community of some 650 hearty souls located on the southern tip of Great Bear Lake in the Canadian Arctic. Deline's case is based on a reference to hockey in the diary of explorer Sir John Franklin. Franklin writes about how in the winter of 1825 his crew played hockey to pass the time. No mention is made of skates being used in these games, although skating is mentioned as a separate activity. The Deline argument received support when a group of former NHL players, organized by former Pittsburgh Penguin, Montreal Canadien, and Detroit Red Wing John Chabot made the trek north to promote the community as hockey's birthplace.

Why is this designation so important to so many Canadians? Paul Henderson has a theory. "Anytime that your little area might have originated something, it's awful significant. Like my little community of Lucknow, Ontario. When I was growing up, there was a Chinese family called the Chins and George, the older boy, got a tryout with Detroit. They were too small and none of them ever made pro, but man, I mean we would fill the rink for intermediate games. I was so proud to say that I was from Lucknow, the home of the Chin boys.

"We were less than a thousand people so obviously I think that if Lucknow had ever been in the running as the birthplace of hockey I would have been elated. I'd have said, 'Holy smokes, is this any good! Man, what a heritage I got in my town.' That's where the factual part gives way to the emotional part. We all have our little biases or identification marks that we can hang on to."

How Hockey Explains Paul MacLean

He's a humble hockey player from small-town Nova Scotia who played junior hockey in the Quebec Major Junior Hockey League and scored more than 35 goals as an NHL rookie. In his first five professional campaigns, he netted 176 goals, an average of 35 per season. He played with pride for Canada at the Olympic Games. Sound familiar?

Oh yes, for you trivia buffs, he's also the highest-scoring French-born player in NHL history.

Paul MacLean was a 6'0", 205-pound forward from Antigonish, Nova Scotia, who played a decade of hockey for the St. Louis Blues, Winnipeg Jets, and Detroit Red Wings

A 6'0", 205-pound forward from Antigonish, Nova Scotia, Paul MacLean netted 176 goals in his first five NHL seasons, an average of 35 per season.

Bruce Bennett Studios/Getty Images

Paul MacLean fights his way through the Netherlands' goal mouth after teammate Terry O'Malley scored the final goal of Canada's 10–1 win in their first game of the 1980 Olympics in Lake Placid.

AP Images

from 1980–81 to 1990–91. Playing with the Jets on a line with high-scoring centre and future Hall of Famer Dale Hawerchuk, he found his own scoring touch.

Among his many more serious achievements, he was recently honoured on an Internet sports blog titled "Real Deal On Sports" for what the blogger described as "one of the greatest mustaches in history—period—transcending sport."

MacLean's most productive season came in 1984–85 when he lit the red light 41 times and finished 12th in the scoring race with 101 points (a guy named Gretzky led the league with 73 goals and 135 assists for 208 points). In all, he scored 324 NHL goals.

In June 2011, after several seasons as an assistant to Mike Babcock in Anaheim and Detroit, Paul MacLean was named head coach of the Ottawa Senators. He was born in Grostenquin, France, where his military father was stationed at the time. MacLean spends part of each summer at his home in Antigonish.

Despite the success he achieved, MacLean's route to the NHL couldn't have

been more different from that of Sid the Kid from Cole Harbour, Nova Scotia. Unlike Crosby, MacLean had to fight to get attention. He was selected 109th overall in the 1978 NHL draft, the sixth pick in the seventh round. His Olympic experience also fell somewhat short of Sidney Crosby's, as Canada finished well out of the medals at the 1980 Lake Placid Games.

There were no agents waiting in line to offer their services to this promising easterner. "The only representation I had was myself and my dad," MacLean said. "I had never even heard of an agent. I had no idea at the time what that would be."

MacLean is often omitted from the list of great Bluenose players for the most technical of reasons. Paul MacLean of Antigonish was born in France, the son of an air force father. He celebrated his second birthday aboard ship on the voyage back to Canada.

In 1979 MacLean was invited to Calgary for the Canadian Olympic team training camp. He ended up making Father David Bauer's squad, the only player on the 1980 Olympic team from east of Montreal. He travelled the world playing hockey at the highest of levels, against future NHL stars from Czechoslovakia and other emerging hockey powers.

Father Bauer's influence extended well beyond the ice. "We were cautioned not to swear and to be fine young men and not to be incorrigible. Apparently previous Canadian teams did not follow that example.

"He thought the game was supposed to be played as gentlemen and not carried away like typical Canadian hockey can sometimes be, with fisticuffs and all that. That year probably made a difference [between] me playing in the NHL and not."

Nova Scotia fans are glad that he stuck to it and became part of the legacy of distinguished players from the birthplace of hockey.

How Hockey Explains Brad Marchand

The name of Brad Marchand can now be added to the list of renowned East Coast players to incubate in the birthplace of hockey. The Bruins' rookie sensation from Hammond's Plains, Nova Scotia, won the hearts of all New England and much of the Atlantic Provinces with his spirited play. His name can also be added to the Stanley Cup because Marchand won that, too.

Marchand made a statement throughout the 2011 playoffs and added two giant exclamation points in Game 7 of the Stanley Cup Finals against the Canucks in Vancouver. The two goals, one an empty-netter, brought his postseason total to 11, the second-highest total in the playoffs. Only one rookie in league history—Dino Ciccarelli with 14 for Minnesota in 1981—had more (Marchand and Jeremy Roenick are tied for second). His five goals in the Finals was two more than any other player on the Bruins or Vancouver Canucks.

"I wanted to come in and I didn't know what to expect. I just wanted to produce. Luckily, I did," Marchand said. "It is surreal. You don't realize it. It just doesn't kick in. I don't know if it ever will. I'm just at a loss for words right now. Obviously, you dream of it as a kid, but I never thought it would happen. Some guys go their whole career without winning it, and to win it my first year is unbelievable."

Drafted by the Bruins 71st overall in 2006, Marchand plays the game with passion and it showed against favoured Vancouver. "We hated them so much," he said after the final game. "They were so cocky. They thought they were just going to roll over us and we prevailed. We went out there and kept our mouths shut and we won."

Some members of the Canucks might take issue with him on the keeping his mouth shut assertion, but technically he's right. In truth the feisty 5′9″, 183-pound winger did his talking with his hands, "dusting" them contemptuously as he skated past the Canucks bench and throwing and connecting with a punch at Daniel Sedin during a dust-up in Game 6.

Marchand used a controversial hit on Bruins teammate Nathan Horton to fire himself up against Vancouver, although Boston general manager Peter Chiarelli suggested that he hates every team he plays. "That's part of his magic too," he added. "He's learning how to draw the line between going over the line and playing an aggressive, agitating game. I have to give him credit. He's learning how to do that on the job."

With the countless historic and social ties between New England and Nova Scotia, it's not surprising that there are lots of Boston fans in the province or that Brad Marchand became the newest link binding the two regions.

On the long flight back to Boston from Vancouver, Marchand couldn't sleep. He told the *Halifax Herald*: "Different guys were sleeping and me and [Gregory] Campbell just sat there with the Cup for about an hour and just went over every name on it."

Marchand's freshman season produced 21 goals and a plus/minus well above zero. He scored five short-handed goals and was voted the prestigious "7th Player Award" by appreciative Boston fans for his two-way contributions and performing beyond expectations.

Meanwhile yet another Nova Scotian is about to explode onto the hockey scene. Fifteen-year-old Nathan MacKinnon from Dartmouth has established himself as a star of the future. Among a long list of Sid the Kid–like accomplishments, he registered 200 points in Atom League play and caught the attention of *ESPN: The Magazine*. Like Crosby, MacKinnon is a product of the Shattuck-St. Mary's prep school in Minnesota. Last season he amassed 96 points in just 40 games.

MacKinnon is in hot demand. He was drafted first overall by Baie-Comeau of the QMJHL but may decide to compete in the NCAA after finishing high school. Whichever route he decides to take, the NHL is the destination and fans can't wait for him to arrive.

How Hockey Explains Quantum Physics and Time Travel

"It is well known that the space-time continuum is curved. The curvature occurs as a result of the influence of mass against movement in time. Recently, it has been possible to detect this curvature. As three-dimensional beings, we perceive time only as a result of memory. We remember what was as a variable interval from what is now. If we had zero memory, we could not detect time—we would exist only for the moment. The result of this is our apparent perception of time as a linear line, always going forward." —David Faige

Conrad "Connie" MacNeil claims that he's been shortchanged by Andy Warhol. The late pop artist had promised that everyone on earth would be famous for 15 minutes and MacNeil wonders what happened to his remaining 14:54.

Self-deprecating humour is a trademark of the modest 81-year-old former educator and real estate agent. He uses it to deflect or at least diffuse the spotlight from one of the most incredible feats in hockey history: three goals in six seconds. No, it's not a misprint. MacNeil scored three goals in six seconds (the approximate time it took for you to read this paragraph).

On the night of February 27, 1950, MacNeil was a fresh-faced 19-year-old freshman at Acadia University in Wolfville, Nova Scotia. A resident of Reserve Mines, Cape Breton, the 5′9″, 160-pound left winger usually toiled on the third line for the varsity Acadia

Connie MacNeil scored three goals in six seconds for the Acadia University Axemen of the Annapolis Valley Senior B Hockey League in February 1950.

Courtesy of Connie MacNeil

Axemen of the Annapolis Valley Senior B Hockey League. On this night, however, the Axemen were shorthanded, the campus having been hit hard by a flu epidemic. "Our team was decimated," MacNeil recalled. The coach was forced to juggle lines and mix and match the remaining players. The speedy MacNeil, who describes himself as an opportunist, was therefore paired with talented second line centre Gint MacKenzie, a fine stickhandler and superior faceoff man.

The Acadia Arena, known locally as the Ice Palace due to the fact that it was invariably colder inside than out, boasted the only artificial ice surface in the Annapolis Valley at that time. It was also unique in that the ice surface was only 180 feet in length. On this night the Axemen were hosting the nearby Kentville Wildcats in the seventh and deciding game of the playoff semifinals and the arena was packed well beyond its 1,400 capacity.

"I wasn't getting a lot of ice time my first year but that night the coach sent me out in a coincidental penalty situation in the first period," MacNeil said. "I guess he thought that playing four a side with all that open ice, my speed might help. I picked the puck up in our own end of the rink and I carried it out. I usually didn't carry the puck but I had lots of room so I carried it through the centre ice zone and over the blue line. I was looking for someone to pass the puck off to. I guess the Wildcats didn't think I was much of a threat because no one came to check me. Finally I looked up, and I thought I saw [Kentville goaltender Al] Tomori saying something to one of his defenceman about covering MacKenzie, who was our big scorer. I just put the puck on net hoping that we'd get a rebound—and it went in. Just a wrist shot, the only kind I knew—from 25 feet or 30 feet. The time of the goal was 7:35."

Time travel is one explanation of what followed. It is conceivable that MacNeil, who

later taught advanced science, among other subjects, used his freshman knowledge of quantum physics to go back in time.

"I went back to take my position while the referee reported the goal over at the scorer's box. Bruce Dunlop, our left defenceman, was giving me a hard time about not passing the puck on the previous play. He called me a puck hog and a few other things, just giving the new guy a hard time. 'Who do you think you are carrying the puck end to end, rookie? Pass the puck!' I jawed back a bit and glanced up from the discussion just in time to see the referee come over and raise his arm. I took three quick steps and cut through the circle just as Gint won the draw and pushed the puck in front of me. I was just hitting my stride and I skated on it and picked it up in full flight. I looked up and their right defenceman was closing on me fast so I just fired it through his legs and I knew the goalie didn't see it. He was completely at sea, and it just caught the corner maybe two feet up in the net at the 7:38 mark. I couldn't believe it. Bang, bang—two goals very quickly.

"I went back and thought I'd have another little talk with Dunlop to see what he thought of that one. We exchanged some pleasantries but by now I sort of had the upper hand with him. The referee was over recording the goal, and I kept my eye on him as he skated back to the centre ice. I stayed just off the circle by myself, sort of lying in the weeds. Just as he was ready to drop the puck I took three or four quick steps through the circle and the puck appeared magically on my stick. I took a stride or two and shot it in the general direction of the net, again through a screen of defencemen. I saw that the puck was going directly at the goaltender. It would have hit him right in the belly button if he'd stayed still, but he couldn't see it! He moved away from the post, from the near side to cover the wide side, and as he moved the puck went right past him under his arm at 7:41. I remember watching Tomori shredding his stick over the crossbar of the net. The same defenceman had blocked his view twice and he was giving him an etiquette lesson.

"When the line finally returned to the bench, I remember the manager saying to me, 'Mr. Wrigley—he called me that because I was always chewing gum—those must be the fastest three goals you ever had.' I was probably too shocked to answer."

The final score was 13–11 for Kentville, despite Acadia's 55–22 advantage in shots. Almost forgotten is the fact that Allie Carver, an import from Prince Edward Island, scored five third-period goals for the visitors that night against a replacement goalie. MacNeil went on to capture the league's MVP award. But, more than 60 years later, what people remember is that six-second span. The term *hat trick* doesn't seem to do it justice. Perhaps *lid legerdemain* would better capture its uniqueness. There are skeptics, but MacNeil doesn't let that bother him. "People say that I must have been playing against the Wolfville Nursing Home or the Halifax School for the Blind," he chuckled.

Contacted the day after MacNeil's achievement at his Montreal office by Halifax newspaper columnist Alex Nickerson, NHL president Clarence Campbell said that the feat was "fantastic." "I was never sure whether Campbell meant fantastic as in *great* or fantastic as in *bullshit*," deadpanned MacNeil. "It could be interpreted either way."

Even NHL legends are genuinely interested in the details of how it was accomplished. "I met Jean Beliveau at a fundraiser," MacNeil said. "A friend tapped me on the shoulder and I was introduced as the guy who scored three goals in six seconds. It took me completely by surprise." At this point it must be said that Le Gros Bill was no slouch at scoring rapid hat tricks either. On November 5, 1955, he netted three in 44 seconds against Hall of Famer Terry Sawchuck of the Detroit Red Wings. The performance was responsible for an NHL rule change whereby a penalized player could leave the penalty box once a power play goal was scored. Rule 26(c) is better known as "The Canadiens Rule." MacNeil knew the scoring connection that they shared but deftly sidestepped any talk of comparisons. "Beliveau shook my hand and said, 'How did you do that?' I certainly didn't want to blow my own horn to the great Jean Beliveau. I said to myself, 'Lord give me some words here.' At last I managed to say, 'Small rink, poor lights, slow clock.'" Three rapid verbal shots that scored big with a laughing Beliveau.

Sadly, there is no central repository for such records. They are strictly up to the league to document and maintain. The NHL record for a three-goal outburst is 21 seconds held by Chicago Blackhawks' legendary Bill Mosienko in a 1952 game against the New York Rangers.

As a former school administrator and teacher of physical education, math, and physics, MacNeil fittingly can counter suggestions that three goals in six seconds is physically impossible. "It is definitely possible," he said. "Sixty mph is 88 feet per second if you break it down mathematically and your grandmother can shoot a puck 60 mph." For those who remain skeptical, in 2010 the *Halifax Chronicle-Herald* asked two members of the current Acadia Axemen hockey team to reenact the hat trick on their Olympic-size ice surface. The results confirmed MacNeil's feat as doable. "If people still aren't convinced, I tell them that time went a lot slower in those days and you could get a lot more accomplished."

HOW HOCKEY EXPLAINS DON CHERRY

Ron MacLean, Don Cherry's long-suffering straight man, punching bag, and *Coach's Corner* chaperone on *Hockey Night in Canada*, was addressing a gathering of some 2,000 educators at the PEI Teachers Federation's annual meeting in Charlottetown, Prince Edward Island. MacLean had been informed just prior to his keynote that part of his audience would be French Immersion teachers.

"Don [Cherry] believes in French immersion," deadpanned MacLean. "He just thinks they don't hold them under long enough." There was an audible gasp from the packed auditorium, followed by an uncomfortable pause as they digested it, and then laughter. After all it was a Don Cherry story, and as Yogi Berra once said of his own reputation, "I didn't say everything I said."

The teachers were content to know that it was something Cherry *might* well have said. He has become so famous and so stereotyped that many quotes that are attributed to him didn't emerge from his mouth at all. The audience knew that, and MacLean knew that, and MacLean knew that the audience knew that. The humour was in the image. Who hadn't witnessed a Cherry rant about Frenchmen, Europeans, or media "pinkos"? Even nonhockey fans knew Mr. Cherry's rap sheet.

"There, the joke is about Don," confirmed MacLean. "It's not about the teachers. He's Archie Bunker and I'm Meathead. I wish that we could laugh at ourselves more. We need to stay in that state of laughter because that's all it is, but political correctness and fear of fallout intervene. There's an old saying that insult is the price of clarity." MacLean pays that fee generously most

A resplendent Don Cherry stands on the ice before the start of Game 3 of the 2008 Eastern Conference Finals in Philadelphia.

Bruce Bennett/
Getty Images

16

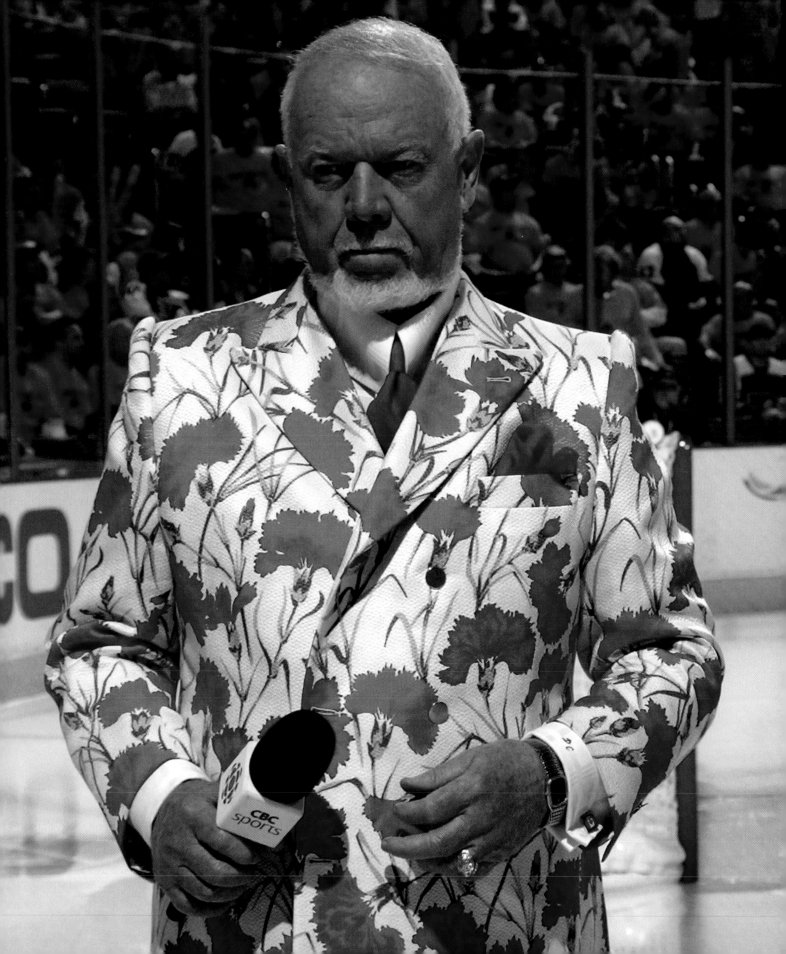

> **"Don Cherry is the reason why all the prisons are in Kingston. They put them there because of Don Cherry specifically. His suits are a sartorial crime. Anyone who'd wear outfits like that has to be a criminal."**
>
> —Bill "Spaceman" Lee, former major league pitcher and hockey fan

Saturday nights and the opinions that he gets from Cherry in return are crystal clear.

Depending on whom you ask, Don Cherry is a bully, a straight-talker, a xenophobe, a patriot, a sentimentalist, a shit-disturber, and a walking faux pas. He is short-tempered, passionate, politically incorrect, fearless, loyal, stubborn, boorish, pompous, shrewd, stubborn, and insufferable. He has played hockey, coached hockey, analyzed hockey, hurt hockey, and helped hockey. He knows everything about the game and he knows nothing about the game. He sees beauty in the ugly or mundane parts of the game and often seems to recoil at the artistic efforts of skilled players. He wasn't good enough to make the NHL but wears his minor league status as a badge of honour. He has legions of fans who hang on his every word. He has legions of detractors who would prefer listening to fingernails scraping across a chalkboard. Several media profiles of Cherry have suggested similarities to American right-wing talk show know-it-all Rush Limbaugh. ESPN suggested that he was equal parts Rush and John Madden, but as the ultimate Canadian patriot, the least Cherry deserves are Canadian points of reference.

Cherry has the sentimentality of Celine Dion, the boorishness of Howie Mandel, the gall of Conrad Black, and the balls of Pierre Trudeau. He also has the loyalty of his late canine friend Blue and the patriotism of Pierre Berton. All in one 5'10", 185-pound package encased in suits so garish that they would make Toller Cranston blush.

Roots of Grapes

Ever wonder what it would be like to put Cherry on the psychiatrist's couch and ask him about his childhood? Was he dropped on the head by a Swedish midwife? Did his mother run off with a travelling visor salesman from Quebec? Was his finishing school bombed by the Russians? Perhaps he was potty trained at gunpoint?

Cherry's childhood seems to have no such skeletons. He was born in Kingston, Ontario, a city that claims to be the birthplace of hockey, although DNA tests have ruled Cherry out as the father. His mother Maude worked as a tailor at the nearby Royal Military College. Cherry has called his mother his "guiding hand" and even later in life she was able to reel him in when he got too big for his carefully tailored britches. His father Delmar, a master electrician, was a tall, athletic man, a larger-than-life figure to his doting son. "His size reminded me of Gulliver, while the rest of us were Lilliputians," Cherry said in his book *Grapes*, the title being a reference to Cherry's nickname dating back to his playing days.

It's obvious that this particular pit didn't fall too far from the Cherry tree. His father instilled in him the importance of exuding a positive, even commanding attitude. To that end, he was a meticulous dresser and carried himself with a natural authority.

Cherry's working life before *Hockey Night in Canada* was hockey, hockey, and more hockey. He was what is known as a journeyman player—solid and versatile but not good enough for the NHL in the days of the original six. He toiled in the AHL from 1954–72, a minor league odyssey that shaped his value system and impacted his political views. It was playing in outposts such as Hershey, Springfield, and Rochester that that he came to appreciate character, hard work, integrity, and heart.

Former Leaf Brian Conacher (son of the great Lionel Conacher) played parts of two seasons with Cherry in Rochester. "Don recognized that when his hockey career—whatever it amounted to—was over, he was going to have to work the rest of his life. He sure never anticipated the gig he's got now," Conacher remembered.

"He worked in the summers at Kodak in Rochester so he didn't just sit around in the off months. You really couldn't afford to do that because you didn't make enough money playing hockey."

Former Leafs defenceman Jim McKenny was able to observe Cherry up close and personal when the two roomed together as members of the Rochester Americans. "Don was a real hard player," he recalled. "He wasn't a dirty hockey player—just hard. He played hard every shift of every game that he played. He blocked shots and he'd rush the puck and he tried like crazy."

McKenny suggests that even back then there were subtle signs of what was to follow. "He was outspoken then too—all the time, all day long, although there was no indication of him being a coach or commentator," he said. "He was always complaining that he didn't get enough meal money and that he was always getting shit on. Nobody wanted to room with him. I was the 19-year-old alcoholic on the team and no one wanted to room with me so they put us together.

"He came by his blue-collar attitudes honestly, working on heavy machinery in

the summers at Kodak. Then Kodak moved half their action to Denver, and Don's job went with it. He retired and had no job. Then he went and sold Cadillacs and in a year he made *no* sales. He got dressed up every day and *never made a sale!* He was on the verge of going on relief, on welfare."

Desperate for employment, he attempted a comeback with Rochester. Soon they fired the coach and replaced him with Cherry. "He phoned around to all his buddies in the American League that he used to play with," McKenny said. "Now they're all coaching in the International League and he said if you've got any goons there you want to get rid of, I'll take them and I'll pay the bus fare. So we got about five or six of them and from then on we won."

Former Toronto Maple Leafs defenceman Jim McKenny (right) roomed with Don Cherry as a member of the Rochester Americans in the late 1960s.

Frank Prazak/Hockey Hall of Fame

19

Loved or Hated

Instead of delving into Cherry's past, it might be even more interesting to delve into the minds of those who tune in to watch him every Saturday night. After all, the viewers are the ones who have made Cherry the media darling—and millionaire—that he is. The fact is that Grapes has, accidentally or otherwise, tapped into a strong wellspring of Canadian sentiment. Lest you think that his fan base is limited to blue collar aficionados of hockey violence and mayhem, think again. His is a broad demographic that includes the disgruntled, the gruntled, and the not-gruntled-at-all-but-willing-to-be-convinced-that-they-should-be-gruntled. Included in this fan base are professors, doctors, lawyers, and politicians.

Canadians are not a people who wear their emotions on their sleeves, and so apparently we do it vicariously through Don Cherry, who gets choked up about dump-ins. When Cherry gets hot under his collar—and who wouldn't get hot under such a yoke—we all know where he stands.

How can a man who is the antithesis of the typical Canadian be so damn Canadian? He is downright American in expressing his Canadian-ness. If we are the silent majority, he is the lone loud voice of all that pent-up opinion and passion.

Richard Johnson is curator of the New England Sports Museum and a respected author. He is also a devotee of *Hockey Night in Canada.* Despite his impressive university background and liberal views, he's an unrepentant Cherry fan. "He realizes that sport is entertainment," said Johnson. "He's a wonderful entertainer and colourful. Certainly the sport needs more characters—and he's a character. He exudes spirit, love of the game, and has a Canadian flag tattooed on his chest! I think it's great. In the US he'd probably be a right-wing blowhard, and I couldn't stand him. But the fact is, coming from a Canadian, it's so rare that it's refreshing."

Perhaps no one outside of his immediate family knows more about Don Cherry than Ron MacLean, his *Hockey Night in Canada* partner and one of the most insightful and erudite broadcasters in the country. The pairing of Cherry and MacLean is unique, not to say bizarre. But they're no *Odd Couple*, not in the Oscar and Felix sense. Cherry, the abrasive jock, is anything but slovenly in his dress, and MacLean, while intelligent, is no prig, in fact quite the opposite since he's a jock himself. MacLean offers a comparison from the classics. "I could sort of see us as Sancho and Don Quixote," he said, "but I can never quite decide who's which."

Early on in Cherry's broadcast career, *Hockey Night in Canada* executive producer Ralph Mellanby realized that his new recruit was going to need help. Without it, his commentaries would turn into one nonstop rant. This person would have to have the skin of a rhinoceros. It had to be someone who could give Cherry just enough freedom before reining him in. After a brief but unsuccessful stint with Dave Hodge, Mellanby found MacLean, who was brought on board as ballast for Cherry's boat-rocking antics.

Where the consummately professional Hodge would not tolerate Cherry's unfocused ravings, MacLean saw the potential to be indispensable. The genius lies in Mellanby's intuitive conviction that this odd coupling would work. "Don was a cold beer on a hot day while Ron was vintage champagne," Mellanby said.

Calling MacLean an enforcer will no doubt invite derision from Cherry. But in essence that's what the mild-mannered co-host of *Coach's Corner* is. He protects Cherry—mostly from himself. He does this not through intimidation—perish the thought—but through distraction, humour, bad puns, and a litany of other improvised survival strategies. Mellanby prefers to use a hockey term to describe the relationship. "MacLean is the referee," he said.

Often his interventions make MacLean the object of Cherry's anger and scorn, but he seldom seems flustered. He's like a rodeo clown after the cowboy has been thrown from the bull, except that MacLean's job is also to protect the bull. More often than not, MacLean succeeds in steering the unpredictable star in another direction and away from trouble. There are many notable exceptions.

MacLean laments the fact that the real insider hockey talk takes place after the camera lights go off. "With Don, as wonderful as *Coach's Corner* is, I often feel that when we go back and sit in the hotel room over a pail of beer those conversations are where I really get an understanding. The problem is that you could never jam that into a six-minute *Coach's Corner*."

MacLean's *Don Quixote* comparison is apt, although the idea of *Hockey Knights in Canada* conjures up some interesting images, not the least of which is Cherry's choice of armour. Certainly the current show features its share of jousting between the two. MacLean claims that it is Cherry who picks the time and place for this verbal sparring. "I think he has a real sense of *This is boring. These two guys are too happy, too pleased with themselves. This is flatlining. I'm going to kick it up a notch here and for the sake of the show make Ron look bad or make myself look bad.* He's smart enough to know that he himself is looking bad sometimes when he's being the bully," MacLean said.

Not everyone agrees. For those who can't imagine a time when Don Cherry wasn't the resident mouthpiece of *Hockey Night in Canada*, he did have a predecessor. Remember back to 1968, or about 12 years

BC (Before Cherry)? There was a time on *Hockey Night in Canada* when the between-period analyst was a high-tech master of the telestrator, a time when the hockey guru wore a light blue coordinated suit that didn't have viewers running for the sunglasses and Visine. It was a time when Howie Meeker was the colourful, outspoken, emphatic, and passionate voice of the game.

"My first big star was Howie Meeker," said Mellanby. "Howie was my national guy and he became a household name. And then Don came in and unexpectedly became the next big star. They were very different personalities. The two really dislike one another. I think there was jealously there when Don took part of Howie's mantel and his airtime."

Meeker, now in his late eighties and living in British Columbia, recently received the Order of Canada. Still refreshingly outspoken,

Howie Meeker waves to fans during a pregame ceremony in Toronto in March 2011. Meeker, a Hall of Famer, was *Hockey Night In Canada's* star personality in the late 1960s and early 1970s.

Abelimages/ Getty Images

he is reluctant to be quoted on the subject of Cherry. "It's a ticklish subject," he said. "I hate to get involved in a fight with a skunk because he has access to millions of viewers. I give him full marks for having the best circus act—clown act—in the history of hockey. I give him full marks for being entertaining to a certain group of people in the country.... Without MacLean, he'd be in trouble. He sits there and takes insult after insult. I guess for half a million dollars a year, I might too.

"I don't think he's good for the game. The guy who said that he appeals to the lowest common denominator is dead on. He does very well financially and whoever is advising him has him dressed like the person he is.

As for Cherry's monologues about the Canadian military, Meeker thinks the setting is all wrong. "I tune in for a hockey game," he said. "I don't want to hear his opinion on the military. Or all his friends. 'He's a great friend of mine' and all this and that. Tell me *what's going on*—on the ice!"

For his part, Cherry once said of Meeker, the former NHL Rookie of the Year, four-time Stanley Cup winner, and Hall of Famer, "Aw, what does he know?"

The bigger question is whether Cherry has been good or bad for hockey, whether his glorification of the violent side of the game has set it back in its evolution.

"I don't buy that at all," said MacLean. "If you were to talk to Bobby Orr, and he would be the greatest player of his time, or Gretzky who's not far behind, those guys understand that you can't eliminate that part of the game."

One thing is certain. Those who think that Cherry's remarks are off-the-cuff explosions with no thought behind them are totally wrong, says MacLean. Cherry's opinions, misguided or not, come from his own hardscrabble background and observation, not from a desire to shock.

"Grapes speaks from experience," MacLean said. "Even his whole thing on visors was a carefully considered argument. All that really bothered him about visors is that once you start hedging and putting safety first, you're not really committed, and there's something really profound in that. In life if you're focusing so much on safety, how can you be a life force? Grapes is a real spokesman for—without saying it in the most sophisticated way—not putting safety first all the time.

"He's got a weird and wonderful way of looking at a check stop and being bothered by the fact that the police are invading your privacy. Now again, who in their right mind would say it's a bad idea to have a check stop? But I understand how Grapes looks at things and he sort of says, 'Okay, is that good, is that right?' I'm glad someone's sitting back and critically looking at these things and saying, 'Okay, is that an invasion of privacy?', because if you take it to the next level, is George Bush allowed to violate the rule of law and walk into Iraq? Of course, he's not. But he is! So those kinds of deep arguments have to have micro levels. Of course he'd be the first to want to go to Iraq, and we had a vehement disagreement over that subject. So there you go. He, on the one hand, is looking at something and saying, 'I wonder about this' and on the other he's saying, 'Ok, for the sake of law and order…'"

MacLean feels that there are many misconceptions about his partner, and he's more than willing to dispel them. "Don is so well read," MacLean said. "People don't know that. He's obviously a huge fan of Drake and Nelson and all the naval history, but he's also a huge fan of T.E. Lawrence so he knows the state of the Middle East from before World War I. He knows the state of Afghanistan. He just brings so much to the table that I sit there sometimes in just amazement at how well-read and knowledgeable he is. He has everything. He has originals of T.E. Lawrence, and it goes way beyond that. He's pretty good on Shakespeare, he's good on pop culture, Oscar Wilde, you name it."

One of the frequent complaints against *Coach's Corner* is that it is Toronto-centric. Despite the team's lack of on-ice success in recent years, the Maple Leafs get much more attention than the Vancouver Canucks, Montreal Canadiens, and other Canadian teams. MacLean bridles at the idea that there is any bias on his part. "Ask Dick Irvin about that one. Ask Dick if he was accused of being pro-Montreal? Grapes makes no bones about being a guy from Toronto and he's cheering for the Leafs, but he knows where his bread's buttered too. I don't know if that enters his mind but it wouldn't surprise me, knowing how clever he is. It's not a bad idea playing to your audience."

Ralph Mellanby suggests yet another reason why Cherry might be partial to the Leafs. It seems that Maple Leaf Gardens served as his "safe house" for a while, and Harold Ballard was his warden. "I loved Harold Ballard," said Mellanby. "He kept suspending broadcasting guys but always got them back—guys like Brian McFarlane. But he loved Don Cherry. When Don kept getting barred from different NHL buildings, the satellite hadn't yet been invented so I had to have a place where I could send him out for a couple of years. That place was Maple Leaf Gardens, because Harold hated all of the other owners and was happy to have Don around."

Nevertheless, we don't have to agree with everything he says. Many of his supporters think he has harmed the game with his blinkered vision of it. It's the vision of a scrapper and an underdog, a career minor leaguer who identifies with and appreciates the grinders of the game. Johnny Bower, then goalie with the AHL's Providence Reds, recalls facing Cherry when he was a member of the Hershey Bears. "I think he scored one goal against me," said Bower with a chuckle. "I was screened. It hit about six guys before it went in. I tell everybody that he couldn't break a paper bag with his shot. I tease him like that, but he had a pretty good shot and he was a very aggressive defenceman too.

"I don't mind listening to him once in a while. He's a big blow bag of coco but boy he knows his hockey. The only thing that gets me is those outfits he's wearing! 'Oh gosh,' I said to my wife, 'Look at him. He looks like he got that from the Salvation Army.'"

In what other profession, with the possible exception of a Canadian Senator, could you work a few minutes a week, be paid an enormous amount of taxpayer money, and have a huge impact on Canadians coast-to-coast? How does he manage it? "He's just honest," said McKenny. "Anything he says he will stand behind. Canadians simply love his honesty. If that's the way he feels then he'll say it. He's only on for 10 minutes a week, but everybody watches it so they think he's on all the time."

McKenny thinks that CBC is wise in the way they use their big gun. "He decides what he wants to talk about so he'll get the counter time and he'll talk about certain plays and players that he likes," McKenny said. "They don't ask him about the whole league, just certain things that he wants to talk about. He's smart enough to focus on that. He knows he doesn't know the whole league. He never touches on the business side, the salary cap, or that kind of stuff. It's just the heart of the players that he watches for. That's the way he coached too. He wasn't a real technical coach. He would more or less pump the players up and get them to go out there and if they didn't try hard every game he'd dislike them. And it would take a lot of work to get back in his good face, so you might as well do what he wants. He was a great guy to play for. He brings that same heart to *Coach's Corner.*"

From the Bench to the Mic

Even before Sidney Crosby entered the NHL he had drawn the ire of Cherry, who saw the budding star as a hot dog. This was largely based on a single amazing goal that the junior phenom scored by scooping the puck onto his stick behind the net and depositing it past the goalie. For some reason this provoked Cherry, who often equates skill with being a prima donna. When Crosby declined to play in the Top Prospects Game in 2005, Cherry again slammed the young Nova Scotian.

Once Sid the Kid was in the NHL, Cherry felt that he whined to the referees too much. When confronted by the Pittsburgh media about an apparent bias against their youthful star, he pointed out that it was a charge that he had previously levelled against Gretzky and Mario Lemieux.

Cherry's early criticism of Crosby seems to have disappeared. "It took a while for Don to realize that Sid Crosby's the same kind of kid as Bobby Orr was," suggested McKenny. "He's the hardest working kid on the ice every day. And he loved Bobby because Bobby worked like a dog. He loved the pluggers—Dennis O'Brien and all that shit. He'd tell them what to do, and they'd go right out and do it. That's Sidney Crosby."

To his credit, the 76-year-old former executive director of *Hockey Night in Canada* takes full responsibility for his media creation. "I inflicted Don on an unsuspecting Canadian public," Mellanby said. "When I brought Don in he'd been Coach of the Year twice. I knew he was showbiz, although I must say he didn't dress then like he does now. He's great entertainment. If you like him or hate him it doesn't matter. It's great Canadian entertainment."

The actual genesis of Cherry's broadcasting career can be traced back to May 10, 1979. It was the seventh and deciding game of the Stanley Cup semifinals with the Montreal Canadiens at the Montreal Forum. Going into the third period, Cherry's underdog Bruins held a 3–1 lead. But before the frame had reached the halfway point the Canadiens had pulled even at 3–3 and things were looking dark for the Cherry-coached Bostonians. Then, with 3:59 showing on the clock, Rick Middleton took control of the puck behind the Habs' net, deftly moved in front, and backhanded the puck past a stunned Ken Dryden. As play resumed less than four minutes stood between the Bruins and advancement to the Stanley Cup Finals. And then disaster struck. Trying desperately to preserve the tenuous 4–3 lead against the swarming Canadiens, the Bruins committed the most unpardonable of hockey sins at such a time: too many men on the ice.

Again play resumed and for 1:10 the Bs weathered the storm from the desperate Canadiens. Then a streaking Guy Lafleur, the guy that Cherry most feared, took a drop pass from Jacques Lemaire just inside the blue line and let go a blistering shot that eluded goalie Gilles Gilbert. In the subsequent overtime, the Canadiens rode the wave of momentum to victory, Yvon Lambert scoring the winner 9:33 into the extra frame. Later Cherry would take full responsibility for the blunder. "I deserved to be court-martialled," he admitted.

Cherry had been coach of the Boston Bruins under general manager Harry Sinden for five seasons, but within a month he was gone, taking over the reins at Colorado for a year before moving on to *Hockey Night in Canada.* Cherry's relationship with Sinden had initially been strong but a series of disagreements—some major, most minor—had created a rift that continued to grow until the

Don Cherry was the head coach of the Boston Bruins from 1974–75 through 1978–79.

Bruce Bennett Studios/Getty Images

"too many men on the ice" debacle sealed his fate. When Cherry was firmly entrenched on his CBC soapbox, he used every opportunity to take shots at his former boss and friend.

Sinden strikes a conciliatory tone when he talks about events before and after the Game 7 deal breaker. "The differences that Don Cherry and I had mainly came from him to me and not me to him," Sinden said recently. "I was a target when he first started on *Hockey Night in Canada* and for a long time after, and I resented it of course. No one likes to be ridiculed like that without any real chance of answering back. But when he was here as our coach I was very friendly with him, and we were very good friends."

Sinden finds it difficult to reconcile those happy times with the bitterness and acrimony that followed. "I don't know why really, when I look back, why it kind of fell apart...mainly it was after that Montreal series where we had too many men on the ice. As outrageous as he is, and I get the program here most Saturdays, I turn him on because I want to watch him too. His work has been unbelievably interesting up there. His knowledge of the game is reasonably good—it's not great, but it's reasonably good—and his interest and his bravado about Canada is worth the price right there. He is Canadiana."

Unfortunately this patriotic bravado sometimes comes at the expense of non-Canadian hockey players. He once dismissed Alpo Suhonen, a native of Finland who was then assistant coach of the Winnipeg Jets, as "some kind of dog food." Jets owner Barry Shenkarow was so incensed that he was prepared to sue.

"His comments about Europeans are all bad, all bad," said Sinden. "He's compulsive that way, and his opinions of how a player should play and what a player should be like are not valid. He has the forum, and a lot of the things

he says and does are not right and he gets away with talking that way. I think he was even chastised by Parliament once for comments he made about the country not getting involved in Iraq. I might have agreed with him then but I don't think I'd have ever said it on TV."

On March 23, 2003, viewers who tuned in late to *Coach's Corner* may well have thought they had stumbled onto *Question Period* instead. Cherry and MacLean used the entire spot not to discuss ice wars but real ones, specifically Canada's decision not to participate in the invasion of Iraq. Among other targets, he chastised Montreal fans for booing the US national anthem before a recent game. Uncharacteristically, MacLean had opened the floodgate by suggesting that "everybody wants to know what you think." With that invitation, Cherry made it abundantly clear that he was in favour of the US invasion and that every right-minded Canadian should be as well. He expressed his dismay that Canada would not support the United States in the operation in Iraq and took a swipe at MacLean for his neutrality.

Even though the rationale for invading Iraq has been largely discredited, Cherry's passion for righteous military engagement remains, as does his unwavering support for Canadian troops in Afghanistan. In an April 23, 2010, post on his site What's Left, Stephen Gowans raged against Cherry, calling him "a pugnacious, inarticulate, and bigoted blowhard" who believes that "Canada distinguishes itself on the world stage in two ways: by producing the world's best hockey players and the world's best soldiers." The context in which the column appeared was a discussion about whether Canadian troops in Afghanistan had been complicit in the torture of captured Afghans when they were turned over to state officials. It was Cherry's "unquestioning support of the Canadian military's role" in that country that

"Ron MacLean has great respect for Cherry. He really does. They get along really, really well. They know to a certain degree it's showbiz. Once they get off air they're pals, but Don, he's very caustic and MacLean knows how to pull his chain too. And when to pull him back. MacLean's a master at that, he really is! Cherry wouldn't be nearly as good without MacLean. He's a very knowledgeable straight man."

—Paul Henderson

so infuriated Gowans. That and presumably the fact that he had been employed by the tax-supported CBC to talk about hockey.

Cherry has been instrumental in bringing Canadian patriotism to the fore, many would argue. "He's brought so much respect to the armed forces and our veterans and everything like that," said Paul Henderson. "That's the Canadian aspect of it, that's what the real Canadians think."

Ron MacLean suggests that Cherry's love of the military and respect for authority informs his commentary. "My take on that is: it's Don. Don is a columnist and the finest traditions of that job demand that if you don't reveal something of yourself, it's all superficial. To his credit, Don has given you the best of himself, whether you agree with it or not is up to you. And there will be cries of jingoism and all these other complaints, but the fact is that this is a guy who doesn't delude himself one iota that a hockey player isn't a soldier—but he likens the battle-testedness needed in both professions."

Rick Salutin thinks that CBC elitism, and not Don Cherry, creates many of the problems. In a February 13, 2004, column Salutin points out that the mother network was founded (radio in 1936; television in 1952) by people, "who saw it as their mission to elevate Canadians above the benchmarks of hockey, beer, and doughnuts." He added that although

these experts were supposedly savvy in mass media, "they had an uneasy relationship with the masses. So they built *Hockey Night in Canada* [created by private broadcaster Foster Hewitt], but positioned it as an element of national culture and unity."

Given this great divide, it's little wonder that Cherry and the CBC have clashed on several occasions. In short, he may occasionally be way off base, but never in the eyes of his base. Serge Savard thinks that Cherry's popularity is at least partly due to the motherhood and apple pie causes that he embraces. Savard got to know Cherry when he was an assistant with Team Canada in 1976, in charge of the defence. A perennial all-star defenceman for Montreal before moving on to the Canadiens' front office as president, he has a fundamental disagreement with Don Cherry's philosophy.

"Now he's become more popular because he took this stance on armies and soldiers—which everyone agrees with," Savard said. "If I mention the name of a soldier who died last night, everyone starts to cry, and everyone will end up beside me, you know? We'll have a moment of silence. He took that really nationalist stand and he's an icon in English Canada. Not in French Canada because they don't watch him as much."

Little wonder. In January 2004, Cherry ridiculed "Europeans and French guys" for

Don Cherry poses in front of the Canadian flag with a replica of his beloved dog Blue during a 1993 photo shoot. Cherry's support of Canadian players and the Canadian military has drawn the broadcaster criticism.

Rick Stewart/Getty Images Sport

wearing hockey helmet visors and suggested that such equipment promoted more high-sticking by users against nonusers. The strong implication was that only cowards and/or wimps would wear such protection. CBC Television vice president Harold Redekopp called his comments, "inappropriate and reprehensible," and had, "stepped beyond the role." He announced immediate plans to put Cherry on a seven-second delay. Studies later showed that Cherry had been statistically correct: 22 percent of North Americans from outside of Quebec used them, compared with 40 percent of Quebecers and 50 percent of Europeans. However, Cherry's thesis about increased stick work by visor wearers proved false.

This was only the most recent of many such incidents. Upset that Quebec gold-medalist Olympian Jean-Luc Brassard had been chosen as Canada's flag-bearer at the 1998 Olympics in Nagano, he referred to him as "a French guy, some skier that nobody knows about." Delving into politics, he had also voiced his opinion on Quebec nationalists. "They don't like the Canadian flag but they want our money," he said. "We bail them out. I've never seen such a bunch of whiners in my life."

Dino Sisto, in an interview on *CBC Newsworld*, praised Cherry's hockey commentary but suggested that he has an ongoing problem with "ethnicities." When the controversial remarks made it to Parliament Hill, the Bloc Québécois went even further, calling Cherry's remarks racist. Predictably politicians were quick to weigh in, either condemning or defending the embattled icon. Speaking for the NDP, Jack Layton found the tirade offensive and waxed eloquent about watching great Francophone players of the past.

> "Don Cherry has brought a real flair to the game. They did a survey about 10 years ago on CBC—most influential sports personality in the country. MacLean was 8 percent and Cherry was 70 percent and then Brian Williams. No one else was over 10 percent. There are a lot of people who don't even watch the game anymore, but *Coach's Corner* comes on and the ratings go right up." —**Paul Henderson**

Conservative MP Peter MacKay felt that the whole episode had been blown out of proportion. "It seems to be more of a commentary on their style of play, as opposed to anything to do with their language or ethnic origins," MacKay argued. With his rap sheet, it wasn't surprising that the visor remarks were treated seriously. It was suggested that he may even have violated the Official Languages Act.

Not surprisingly Cherry's comments have earned him the reputation as being anti-French and anti-Quebec, although he denies the charge. A November 7, 2006, appearance at the House of Commons was greeted with enthusiastic cheers from many and jeers from Francophones when he was introduced by the Speaker of the House. "You can't please everybody," said Cherry afterward, clearly happy with all the attention. After a brief meeting with Prime Minister Harper, he divulged that he had been asked to run for office. "I'm too great on television," he claimed to have told the Prime Minister. He then gave Harper his highest compliment, calling him a "grinder" for supporting the troops.

Often the emotional impact of what Cherry says obscures the fact that he is factually correct. However in the Canadian political climate, facts often don't matter. Cherry will never be knighted for his diplomacy.

Darryl Sittler, a skilled player who is the embodiment of class on and off the ice, thinks that, on balance, Cherry has been good for the game. "He says things that sometimes other people might be thinking but Don has the nerve to say it," Sittler noted. "He's very colourful, his whole schtick is that, and he loves Canada, he loves our troops, and he's a passionate, sentimental guy and I think most hockey fans feel a connection with him because of that."

Former Leafs star Ron Ellis appreciates Cherry's support of Canadian players and sees shifts in his attitudes toward non-Canadians. "He's mellowing on the European players," Ellis said. "It's changing and they are becoming a force. I have no problem with him saying, 'Hey these guys are taking away a lot of jobs from Canadian players.' There's some truth to that. But it's an open market now, and a lot of our Canadian players are playing in Europe, so it's a two-way street. You love, love, love him or you hate him, but I do respect him."

Perhaps part of the "mellowing" process had to do with Swedish defenceman Nicklas Lidstrom captaining the Detroit Red Wings to a Stanley Cup championship in 2008, something Cherry said would never happen. In addition to Lidstrom, the Wings featured talented Europeans at every position except goal.

In fact Savard's biggest complaint about Cherry has nothing to do with language or ethnicity. He feels that Cherry is quite simply out of step with the times. "I know Don a lot," Savard said. "He's a very likable guy when you know him very closely but I just don't agree with the stance that he's taken all his life about hockey. He became very popular so people really listened to him and . . . that was not my view of the way hockey should be.

"Hockey changed in a bad way with the Flyers. Before that each team had an enforcer to protect the smaller players. We had John Ferguson, Boston had Ted Green, and so on. Those guys would fight once in a while but all enforcers in the league were playing regular, including Ferguson and Green. And then Philly took hockey back 20 years because they put three or even four enforcers on the team, and they won two Stanley Cups that way. Then minor hockey started to play like that.

"We had a tough time to get rid of that. We're just going through that right now. There's no more fighting in the game. It's too bad because most of our NHL leaders were American, and they thought fighting was part of the game. Many times in meetings they'd say, 'If you want to solve that, it could be solved in five minutes.' When we played the Flyers we, Montreal, didn't want to fight with them but we had to. They were jumping on you, and both teams would be penalized five minutes. They weren't penalized for being the instigator, and then the league brought in the instigator rule. They brought things in slowly, slowly. They allowed them to fight three times before they were kicked out of a game. It was ridiculous, and I kept saying, 'we're the only sport on earth that allows fighting in a game.' Now there's almost no fighting and the Canadiens have the best TV ratings they've ever had. Skill, that's what people like."

While he concedes that there will always be an intimidation factor in hockey and every other contact sport, Henderson agrees that Cherry's concentration on that aspect of the sport has been counterproductive.

"I think he goes overboard with the talk about rough stuff," Henderson said. "He says

nobody ever got hurt by a punch in the face. Are you kidding me!? Ask Nick Kypreos that! [Kypreos sustained a career-ending concussion in a fight with Ryan VandenBussche of the Rangers in a 1997 preseason game.] There are a lot of guys like that."

"Personally—and I've thought this for a long time—I don't think there's any place in the game anymore for fighting. Guys are too big and too strong. Guys who are 6′4″ or 6′6″ and weigh 235 pounds are going out there and grabbing someone who is 180 pounds. I mean, that doesn't make sense to me. That time in our society has gone. When we grew up you'd get into a fight, and when the fight was over we'd shake hands with the guy. In today's society you pull out a knife and knife a guy or shoot the guy. It's just a whole different world with these video games and everything like that. We've got a culture that needs to change."

It is no surprise to anyone that Dave "Tiger" Williams, the most penalized player in NHL history, is in Cherry's corner all the way. Tiger is practically a cover boy for Cherry's brand of rock 'em, sock 'em hockey. "I love Don Cherry," said Tiger. "Don Cherry is what we should tell our kids to be like as Canadians."

Reminded that Cherry has criticized Europeans, some of whom were his teammates in Toronto, Tiger is able to rationalize. "You can't be right all of the time. Canadians come first—that's all that Don Cherry always says. He's not asking for any more or any less. Cherry's not going to pick out a Canadian to criticize, so he may as well pick out a non-Canadian and if that happens to be your buddy boy Borje Salming or your buddy who played in Russia, that's life, man. That's just the way it goes. It's not very often that he's in left field—not very often."

"To me he's been great for hockey, and if a guy doesn't know otherwise then he just

> "Don is Don! He has an amazing following and his outspoken views on fighting sell more *Rock 'em, Sock 'em* videos and make him money, so don't expect any change. He is a TV personality, loved by many, reviled by many."
>
> —Alan Eagleson

doesn't know hockey. And the guy's not a Canadian he's just a typical—in Grapes' new word—he's just a typical Canadian pinko! And too many of those bleeding liberal hearts people live in this country, and it's too bad they don't move on."

Brian Conacher is the son of the great Lionel Conacher, generally acknowledged as Canada's greatest athlete. He's an astute student of the game of hockey. "In reality as a commentator I think he appeals to the lowest common denominator of fans, and he's become a little bit of a cult," Conacher said of Cherry. "Certainly I don't begrudge him his success. But to me, the thing I haven't liked about it is that it has turned hockey a little bit into *World Wrestling Entertainment*. It's made it almost at times like a circus and I don't like that.... The European influence in the National Hockey League has been largely positive. Don's is a bit of a T-shirt mentality. The other thing that I've always found kind of curious is, I don't think he's ever completed a thought. It's almost stream of consciousness."

How Hockey Explains Ron MacLean

In 2008, CBC faced off against Ron MacLean and lost. MacLean scored a $500,000 salary, with a huge assist from the Canadian viewing public. Average Canadians thought that their taxes would be well spent in providing a generous raise for MacLean. CBC switchboards were deluged with calls of support of the mild-mannered *Hockey Night in Canada* host. Emails arrived by the tens of thousands

and sports call-in shows were overwhelmed with calls. Boycotts of sponsors such as Labatt Brewery were threatened.

MacLean ended up with a reported $500,000 per year package. Since it's reasonable to assume that most petitioners were hauling in less than half a million, they must have seen something very special about the other half of the *Coach's Corner* tandem. They seemed to be saying, "If Cherry is making $700,000, then MacLean deserves something approaching that—perhaps in hardship pay alone." Indeed, an online poll conducted during negotiations indicated that 52 percent of viewers would cease to watch the show if MacLean were cut adrift.

This is not the kind of outcry that is precipitated by a foil, a flak, or a stooge. It was tangible recognition of a kind of genius that is rare in today's sports media: the ability to listen, to question, and to analyze in a cogent and articulate manner.

"My dad was stationed in Zweibrucken, Germany, and that's where I was born," MacLean said. "He then came to Nova Scotia for a brief stint and was stationed at Gorsebrook in Halifax. I was a year and four months old at the time. After a year's stay in Halifax, we went to Victoria and then dad was stationed in Whitehorse, Yukon, and that's where I got introduced to hockey.

"I was in Whitehorse from 1964 to 1968. When I was four or five years old, we had a neighbour across the street with a backyard rink. The family name was Clement, and I think the young guy's name was Bill. He

Ron MacLean has shared the *Coach's Corner* with Don Cherry for more than 20 years. MacLean often refers to his role as that of a referee, steering the unpredictable Cherry away from trouble.

Dave Sandford/ Getty Images

do to control that. We tend to be isolationists, we tend to look out for our own backyard but it's certainly not something I'm comfortable with. I'm not even comfortable with being Canadian only. I'm grateful to be Canadian but I'm one of six billion. I can't solve the perception, and that's where Don is right. If you're hosting from Studio 42 in Toronto, what is a person from Vancouver to think?"

Sometimes they think the worst. In 2010, MacLean became embroiled in a controversy centred on allegations that he had unfairly taken sides in a *HNIC* interview with NHL senior vice president of hockey operations and chief discipline dispenser Colin Campbell.

MacLean and Campbell were discussing the Vancouver Canucks' accusation against referee Stephane Auger that Auger had issued retaliatory penalties against forward Alex Burrows.

introduced me to the game along with a kid next door named Dwight Riondeau, and those two kids got me on skates when I was four in Whitehorse and I just took to the game."

In a sport often touted as the great Canadian unifier, MacLean is acutely aware that it can also be divisive and polarizing. Charges of bias toward one team or another are par for the course—and usually aimed at Cherry for his blatant cheering for Toronto and Boston. "You just can't win that one," MacLean admitted. "That's one of my deep concerns about our parochialism, our willingness to paint ourselves in our flag. It also tends to show up in provincialism and all those borders really bother me. There's nothing I can

Burrows charged that Auger had promised such revenge because he felt he had been "shown up" by the player in a previous game.

Vancouver players, coaches, fans, and media saw the interview as a blatant attempt to discredit Burrows and exonerate the referee. They were especially critical of MacLean, who they felt should have approached the topic with more balance and less editorial commentary. Ironically, MacLean, the Level 5 referee, was being accused of supporting a fellow referee with a bias that belies the impartiality of a referee. "I can't imagine [Auger] said, 'I'll get you,' we all agree on that," MacLean said at one point.

During the controversial *HNIC* spot, video

clips were played of Burrows purportedly feigning injuries and provoking other players into fights. After one clip, MacLean could not contain his sarcasm for what he believed to be an Academy Award worthy performance by Burrows. "Obviously when Burrows went down we all thought he was dead," MacLean said. But the comment that drew the most ire from people west of the Rockies was the one that followed: "And you can see Burrows say, 'Don't worry. Has he signalled five yet?'" suggesting that his injury was nonexistent.

On hearing the exchange between Campbell and MacLean, Canucks coach Alain Vigneault was indignant when interviewed on *HNIC's After Hours* postgame show. "I think it's really quite unfair for your boy Ron MacLean to go after Alex the way he did tonight, and [show] the footage that he did tonight," he said. Vigneault argued that the negative clips should have been balanced with footage of "Auger and Burrows skating 31 seconds together prior to the game." This was the period when the alleged threat from Auger was supposedly made.

Some in the media even referred to MacLean as a "shill" for the NHL. A *National Post* reporter turned MacLean's own words against him. MacLean had opened the interview with Campbell by saying, "Obviously ethics, integrity, competence, fairness, and a lot of issues were raised in the mix of that discussion." Said *Post* columnist Bruce Arthur, "You could have said that about [the *HNIC*] discussion too."

The unflappable MacLean dissects the incident and concedes that it might have been handled better. "If I had that one to do again I would have been just a little less cutting in what a referee might think the guy is doing as he looks for the call," he said. But like any good referee, MacLean sticks by his call. "There's no doubt in my mind that I built a case," he said. "We didn't run the clips completely smoothly either, but the point was I was building a case where this guy was a chronic offender and the league hasn't really been able to curb him of that."

Although hockey has brought him fame and fortune, MacLean is surprisingly grounded, careful to keep the game of hockey in perspective. Unlike his *Coach's Corner* partner, MacLean's form of patriotism is very Canadian.

"I'm grateful to be Canadian, always have been grateful," MacLean said. "But that's such happenstance, right? I take pride in the fact that hockey's what we're known for, but I really treat it more with a sense of great gratitude. Paul Henderson probably articulates it better than anybody. 'Okay, I scored the winner in Games 6, 7, and 8 and we won and so what? Is that all there is?' There were tens of thousands of Canadians in the stands in Buffalo at the 2010 World Juniors. There were 3,000 who trekked to Moscow in 1972. So we've always had that sense of joy about the game. It's nice when you win; I'm not downplaying the fact that somebody wins. But it's more a game of *try*. It's such a game of *try*. I love that about it.

"Sports, music, and the arts have the ability to do such wonderful things. They unify so you don't want to throw up borders; you don't want to throw up fences as to who the game belongs to. It's cost reliant and weather reliant, so it's hard to make it the world's game. So it is what it is. David Adams Richards, an author from New Brunswick, had a great saying: 'When are we most Canadian? When we drop the puck.' I just like that. I just think that sums it up."

Don Cherry may be Mr. Winter for many Canadians, but Ron MacLean is truly a man for all seasons.

3

HOW HOCKEY EXPLAINS MARSHALL McLUHAN

I**N ALL LIKELIHOOD,** Marshall McLuhan wasn't talking about hockey when he informed us that "the medium is the message." Nor was his prediction of a "global village" of collective identity a reference to the unifying effects of our national game. Born in Edmonton but raised and educated in Winnipeg, the eminent philosopher-scholar became the world's foremost communications theorist. He argued that the medium that allows society to interact is more significant than the actual message. But what if the medium for communication in Canada is hockey? In other words, did Foster foster hockey, or did hockey foster Foster?

In 1923, or approximately 55 years BC (Before Cherry), Foster Hewitt broadcast his first hockey game. For Canadians of subsequent decades, it was Hewitt who introduced them to hockey. Former Bruins coach Harry Sinden's experience was in many ways typical. "It was the radio at my grandmother's house. Traditionally in those days you'd go to Grandma's house for Sunday dinner. We didn't live that far away but we had to take a streetcar in Toronto and the game came on late and I don't think they did the first period. Sometimes it would come on with five minutes left in the first period. After dinner all the grown-ups would play cards on a big table and we'd have the hockey game on and I think there was a prize if you picked the winner. My sister and I could win 10 cents or 20 cents. I remember sitting there and falling asleep in those chairs listening to those games—and then waking up and finding out the Leafs lost and start crying. That's my first memory of the NHL."

Foster Hewitt was Canada's premiere hockey play-by-play broadcaster from the 1920s through the 1960s.

Toronto won the Cup in 1947, '48, and '49 and was the team of choice for most Canadians. Recalls Sinden: "That was the only game you could get on radio across Canada, west of Cornwall. So everyone was Foster Hewitt, Maple Leaf–oriented."

Ralph Mellanby, who as executive director for 19 years brought innovation and quality to *Hockey Night in Canada* and is largely responsible for its iconic status, has a similar story. Mellanby was enticed into hockey broadcasting by the unlikely siren call of Hewitt, the voice of the Leafs. As a child he would sit by the fire at his grandparents' home in Hamilton, Ontario, listening to the Leafs game on Saturday night. "There were no local hockey games on in those days," he said. "It was the only night that hockey was on and it was a great unifier of the country."

Little did young Ralph know that in a few short years he would team with Hewitt to bring hockey to a new generation of Canadian fans from coast to coast. "Foster and I did radio on CBC," Mellanby said. "Regional radio had just started when I began, with Montreal and Toronto. We *were* hockey on TV. The only hockey that was on was Wednesday night on CTV, and Saturday nights on CBC. Two nights a week you could watch hockey. That was it. That went on until Vancouver arrived in 1970.

"In the mid-1970s all that changed. But we still controlled even all the regional broadcasts in Edmonton and Calgary as part of their entry into the league. *HNIC* was the major domo anyways. For instance, I gave Ron MacLean his start on local TV at CITV in Edmonton. That was our farm system. . . . So if you were in Toronto when the regional telecast came on, it was still Bill Hewitt, Brian McFarlane, and Dave Hodge even though it was on CHCH Television. It was still *HNIC* and local. We were the image of the NHL.

We could control the programming. The same people who were doing *HNIC* were doing the Edmonton Oilers. In Vancouver it was Jim Robson. He was doing local television and also their national broadcast with Ted Reynolds and people like that."

Future *Hockey Night in Canada* mainstay Dick Irvin grew up far removed from Toronto in Regina, Saskatchewan. But Hewitt was still a household name. "By the time the game came on air the first period was just about over. Finally Foster's voice would come on and my mother would claim that as soon as he said, 'Hello Canada and hockey fans in the United States,' she could tell by the tone of his voice if the Leafs were ahead, behind, or tied. And she was darn pretty accurate."

Irvin's dad, Dick Irvin Sr., had been coach of the Leafs for nine years before taking over the reins of the cellar-dwelling Montreal Canadiens in 1940. Back home in Regina, young Irvin was frustrated by the lack of coverage of the Canadiens. "That was the worst part of the Leafs broadcast for me. I'd get so nervous when they looked at the out-of-town scoreboard. There were only two other games maximum at that time of course (in a six-team NHL). I was always afraid that they were going to give news that the Canadiens were losing."

The influence of those radio broadcasts was far-reaching. "My dad told me that in the mid-1930s, the Leafs and Red Wings took a barnstorming trip after the season and played a series of exhibitions in western Canada," Irvin recalled. "The CPR gave them two special cars on the Transcontinental and they would advertise in cities and towns where they were passing through that the train would be arriving at 3 in the afternoon and players would be available for autographs on the platform. The Leafs would be mobbed and the Red Wings were ignored. They didn't know who in the hell the Red Wings were but they all knew the Leafs. They wondered about this for the first couple of stops and then suddenly realized what it was—it was radio. They knew all these guys from radio, guys like Syl Apps. All Canadian kids wanted to be Syl Apps and most of us had never even seen him."

So great was the power of *Hockey Night in Canada* on radio that when Hewitt made a plea for wartime supplies or anything that would aid the war effort, the response was overwhelming. After the Japanese invaded Pearl Harbour, there was genuine fear that Canada's west coast was vulnerable to attack. The Defence Department was in desperate need of binoculars but the suppliers were overwhelmed with orders. They turned to Foster Hewitt for help. Foster made a single on-air appeal that garnered more than 1,100 sets of binoculars. So successful was the strategy that Hewitt made another plea the following Saturday night: "That's enough binoculars!" Keep in mind that this was radio— and then only once a week on Saturday night. "What was the country doing?" Dick Irvin asked rhetorically.

There are countless stories of lonesome Canadian soldiers stationed overseas being heartened by condensed recordings of Leafs broadcasts. Hewitt often worked on them until 4 in the morning to make sure they were just right.

The advent of television only added to the passion for the game across Canada. The first TV broadcast of a game was on October 11, 1952, from the Montreal Forum—and it was in French. The first telecast from Maple Leaf Gardens took place on November 1 of that same year. The arrival of televised hockey jump-started sales of the newfangled gadgets across the country. The symbiotic relationship between the sport and the small screen has thrived ever since.

This ushered in an era when Saturday night was the highlight of the week for many Canadians. A time when an entire country sat in the warm glow of the Dumont or Emerson or RCA to hear those much anticipated opening words: "Hello, Canada and hockey fans in the United States and Newfoundland." Soon the flickering black and white images appeared, accompanied by the familiar voices of Foster Hewitt or Danny Gallivan. It was a scene played out from seaside villages like Heart's Content, Newfoundland; and Briar Island, Nova Scotia; across the cities and towns of Quebec and Ontario; to the farmhouses of Manitoba and Saskatchewan; to the Alberta foothills and downtown Vancouver apartments.

The opening *HNIC* theme music was all that was needed to raise the hairs on the necks of countless Canadians, young and old. Music also signalled the end of the show. The expression "It ain't over till the fat lady sings," may have referred to Kate Smith, but in Canada, you knew that the game was over when a shapely and elegant lady named Juliette began to sing. No offense to "Canada's pet," but that's when many of us trundled off to bed.

Hockey Night in Canada has added much to our culture, even to our vocabulary. Hewitt's simple, "He shoots, he scores," quickly became the call heard in pickup and road hockey games everywhere. And then there was the "gondola." Who knew that a gondola could be more than a strange craft poled along Venetian canals by men in striped shirts and funny hats? And if Foster broadcast from a gondola, did that make him a gondolier? Young minds boggled at the very idea.

When it came to vocabulary building, however, Danny Gallivan was the Daniel Webster of the game. If you were a high school student, you quickly learned to emulate Gallivan and not Howie Meeker or other

Bill "Spaceman" Lee, who once pitched for the Montreal Expos in a city devoted to hockey, agrees about the unifying power of the game. "If it wasn't for *Hockey Night in Canada*, the population of Canada would be about one half," he suggested. "Every husband and wife would fight at the end of the hockey game and then they would patch things up by going to bed and producing another Canadian."

Dick Irvin Jr. (left) and Ron MacLean share the stage at the 2006 NHL TV Awards Show. Irvin's career on *Hockey Night In Canada* spanned from 1966 to 1999. MacLean joined the program in 1986.

Dave Sandford/Getty Images

commentators. "Jumpin Jehoshaphat" does not impress teachers, nor do terms such as "Gee Whiz" or "Gee Willikers." Gallivan was a wordsmith. When you had a book report due on Monday morning, just listening to Danny would arm you with enough descriptors to convince any English teacher that you had spent the weekend with your head in a book and not, perish the thought, wasting your time watching hockey on television.

Say that, for example, Ken Dryden made a stop that Gallivan termed a "scintillating save." Thus your review of *To Kill a Mockingbird* became a "scintillating novel of prejudice in the American south." And when author Harper Lee's villainous bigot Bob Ewell tried to stab young Jem at the book's conclusion, his knife "failed to negotiate contact" with the boy. Gallivan also gave us "cannonading drives," "larcenous saves," "rapier-like grabs," "yeoman service," and the immortal "spin-o-rama."

During his career from 1952 to 1984, Gallivan was doubtlessly responsible for a good many passing grades in English and the successful careers of God-knows-how-many members of Canada's literati. I call it the Gallivanization Effect on Canada and I like to think that Danny, if he were alive today, would approve of that term.

In fact, between Gallivan and his French counterpart Rene Lecavalier, the Montreal Canadiens and *HNIC* helped to pioneer the cause of bilingual education in Canada. Lecavalier educated the English-speaking audience of Quebec by using French terminology for all aspects of the game from puck (*la rondelle*) to "He shoots, he scores" ("*Il lance, il compte*"). In addition, Lecavalier was often the only voice of Les Canadiens for English-speaking fans of that team outside the belle province. Those fans had what teachers would love to bring to their classrooms: the ultimate motivation to learn the language.

Today the language on *HNIC* is uneven at best. There are still linguists in the booth, but few poets. Ron MacLean is an artful punster and a great communicator, but Don Cherry is challenged to rise above hockey lingo and "everythink like that." The thought of any student using Don as a model would make teachers rethink their choice of professions.

Richard Johnson, an American sports historian and fan of *Hockey Night in Canada*, thinks that the United States has nothing to equal it in terms of quality and impact. "There is no US sporting broadcast that would even compare. Just the introduction to the broadcast is unique. The new song is growing on me. The bagpipes. I'll get teary-eyed watching that. Bobby Orr skating in. Jean Beliveau. It's basically this pantheon of Canadiana. You pinch yourself if you're older because you saw these guys and they pay homage to the past. I like the fact that when they do a lead-in to a broadcast they show the city first—the river in Montreal, the lake in Toronto. They show what it's like outside, the people going in the arena, the human perspective, the grassroots

perspective. The broadcast doesn't have the personalities of the ESPN people. *Hockey Night in Canada* maintains its cultural integrity. Before anyone ever saw an NHL game they imagined themselves introduced by Foster Hewitt, having their abilities described by him to the country. The TV broadcasts had this wonderful British eccentricity about them because they started at 8:00 and it was halfway through the first period before the network picked it up. The Imperial Oil guy was as much a Canadian icon as anyone, as famous as anyone in the country."

A show watched by millions of rabidly partisan viewers is bound to produce critics, and *Hockey Night in Canada* is no exception. When there were only two Canadian franchises, accusations of bias were either from Montreal or Toronto fans.

"We were all accused of being homers," said Dick Irvin. "You should have seen the mail Danny and I used to get. When I started on the show in the mid-'60s, some of it was great and some of it was just awful. Then along came Vancouver, Calgary, Edmonton, and other Canadian teams and the mail dropped off because the country was no longer polarized. You were either a Leafs fan or you were for the Canadiens whether you lived in Montreal or Saskatoon. It really showed in the reaction; it was quite obvious. Once those other regions got teams to cheer for it changed."

As executive director, Mellanby got it from both sides and in both official languages. He was sensitive to the charges and took steps to eliminate any perception of favouritism. "I fielded much of the feedback myself, although not necessarily the French," Mellanby said. "There were messages from people who were mad at Dick Irvin and Mickey Redmond up in the booth or with Danny Gallivan. Montreal would win four straight in the Stanley Cup series and they'd all be mad because they were Toronto fans or Red Wings fans. It was always the bias issue, but there was never any bias. When Danny and Bill [Hewitt] retired, that's when I brought in Bob Cole, who's been there for 30 or 40 years. I wanted a national crew and a national announcer so they couldn't say, hey that's a Toronto guy or he's a Montreal guy. That led me to the Ron MacLeans and to the Bob Coles. It changed the face of *HNIC* into a national broadcast."

Mellanby wasn't afraid to take chances, to shake things up and innovate. Some things worked and some didn't. He recalls one failed experiment. "We put a mic on the bench once. I had always wanted to do that. The first time we used it to listen on the bench, my friend Bobby Clarke called referee Bruce Hood 'a —ing ——'. We had to get rid of the mics, although I did have a priest write me a letter that was very interesting. He said don't get rid of the mic, just tell the players to stop swearing. Well, that was impossible. Those were the days of 'Give me a Pepsi ——ing Cola.' Those guys didn't know how to *speak* without swearing. They spoke profanity."

One experiment that did work well for Mellanby was Howie Meeker. He hired the former Toronto Maple Leaf because Meeker was passionate about the game and how it should be played. He was smart enough to just turn him loose without a script. "Mellanby has a lot of positive things about him," said Meeker, "but the most positive was that he left me alone. He used to say, 'Howie, I don't care what you say but don't hang us.' He would come in some nights and there'd be players coming on and he'd say, 'Howie, what are you looking for tonight?' I said, 'Ralph, I sit there and I don't look for anything. If I see it and it's interesting, I do it. If I look for it, I never see it. Mellanby was very, very good with me. It didn't pay us any money in those days related to what they're getting now but it paid off in other aspects of life."

Meeker used *HNIC* as his pulpit to preach the importance of skills to young hockey players. One of his best students was Mellanby's son Scott, who went on to a stellar NHL career. If Meeker owed Mellanby anything for hiring him it was repaid a thousand times by the hockey knowledge he imparted to Scott at his hockey schools. "He played 20 years in the National Hockey League," Meeker said proudly.

Hockey Night in Canada was a rite of passage for generations of young Canadians. Indeed youngsters in Newfoundland outports and Vancouver high-rises were sharing the same experience.

The list of Mellanby hires that became household hockey names is long and distinguished: Howie Meeker, Dave Hodge, Dick Irvin, Dan Kelly, Ted Darling, Gary Dornhoefer, Mickey Redmond, Jim Robson, Ted Reynolds, Babe Pratt, Don Whitman, and Don Cherry.

"There was nothing like *Hockey Night in Canada* in its prime," said Mellanby. "The only thing that can compare—and I did 13 of them—were the Olympics. *Hockey Night* bought everyone in the household together across the country. I don't think there will ever be anything like that again.

"It's changed dramatically with the growth of TSN and Sportsnet. I did it for almost a quarter of a century and it isn't the Holy Grail anymore. It doesn't get the same numbers; it's just changed so dramatically. It isn't the influence it used to be. Those days are gone.

They are totally obliterated because with Calgary, Edmonton, and Vancouver, and soon Winnipeg and Quebec back, it's become a very regional network. If you're a guy in Calgary, you're rooting for the Flames. You don't root for an easterner.

"It's still an important part of hockey but now if you're a Leaf fan you can get the Sportsnet Leaf package or if you're a Montreal fan you get the TSN or RDS or Montreal package. No longer is everyone watching the same show coast to coast."

Howie Meeker participates in the 1998 Hockey Hall of Fame induction ceremonies. Meeker, a former NHL Rookie of the Year, entered the Hall of Fame as a broadcaster after a lengthy career with *Hockey Night In Canada* and TSN.

Bruce Bennett Studios/Getty Images

41

HOW HOCKEY EXPLAINS QUEBEC

How Hockey Explains the Quiet Revolution

"I T ALL BEGAN in Boston on March 13, 1955," recalls Jean Beliveau. Beliveau was on the Boston Garden ice that night when the Montreal Canadiens were playing the Bruins. With six minutes left in the game and Boston leading 3–1, Montreal removed goaltender Jacques Plante in favour of a sixth attacker. After the ensuing faceoff, Maurice "Rocket" Richard and Bruins 6′2″, 185-pound defenceman Hal Laycoe chased the puck down the ice. "Laycoe was not a dirty player," remembers Beliveau of the Sutherland, Saskatchewan native. "He was a good player—a good defenceman." The two men had been teammates and occasional tennis partners in Montreal a few years earlier. As Richard wheeled toward the net, Laycoe's stick made contact with his head and the referee raised his arm to signal a penalty.

When the Bruins finally touched the puck to stop play, Richard saw red, literally and figuratively. Laycoe's stick had opened a gash and blood was pouring out. The cut would later take eight stitches to repair. Whenever Richard was angry his dark eyes bore holes in the enemy. At least one opponent called it the look of "an escaped mental patient." Sportswriters dubbed it "the Rocket's red glare." He charged toward Laycoe, who had dropped his gloves, stick, and glasses in anticipation of a fight. Richard kept his stick and took a mighty swing at Laycoe, landing a glancing blow to his shoulder and face.

After some further scuffling, it looked like peace had been restored. The players were under control and Richard's weapon had been confiscated. Suddenly the Canadiens star broke free, grabbed another stick, and

Maurice Richard led the Montreal Canadiens to eight Stanley Cups, including four straight from 1957 to 1960. The Hall of Famer was the first player to score 50 goals in a single NHL season.

AP Images

43

assaulted Laycoe two more times. The last blow broke the stick. Richard found a third stick and struck yet another blow against the defenceless Bruin defenceman. With blood in his eyes, Richard grabbed linesman Cliff Thompson, who he felt had been overly aggressive in his peacemaking. He punched him twice in the face. When the ugly spectacle was at last over, Laycoe was given five minutes for high-sticking and Richard was assessed a game misconduct.

Little did anyone at the Garden know at the time, but they had just witnessed the opening salvo of Quebec's Quiet Revolution. The American Revolution had started not far away at the Battles of Lexington and Concord on April 19, 1775, with "the shot heard 'round the world." In the land of Richard's ancestors, the French Revolution had begun with the storming of the Bastille. In typical Canadian fashion, hockey sticks, and not guns, were the weapons of choice in this uprising. In fact, as revolutions go, this one would prove to be largely nonviolent despite the donnybrook that started it and the righteous backlash that would soon follow. Nevertheless, radical social change in Quebec was underway.

Everyone knew that the other skate was yet to drop. The Bruins were rumoured to be asking for a lifetime ban for the Habs star player. Finally, Boston general manager Lynn Patrick demanded an immediate suspension for at least the remainder of the year and the playoffs.

The ultimate decision was in the hands of NHL President Clarence Campbell. For agonizing hours and days, anxious Quebecers awaited the news. On March 16, 1955, after deliberating for several hours with representatives of each team and game officials, the punishment was announced to the hockey world. Richard would indeed be suspended for the remainder of the season—*and* the playoffs.

The outrage throughout Quebec and especially in Montreal was instantaneous and visceral. It was as if all the wrongs committed against the citizenry by the English establishment had built to this one moment in history. The provincial media, both English and French, were united in their rage. With not-so-subtle overtones of the guillotine and the French Revolution, one French newspaper's editorial cartoon featured Campbell's bloody head on a platter. The mood was growing uglier by the minute. A caller to Campbell's secretary said, "Tell Campbell I'm an undertaker and he'll be needing me in a few days." There was even a threat to blow up the Sun Life Building where the NHL offices were housed.

It wasn't the first time that the population of Quebec had rushed to the defence of their beloved cultural icon. When Richard attacked Bob Bailey of the Leafs in a game a few months earlier, his fans took up a collection to pay his fine. Richard in turn gave the largesse to charity. There was little question that Quebec's population felt discriminated against and that Richard had become their martyr. "If Richard's name was Richardson you would have given a different verdict," one fan wrote to the NHL head office.

As fate would have it, the Canadiens were at home to play Detroit the night after Campbell's edict. It was St. Patrick's Day. In an ill-conceived show of bravado, Clarence Campbell attended the game and was immediately confronted with open hostility inside and outside the Forum. Tomatoes, eggs, shoes, bottles, and finally smoke bombs were thrown in his direction. As the smoke shrouded the stands near the NHL president's seat, the panicked Forum crowd rushed the exits. Campbell and his entourage retreated to the referees' dressing room. The game was defaulted 4–1 by the Canadiens, but as their coach Dick

Maurice Richard battles for the puck while being checked by an opponent in the 1940s. Richard played in every NHL All-Star Game from 1947 to 1959.

Bruce Bennett Studios/Getty Images

The night after NHL president Clarence Campbell suspended Maurice Richard for the remainder of the 1955 season and playoffs, Campbell attended the Canadiens–Red Wings game in Montreal. Tomatoes, eggs, shoes, bottles, and even smoke bombs were thrown in his direction. Here a fan is restrained from access to the NHL president. Getty Images

Irvin Sr. conceded later, "the people didn't care if we got licked 100–1 that night."

Outside the Forum, a full-fledged riot was underway. Incensed fans, emboldened by liquor, roamed St. Catherine's Street, breaking windows, setting fires, and committing other acts of vandalism. The unrest continued for several hours, during which a dozen policemen and 25 rioters were injured. There were more than 70 arrests. It was an ugly scene that was etched in the minds of Quebecers and Canadians for different reasons. Most Canadians outside of Quebec saw it as a riot over a hockey game. Many Quebecers saw it as the Plains of Abraham revisited. Asked recently if the riot was the result of another perceived attack on Quebec from English Canada, the ever-diplomatic Beliveau would only chuckle and say it was, "a good combination of things."

The next day Richard made a radio appeal asking that calmer heads prevail but even his mea culpa came with a whiff of burning martyr. Striking a *forgive them for they know not what they do* tone, he concluded with a promise of resurrection. "Because I always try so hard to win and had my troubles in Boston, I was suspended," Richard said. "At playoff time it hurts not to be in the game with the boys. However, I want to do what is good for the people of Montreal and the team. So that no further harm will be done, I would like to ask everyone to get behind the team and to help the boys win from the New York Rangers and Detroit. I will take my punishment and come back next year to help the club and the younger players to win the Cup."

Some 56 years later, Beliveau vividly remembers the implications of the crime and the punishment. "It was when he suspended

Maurice for the rest of the year *and* the play-offs that the fans got upset. They didn't accept that," Beliveau said.

"Then when Mr. Campbell attended the game that's when it all started. Certainly, speaking as a player and a teammate, taking Maurice out of your team for the play-offs was a major blow. We thought maybe for the rest of the year but when the playoff was included…" His voice trails off, no doubt still thinking about the Stanley Cup that got away.

Even today there are very disparate descriptions of the violence that led to the suspension. The Montreal Canadiens' current website scarcely mentions Richard's stick attacks on Laycoe but describes the gash that Laycoe inflicted on him. A recent *Maclean's* magazine article, on the other hand, asserted that "Richard smashed three hockey sticks over the back and head of Bruins defenceman Hal Laycoe…"

After Maurice Richard was suspended for the balance of the 1955 season and playoffs, incensed fans roamed Montreal's St. Catherine's Street, breaking windows, setting fires, and committing other acts of vandalism. A dozen policemen and 25 rioters were injured. There were more than 70 arrests. Getty Images

The 2005 movie *Rocket: The Maurice Richard Story*, directed by Charles Binamé and shot in Quebec in English and French, is surely one of the most fawning biopics in recent memory. A *New York Times* review described his portrayal as "a fighter against discrimination and injustice—a combination of Jackie Robinson and the Gary Cooper version of Lou Gehrig." Charles Foran, in his *Maclean's* review of *Rocket* said: "Richard's a romantic hero assigned the task of building a nation—or boosting the spirit of a nation-in-embryo, perhaps—through his brilliant

---

"When you play for the Montreal Canadiens it's like you got a degree from Harvard!"

—**Chris Chelios, after being traded from Montreal to Chicago**

---

goal scoring and righteous anger alike. As presented in *Maurice Richard*, the fiery on-ice skill and off-ice outrage at the injustices suffered by the French in both the NHL and within their own society are equally intrinsic to Richard's self-definition as a Quebecer, and a man."

Assuming that the injustices that most French Quebecers suffered included the Church, the movie portrayal also ignores the inconvenient fact that Richard and his wife Lucille were devout, lifelong Catholics who raised seven children in the faith. It is patently ridiculous to ascribe all these complex political motives to an essentially simple man who once admitted, "Hockey's the most important thing in my life."

Contemporary reports of the incident and its aftermath were similarly divided. Some accounts had Richard as the villain, plain and simple. Others had the linesman holding Richard's arms while Laycoe was allowed to pummel him.

The front page headline of the March 18, 1955, edition of the *Globe and Mail* screamed "Richard Riot Ends Game" with a subhead adding "NHL Chief Attacked, Mob Loots 30 Stores." The article spoke of crowds "running amok," and the "unbelievable hysteria and violence of revenge-crazed hockey fans." The September 17, 1955, issue of *Maclean's* magazine reported that Richard's attack and his subsequent suspension by the NHL resulted in "the most destructive and frenzied riot in the history of Canadian sport."

A follow-up piece by Sidney Katz in *Maclean's* six months after the riot strongly hinted that there was something much bigger than hockey behind the rioting. The article, titled "The Strange Forces Behind the Richard Riot," described a scene of utter anarchy inside and outside the Forum. After the tear bomb exploded, "the acrid yellowish fumes… sent the crowd rushing to the exits, crying, shrieking, coughing, and retching." The fiery rhetoric continues. "For a time it looked as if a lynching might even be attempted," he wrote, and "rioters were savagely chanting… 'Kill Campbell! Kill Campbell!' The explosion of the bomb was the last straw in a long series of provocative incidents that swept away the last remnants of the crowd's restraint and decency." The scene described outside was "a swath of destruction," and the article reached its hyperbolic zenith with "It looked like the aftermath of a wartime blitz in London."

Quoting criticism from a London, England, newspaper, he finally got to the crux of the matter. "Frank D. Corbett, a citizen of Westmount, expressed an opinion about the riot which many people thought about but few discussed publicly. In a letter to the editor of a local paper, he said bluntly that the outbreak was symptomatic of racial ill-feeling.

'French and English relationships have deteriorated badly over the past 10 years, and they have never been worse,' he wrote. 'The basic unrest is nationalism, which is ever-present in Quebec. Let's face it…the French-Canadians want the English expelled from the province.'"

The aftermath of that incident transformed Quebec. Professor Olivier Bauer of the Universite de Montreal sees it as a defining moment. Said Bauer, "It was definitely the beginning of the moment when Quebec arrived and citizens were proud to be Quebecers—maybe not because of the riot itself, but very quickly the *interpretation* of the riot. It was like the beginning of the great awakening of Quebec identity and Quebec pride. For many it was the beginning of the Quiet Revolution." Of course the ground had been well prepared for such a change. The church had retarded Quebec's economic and social growth and had wielded an influence that was paternal and suffocating. When change did come, it came with the speed and fury of a Richard breakaway, and like the Rocket, once started it couldn't be stopped.

Odd to think that Richard played a role in this massive political and social shift, especially given the apolitical stance that he maintained. Stranger still that Richard, the very Catholic miracle worker, used his biggest miracle to create a decidedly more secular society. At best he was an accidental revolutionary.

How Hockey Explains Toronto vs. Montreal

If the concept of two solitudes was geographical instead of historical and cultural, they would be represented by the cities of Toronto and Montreal. The first is the symbolic bastion of English Canada, with all its wealth and power. The second is the epicentre of French Canada, the fortress that preserves and protects the dreams of a people. In actual fact, both are now cosmopolitan centres with an ethnic diversity that goes well beyond French and English. Actually Quebec City is much more French than Montreal and Calgary is much more English than Toronto.

In the world of hockey, the two ancient franchises were once the only choices for Canadian hockey fans. Sure there were pockets of Bruins fans on the East Coast and Red Wings fans in southern Ontario, but the real national faceoff was between Toronto and Montreal. As their fortunes have risen and fallen across the history of the game, one thing has remained constant. The two teams and their fans do not like each other very much.

Longtime Canadiens broadcaster Dick Irvin Jr. stands next to the pillar honouring his father, the late Dick Irvin Sr., during the unveiling of the Head Coaches section in Builders Row at Montreal's Bell Centre in 2008.
Getty Images

And that's why it's difficult for either Leafs or Habs fans to reconcile the fact that it was the Toronto Maple Leafs who saved the Montreal franchise.

Toronto's anti-French, anti-Catholic Conn Smythe was the key player in keeping the Canadiens franchise alive.

Flashback to another era. Eight-year-old Dickinson Irvin Jr. was crying his eyes out. Slouched in the backseat of his dad's green 1938 Buick, his world suddenly seemed unfair and uncertain. It was April 13, 1940, and the Irvin family had just left Maple Leaf Gardens, where they had watched the New York Rangers capture the Stanley Cup with a 3–2 overtime win against the Toronto Maple Leafs, coached by his dad, Dick Irvin Sr.

Young Dick's love for the Leafs was inextricably tied to his love for his father, and he was inconsolable. Aside from the occasional sobs escaping from the youngster, the car ride was a quiet one. Father, mother, and son drove on a while before the father broke the silence. Keeping his eyes on the postgame traffic ahead, he asked, "Do you think you could cheer for the Montreal Canadiens?" The question came out of the blue and took the young man completely by surprise. It seemed bizarre, completely out of context. Why would his father pose such a ridiculous question? And at a time like this? For one thing the Leafs were not only his team, but they were his father's employer. For another the Canadiens were a truly god-awful hockey team. If the comment had been designed as a joke to lift his spirits, it had failed miserably. *There is no way I could cheer for the Montreal Canadiens*, he thought to himself as he stared out at the city lights. One week later, on Sunday, April 21, the Irvin family left their sublet duplex at 200 Millwood Road in the Davisville district of Toronto to drive back home to Regina, Saskatchewan. "By then, I was a Canadiens fan," recalled Irvin.

What young Irvin hadn't known in the immediate wake of the Cup final was what his father had known for some time—that when the 1940–41 season began, the senior Irvin would be behind the bench in Montreal, coaching the Canadiens.

It is hard for most Canadians to remember a time when the Montreal Canadiens were not a major force on the ice and at the box office, but the aura that is attached to them was not always there. It was once more of a stench than an aura because in 1940 the Canadiens stunk.

How bad was it? The Montreal Maroons had folded in 1938 and the city was now the sole preserve of the Canadiens—and they *still* couldn't draw a crowd. The Depression was still taking its toll and the Second World War was just underway. Hockey was not a

Conn Smythe and Maurice Richard

The one French Canadien player that Conn Smythe not only respected but also coveted was Rocket Richard, probably because he fit Smythe's criteria of being able to "beat 'em in the alley," as well as on the ice. Smythe offered $25,000 for Richard back in the '40s and once, when a reporter asked him his opinion on a famous brawl between the Canadiens' star and Bob Bailey, he offered, "We've got to stamp out that kind of thing, or people are going to keep on buying tickets." On another occasion, Smythe prevented Richard from returning to the ice in a blind rage, saving him from a possible suspension. "I admire the man tremendously," he once said. "Would have given anything to have him play for me..." His admiration didn't get in the way of him offering up verbal abuse. In a game in Montreal, "some joker, no doubt [Frank] Selke," arranged for him to be seated next to Richard's mother-in-law. Pretty soon the two clashed and they continued their verbal sparring throughout the game. Finally, Smythe paused long enough to ask her what she'd been saying in French. "That's where I have it on you, Mr. Smitty," she replied. "I can tell you what I think of you in both languages."

> "It was like there were nine months of hockey and three months of bad ice."

> —Former major league pitcher Bill Lee, after being traded from the Boston Red Sox to the Montreal Expos

priority. Dick Irvin Sr. was called upon not so much for his skills as a coach but for his skills as a miracle worker—to resuscitate the near moribund body of a dying franchise.

For many hockey fans, Dick Irvin Jr. is synonymous with the Montreal Canadiens and *Hockey Night in Canada*. Along with play-by-play man Danny Gallivan, Irvin was the voice of the Canadiens for English-speaking Canada for parts of four decades. Despite describing himself as a "he shoots, he scores kind of guy," the Hall of Fame son of a Hall of Fame father was a smooth-talking analyst and a skillful interviewer. He remains a perceptive student of hockey history and Montreal's place in it.

It's difficult today to imagine a time when the Montreal Canadiens did not draw capacity crowds, a time when they weren't the darlings of the province. "It didn't matter if they were the Flying Frenchmen in 1940," says Irvin. "The team was on the verge of going out of business. My dad came here when the Canadiens were coming off a year [1939–40] when they won 10 games. They almost went out of business. Montreal had lost the Maroons in 1938 for lack of interest and the fellow who owned the Canadiens—Senator Donat Raymond—also owned the Forum. He had previously been a part owner of the Maroons as well before they folded. He had to make up his mind whether he was going to fold the Canadiens or keep it going. They had 1,500 to 2,000 people at the games."

The Forum only sat 9,500 in those days and they still couldn't come close to filling it. "What happened was that the NHL—guys like Conn Smythe and Lester Patrick—got together and said we can't lose Montreal. Montreal is supposedly where it all started [hockey]; *so we can't lose Montreal!* The NHL couldn't go from two teams to no teams in just a couple of years, they didn't want that so they had to keep it going."

There was a decided lack of discipline on the Montreal team at the time. Players would show up to play a game and then go home. "It was just a shambles," said Irvin. "My dad had been coaching the Leafs for nine years—and he and Smythe had agreed that that would be his last year. They got within one or two wins of the Cup in the final year and I always wondered—if they had won the Cup that year, would his run there have kept going? Anyway, Smythe offered my dad a job in the organization somewhere—and there weren't many of them in those days—but my dad didn't want to do it. He wanted to go home to Saskatchewan and get back in the meat business. But Smythe said at this NHL meeting: 'I have just the guy who's going to go in there and straighten that thing out—Irvin.' So he talked to my dad about it. And when my dad was coaching his last game with the Toronto Maple Leafs he knew."

The day after the Leafs' defeat, Irvin boarded a train to Montreal and from there journeyed north to Senator Raymond's home. The two men spent a full day discussing the Montreal situation before Irvin finally signed the contract that would forever change the face of hockey in Quebec. The recovery was far from instantaneous. Before they could get back in the black they would have to get rid of the brown. When the Canadiens skated on the ice they were regularly greeted by a sea of empty brown seats. "The Forum was all brown," recalled Irvin. "They had all brown benches. The so-called box seats were individual chairs and the people used to get mad at the referees and throw the chairs on the ice."

When Irvin took over the reins, there were only two players that he deemed to be of NHL calibre. One was Ray Getliffe, who had played in Boston and had been traded to Montreal that year, and the other was Toe Blake. Irvin promptly brought in Elmer Lach and Ken Reardon. The next year he added Butch Bouchard. And then, in 1942–43, one Maurice Richard joined the team. To top it off, they managed to get the best goalie in hockey from the senior ranks. Bill Durnan had had a bad experience with the Toronto Maple Leafs at training camp and as a result had vowed never to play in the National Hockey League. After an ardent and persistent courtship, the Montreal brain trust finally signed him to a contract an hour before the first game of the 1943–44 season. The additions jelled into a team and the Canadiens did not lose a game at home all year long. "That was the start," said Irvin Jr. "The Rocket became the Rocket that year. You see the league did that. The league had a big role to play in that. Dad came in here and slowly things changed."

From the low point represented by the 1939–40 season, the Canadiens grew into one of the great sports franchises in North American history. People compare them to the New York Yankees and occasionally the Boston Celtics, but in reality there is no comparison because the arena that they skate in is a cultural one.

Irvin Jr. puts the Canadiens' rise in perspective. "From 1944 when Rocket started, they won two Cups in three years and finished first four years in a row. Finishing first meant a lot more then than it does now. There really hasn't been an empty seat at a hockey game since. If you look at attendance figures at the Montreal

Forum over the years, they're different. There would be 18,100 one night and 16,200 the next night. The difference was standing room. There were nights in the '80s and the '90s when Hartford would come in and you could maybe shoot a cannon off in the standing area—but then Boston came in on a Saturday night and they were standing three deep. They were both officially capacity crowds."

The salvaging by Smythe and others of the Montreal Canadiens franchise also kickstarted one of the great rivalries in sport. Jean Beliveau recalls the matchups with Toronto as a number of battles in a prolonged war. "Don't forget at the time before the expansion of the league we used to play each other *14 times*," Beliveau said. "A lot of people from Quebec adopted the Canadiens and we were very successful and they took a lot of pride in being supporters of the Canadiens. Still today, this whole rivalry is still here. Every time Toronto is in Montreal the Leafs have lots of fans, just like the Canadiens have lots of fans in Toronto.

"The rivalry is still there with Toronto, even if the players are all pretty young and they don't know the history and haven't witnessed what it was 40 years ago. But it's good for the sport as long as it doesn't get too crazy."

While Montreal had no problem recruiting from across Canada, the Leafs under Smythe were reluctant to explore Quebec for prospects. Sports historian Richard Johnson elaborates. "The Canadiens took full advantage of signing Protestant, English-speaking players, but Conn Smythe would be *damned* if he'd sign a French-speaking player. He'd rather be fried in his own oil. You could name the French Canadians on his teams on the fingers of one hand."

When Dick Irvin Sr. died in May 1957, his funeral was in Montreal but he was buried at Mt. Pleasant Cemetery in Toronto. Even in death he seemed torn between two great hockey cities. His old boss and friend

Conn Smythe arranged for six members of the 1932 Stanley Cup–winning Leafs to carry the coffin from the hearse to the gravesite. After the brief but moving ceremony, Irvin Jr. was leaving when he was hailed by a man with a harsh voice. It was Smythe. "I was 25 years old and I had never met the man. He said, 'Just don't you forget, your father saved hockey in Montreal.' And, of course, that's something you *don't* forget."

Thus did Smythe send his boy Dick to save the Canadiens. Did the English paternalism toward Quebec finally work in their favour? In the heaven and hell of the NHL, it is sometimes hard to see who is God and who is the devil. The uniforms keep changing. In any case, it is probable that one cannot exist without the other.

How Hockey Explains Quebec Culture

If hockey is culture, Quebec is surely the most sophisticated and aesthetic place on earth. David Asper, businessman and professor of law at the University of Manitoba, posed the question during the 2010 outcry that erupted over Prime Minister Harper's consideration of federal funding of a hockey arena to house a new NHL franchise in Quebec City. Asper argued that such funding was entirely appropriate and consistent with funding within the traditional cultural milieu of ballerinas, actors, and musicians. "To define culture narrowly, without including sports, is elitist," he concluded. In Quebec, where high culture sometimes includes high sticking, this was not news.

It was radio and then television that spread the hockey culture throughout the province. Television came along just in time to showcase Quebec's most exciting and talented teams. Quebecers could see themselves reflected back through these budding hockey legends: Rocket Richard, Jean Beliveau, and the rest. The distinctive joie de vivre, the passion, the graceful art that supports the utilitarian craft of hockey were there for Quebecers and the rest of Canada to see. They saw that their own Flying Frenchmen were unlike any other team in the league, distinctive in style and substance. They were often so fast and so skilled that they made other teams look like lumbering Neanderthals with clubs. The province was enthralled. The people were proud. The hockey culture was entrenched.

There is another divide within Quebec—a third solitude if you like—and this one exists between Montreal and the Rest of Quebec, most notably Quebec City. Montreal has always been the business and power centre. It has always welcomed other cultures and is ethnically diverse. Quebec proudly guards and preserves its Frenchness.

Professor Bauer elaborates, "For me what is very important—and it's not easy to say here in Quebec—is the Habs are the team of Montreal first, not of the rest of Quebec."

5

HOW HOCKEY EXPLAINS RELIGION

Paul Henderson (centre, in the arms of an unidentified teammate) celebrates after scoring the series-winning goal in Game 8 of the 1972 Summit Series between Canada and the Soviet Union. The goal marked one of the great miracles in the history of Canadian hockey.

Melchior DiGiacomo/ Getty Images

Is HOCKEY CANADA'S RELIGION or merely the opiate of its people? Was Paul Henderson's Summit Series goal miraculous or merely fortuitous? Was Alan Eagleson driven from hockey's Garden of Eden for his original sin or was his fall from grace due to garden-variety greed?

"Hockey is the religion of Canada." So speaketh Dave "Tiger" Williams, who in terms of career penalty minutes certainly qualifies as the biggest sinner in NHL history. Williams was a hockey enforcer in the '70s and '80s, most notably with the Toronto Maple Leafs and Vancouver Canucks. He is known to have put the fear of God in countless opponents. He said of hockey: "It is the only common religion that we all agree with in all of Canada—the one faith that ties us together from coast to coast and from the US border to the Arctic Ocean. Whether you're a new Canadian or born here—and we all came here on a boat sometime—it is the religion of our country and it's the fabric that holds us together. It doesn't matter if it's the Olympics, the World Hockey Championships, the Juniors at Christmastime, whatever—it's what we're all about, what we believe in."

Where hockey is concerned, Tiger is a fundamentalist. He remains fiercely devoted to the game and is intolerant of hockey atheists, those who dismiss the game as irrelevant to our daily lives. "Quite frankly the ones who don't agree are, in Don Cherry's words, probably 'pinkos' teaching at a university," said the Saskatchewan native. "We should send them back to where they came from. It is our religion, the fabric and the most important thread in our country, bar none."

Is God even a hockey fan? And if He is, what team does he cheer for? The New Jersey Devils? Unlikely, but then He is renowned for His sense of irony. Of course, some in Quebec still await the second coming of the Quebec Nordiques after they were cast into exile. Are the Nordiques God's chosen people? Their followers certainly claim to be persecuted. If the biblical parallel holds, the Nords should part the St. Lawrence and return to the Promised Land 40 years after leaving for Denver—2035 to be precise. Mark it on your calendar.

Hockey is rife with religious symbolism. Gretzky was known as "The Great One," Mario Lemieux was "The Magnificent One," and Sid Crosby is "The Next One." Like Greek gods, hockey gods are numerous. Practically every team has at least one.

Although he has overseen the spread of this hockey religion to some far-flung places, NHL Commissioner Gary Bettman doesn't have the stature to call himself the Pope of Pucks, so perhaps Don Cherry could assume that symbolic role. His proclamations are unerring, at least in his own mind, and compared to his suit collection, papal gowns seem positively understated.

After Paul Henderson had scored the winning goal in Game 8 of the '72 Summit Series, CBC television producer Ralph Mellanby found him in the Team Canada dressing room. "I'll never forget it," Mellanby said. "Paul looked like a truck had run over him. He was sitting there stunned and I talked to him and he didn't even hear me."

Even today, Henderson has no idea why he called Peter Mahovlich off the ice, or why he jumped on in his place. Was divine intervention involved? "I tell you what," he said. "I was not a Christian in '72. I'm a very devout Christian today and when I get to heaven and have a chance, I'm going to say, 'Okay, tell me about this goal back in '72.'"

Henderson's linemate and close friend Ron Ellis still shakes his head at the events that unfolded in that game. One thing is certain, a couple of players with Bible names—Peter and Paul—changed places at just the right time. Was what followed miraculous? You decide. "Paul calling [Pete] Mahovlich off was not only uncharacteristic of him, it's uncharacteristic of any professional hockey player," suggested Ellis. "But that is exactly true because I was sitting right beside Paul and that is precisely what happened.... Our line came off the ice with a little over two minutes left and Harry Sinden said to us, 'Get ready, you're going back,' meaning after Esposito, Cournoyer, and Peter Mahovlich. So I said, 'okay.' I sat down and I'm trying to get my breath in case Cournoyer comes off and it just so happened that due to the direction that we were going in the arena, Cournoyer was on the far side of the rink, away from the bench. And of course it's an Olympic-size ice surface and it's a long way to come.

"Pete Mahovlich was close to our bench as the left winger. And this is another thing. If Peter had been on the other side, would he have come off? Would he have heard Paul yelling at him? This is amazing stuff! But Paul did stand up, and he started calling to Peter Mahovlich to come off. That is a true story. And Peter had basically just got out there, he was not tired, he was fresh. I don't even know if Peter knows why he came off. I think he probably thought about it—Paul yelling at him—he probably thought, *Well, Paul, I'm going to give you one more chance to score another winner* because he had gotten the two prior. A lot was going on but he came off. Paul would not have been on the ice if Peter hadn't come off."

Alan Eagleson, the genius behind the series and the man who shepherded it to its dramatic conclusion, is equally awed by the way things worked out. He was a witness to events. "Our last three goals were all, in themselves, miraculous. If not miraculous, then memorable. For the final one, I was on the bench," he said. "Paul called Pete off. It happened. There is no doubt about that. My wife Nancy knew Paul and Eleanor Henderson and Ron and Jane Ellis. We were close friends socially. Nancy told Paul, 'I know you're going to score. I just know it.' And there's no question in my mind.... I always said that's the reason Paul became religious. I don't know if there was divine intervention or not but I certainly know that Paul intervened. For whatever reason. There is no doubt that Paul Henderson was *not* put on the ice by Harry Sinden. Something came into him. I remember going in the dressing room and Paul had a beatific smile on his face and his eyes were almost glazed over."

Quebec's New Religion

Sin is up and conventional religion is down, but at the Church of the Montreal Canadiens, attendance is standing room only. At the Bell Centre, where the sin bin replaces the confessional, the Canadiens are sole heirs to a worshipful Quebec public, the only remaining hockey denomination in the province. Of course, zealots believe that the Quebec City franchise represented the true Quebec and that the red-clad Canadiens are false prophets at best, sellouts to English Canada. This heretical faction has yet to rise above the level of cult. Les Canadiens are the high church.

In this evangelical new religion, sports talk radio is the new tower of babble and sermons are preached nightly by TV pundits. "There are 24-hour radio sports talk shows," said former *Hockey Night in Canada* host Dick Irvin Jr. "On the French side that means 24-hour hockey—even in the middle of July.

Last year three separate French language channels had a panel discussion on hockey every single night, Monday to Friday for the whole hockey season plus playoffs.

"There was an English-language all-sports station that I don't usually listen to for personal reasons but it was on my car radio and they were talking hockey and who was going to be the third-string centre for the Canadiens. This was July and it was scorching hot. I switched over to CKAC, a French-language station that's been here for years and has switched to an all-sports format. Know what they were talking about? The Montreal Canadiens. I thought to myself, *Jesus Murphy, this is the middle of July, it's 100 above, and they're talking about hockey!* And people were phoning in—so it wasn't just a bunch of media guys who can't see past hockey. I mean, why? How do you explain it? What the hell do they talk about? I don't know and everyone's mad and they're yelling and hollering." Sure sounds like religion.

There was a time when the Roman Catholic Church was the lifeblood of Quebec. It helped to sustain the original French colonists spiritually and practically in times of severe hardship. As the power of the church grew, it became more oppressive and controlling, culminating in the period from 1945–59 known as "La Grande Noirceur" or "The Great Blackness." The period coincided with the premiership of Maurice Duplessis of the ultra-conservative Union Nationale Party. His government and a veritable army of 50,000 church officials worked hand in glove to suppress the populace and keep them dependent. Church and state were as one and religion was ingrained in every aspect of life from the cradle to the grave. The church ran schools, newspapers, hospitals, and labour unions. It even monitored the cultural content that citizens were allowed to see and hear.

Maurice L. Duplessis, Premier of Quebec, poses for photograph in 1937. Duplessis' premiership coincided with the period known as "The Great Blackness." During this period, religion was ingrained in every aspect of Quebec life from the cradle to the grave.

STF/AFP/Getty Images

So cowed were most French Quebecers that they accepted their lot as second-class citizens without question. Meanwhile English Quebecers, not yoked by the Catholic Church, rose to positions of power and wealth. It was a self-perpetuating system that planted seeds of resentment against the English. The church's influence also extended to the bedrooms of the province. It was expected that every wife should have a baby a year, the so-called "revenge of the cradle." The result was huge families with few resources to support them. The Church, which should have been offering comfort and support, was doing just the opposite.

The dissatisfaction continued to grow, and in 1960 the Duplessis government was finally thrown out of office. Little wonder that when the change came, it came with a vengeance. Under new Liberal Premier Jean Lesage, Quebec awakened and would never be the same again. The Quiet Revolution was under-way. Church and state were made separate and there were immediate changes in every facet of life, from the economy to culture. "It's as if Quebec had been hit by an unreported neutron bomb," wrote Taras Grescoe in his book *Sacre Blues*. "In a single brilliant flash, it incinerated the Catholic faith, leaving the man-made structures intact."

In the 1950s, Quebec had the highest church attendance in Canada at 88 percent. By 2006, that figure had dropped to 20 per-cent and it continues to move downward. A 2008 Leger Marketing poll reported a 6 per-cent rate, "the lowest of any western society." *The State of the Canadian Church in 2006* blamed this on "the massive secularization of Quebec society which began later but has gone farther there than in the rest of the country." Glenn Smith, general director of Christian Direction, a Quebec-based minis-try added: "Quebecers are always late for the train but always go beyond the station." There is no doubt that—like the Nordiques—the theology train has left the province.

Although it no longer ends there, in Quebec everything still starts with religion. The derailed Catholic caboose is still present. Religion is part of the fabric of the province and still lives on in the culture, attitudes, and language. It is ubiquitous. Called "the Quebec anomaly" by University of Lethbridge sociol-ogist Reginald Bibby, 83 percent (according to the 2001 census) of Quebecers still iden-tify themselves as Catholics. To do otherwise would be to deny their history and their heri-tage, since the church has been a cornerstone (some would say millstone) of their evolution as a society. This all but extinct society of devout Catholics has helped to make Quebec a devoutly distinct society. But if they are not practicing Catholicism, what has filled that void? People must have something to believe in and venerate. Nature, even *human* nature, hates a vacuum.

Quebecers have long made reference to the Montreal Canadiens as gods and to their followers as disciples. Olivier Bauer, a theology professor at the Universite de Montreal, has given the time-honoured analogy fresh academic legitimacy by introducing a graduate course titled *La religion du Canadien de Montreal* (*The Religion of the Montreal Canadiens*). Originally from Switzerland, the social scientist and former college goalie was fascinated by the importance and significance of the Montreal Canadiens to Quebec society. After discussions with one of his students—a Catholic priest—he decided that the course offering would create media attention and stimulate dialogue on the subject of religion in today's Quebec. He sees his own role as that of referee—completely neutral, in keeping with his Swiss heritage.

In Toronto, Ottawa, Edmonton, or Boston such religious comparisons would be a tired literary device at best, overblown rhetoric thrown off by jaded sportswriters whose jobs are to create colourful if tenuous metaphors in the face of looming deadlines. Not so in Quebec. In Quebec, the comparisons are valid, or at least worthy of serious discussion. The team does inspire a zeal entirely consistent with the religious history of the place.

In Bauer's theology class, the hierarchy and tenets of the religion of the Les Canadiens de Montreal are studied in detail. He has even penned a 70-page book to support the course. Among the seemingly endless allusions to hockey, he cites Saint Patrick Roy as a canonized Canadien and Carey "Jesus" Price as someone who has been crucified by zealous fans and may or may not rise from the dead. The Habs uniform has long been known as Saint Flanelle ("The Holy Flannel") and it isn't much of a stretch to see the 24 Stanley Cups that the team has successfully quested for (far more than any other NHL team) as the

In the 70-page book he penned for his course *La religion du Canadien de Montreal* (The Religion of the Montreal Canadiens), Professor Olivier Bauer cites Saint Patrick Roy as a canonized Canadien. As a 20-year-old rookie goaltender in 1986, Roy led the Canadiens to the Stanley Cup championship. Bruce Bennett Studios/Getty Images

Holy Grail. Even in the Canadiens famous CH logo, Bauer has discovered the outline of a fish, a well-recognized Christian symbol. Check it out, it really is there!

In Bauer's class nothing is sacred, or perhaps everything is. His premise was that maybe the religious context of Quebec would provide students with new insights into their relationship to the Habs and to God. The Canadiens are to understanding Quebec's religious heritage what parables were to accessing biblical knowledge. "Nowadays in Quebec there is just one big team," said Bauer. "In cities like Boston you have the Red Sox, Patriots, Celtics, and Bruins, and in Toronto, you have the Leafs, the Raptors, and the Blue Jays—so you have many *churches* in those cities. In Montreal and in Quebec you just have Les Canadiens—one denomination. Everything is magnified and attention is drawn to the Habs. For French Quebecers, the kind of religion that you find in the Habs is a very Catholic one, very cultural, and very unique to this place because Quebec remains a very Catholic culture."

The Molson Centre is the high-tech cathedral where hockey services are now held. It has been called soulless and lacking in tradition, of which neither of these complaints is solvable. "So close to heaven, so far from the ice," wrote Taras Grescoe after watching a game there.

In this religion there is no separation of church and skate. Not only do the Canadiens lend themselves nicely to the Catholic metaphor, they also reflect a uniquely Quebec mindset. It's a way of looking at life that starts with the team's official motto, a line from *In Flanders Fields*, the iconic poem of war and remembrance by Canadian Lieutenant Colonel John McCrae. Bauer was struck by the difference in the original English compared with the French translation.

"What is very impressive for me is the English phrase 'From failing hands.' In French

it is: *Nos bras meurtris vous tendent le flambeau, à vous toujours de le porter bien haut.* So first of all it's *bras*—arms and not hands—but the translation is something like 'our bruised arms,' so it's a passive voice. The arms are already bruised, but in English it is 'failing hands.' It's not the same. I think it says something about the kind of suffering you risk for your vision in Quebec. You have to suffer in order to win. *Petite pas.* It is everything."

For the people of a province historically tarnished by the "underachievers" label, the success of Les Canadiens became symbolic of what they might become, and what they can achieve. But in keeping with their history, there was always a price to be paid. That was a given. Originally, this success and this suffering had a direct connection with the teachings and the actions—of the Catholic Church. Said Bauer, "Montreal is a winning team and at the same time there is a lot of sacrifice, there are a lot of victims. Maurice Richard was a victim but also a saviour. I think it fits with the Catholic theology in Montreal and Catholic culture in Quebec." The idea of sacrifice and victimhood hits a distinctive chord with Francophone Quebecers accustomed to a tradition of martyrdom. Studies have shown a spike in the number of suicides by males in those years that the Canadiens fail to reach the playoffs. Through the Habs, however, the righteous anger aroused by past wrongs can be avenged.

Another underlying theme seems to be that hockey is a gift from God to the people of Quebec. To accept this doctrine one would have to accept the premise that the game originated in Montreal. Bauer states this as gospel, although others think it is a leap of faith since several other Canadian jurisdictions make at least as strong a claim to being the birthplace of the game (see Chapter 1). In none of these cases did the birth take

place in a manger. Even the game's Ten Commandments; i.e., the so-called Montreal Rules, were actually the Halifax Rules with a few modifications. The only difference is that Nova Scotian James Creighton, the accepted Moses of the game, codified them in Montreal in 1875. It is not known if he brought them down from Mount Royal chiselled into tablets of stone. In fairness, the province was instrumental in the growth and evolution of the game, if the term *evolution* doesn't offend followers of this fundamentalist religion.

The mix of religion and hockey in Quebec history is undeniable. "In junior hockey it used to be like a monastic existence," said Bauer. "Players used to enter Quebec junior hockey like novice monks into a religious order. Players like Jean Beliveau would have a dedica-tion to hockey but first they would go to Mass. Only then would they play hockey. There was a kind of discipline. The important thing was being a practicing Catholic, and hockey was second. That was the order of things."

Beliveau was in many ways typical of young men who came of age before the Quiet Revolution. "Growing up, it was school, church, and hockey," said hockey's most revered elder statesman. "My parents were very religious."

Beliveau grew up next to a church and credits the Sacred Heart brothers with pro-viding his hockey baptism. "I was an altar boy for three years when I was young. Church and hockey went together. I remem-ber Sunday morning before the high Mass. Without skates, four or five of us would

Jean Beliveau stands among the city cannons in Quebec City in 1952. Beliveau grew up in a religious Catholic family and credits the Sacred Heart brothers with providing his hockey baptism.

Yale Joel//Time Life Pictures/Getty Images

61

be on that little ice surface. Then we'd go to the Mass and after that we had a quick bite, put our skates on, and spend the rest of the day on that ice." Even during the week, the Catholic brothers played hockey with Beliveau. When he was 12 years old, they formed an all-star team and the future star was invited to be a member—a kind of little brother to the brothers.

Later, when Beliveau was starring for the Canadiens in the NHL, the mail he received from fans was very religious in nature. It was Marc Cloutier's job to go through those letters. Cloutier was in charge of public relations for the Habs in the early 1960s before being named assistant to club president David Molson. "The guy that got the most mail was Jean Beliveau," he recalls. "Back in the mid-'60s most of the fan mail, believe it or not, was about the church. They'd say, *We'll say beads for you* or *We'll go to the church and pray for you.* Church was very, very big back then. Not that the players would go to church every day but the Quebec people—the fans—were very much involved with the Catholic church. And the priests and nuns were big fans of the Canadiens."

Even today, Beliveau receives four or five times more letters than any other former player. He still answers each and every one. "Jean Beliveau is like a saint in Quebec," said Bauer. "It says something about his behaviour and the way he is appreciated. He's like a person who is perfect. He and other Canadiens of his time were practicing faith, crossing themselves before skating on the ice. Jean was great player, a good Catholic, and he was always 'Gentleman Jean.'"

If the Montreal Canadiens are truly a religion, there can be only one deity—Maurice Richard. He is a God direct from Central Casting, and a wrathful one at that. Bauer thinks the designation is fitting.

"Everything here in Montreal designates Richard as God because he was very different from any other player in Habs history. I was surprised to discover the kind of passionate faith that people had in Richard, especially after his death."

Bauer makes an unexpected comparison with a near-mythic figure from Quebec's religious past, Frere Andre. Brother Andre, born Andre Bessette on August 9, 1845, was one of the most beloved figures in the history of the church in Quebec. He was elevated to sainthood on Sunday, October 17, 2010, in Rome in recognition of the miracles that he performed during his lifetime. On the surface, he and Rocket Richard would seem to have little in common. A humble, physically frail man, Bessette rose from abject poverty to become doorman at Notre Dame College in Cote-des-Neiges. His humble manner and passivity would appear to be in direct contrast to Richard's fiery demeanour.

A closer look reveals some similarities. Like Andre, Richard at 5'7" and 170 pounds was originally seen as too fragile for his chosen profession. Both were idolized by the public and wore uniforms that garnered instant respect. "You can draw a lot of parallels between Brother Andre and Maurice Richard," Bauer said. He worked tirelessly to erect a chapel to honour Saint Joseph and thanks to his efforts Saint Joseph's Oratory was finally begun in 1924. When he died in 1937, more than a million people filed past his coffin.

"He had incredible motivation and determination to build the things he built—this oratory. There was the same piety around those two guys. Tens of thousands came for their funerals and they both were credited with miracles."

As if to bless this comparison Montreal's Cardinal Jean-Claude Turcotte said on the occasion of Brother Andre's canonization,

The Quebec-born Brother Andre, born Andre Bessette on August 9, 1845, was a highly popular figure among French Canadians and was known for miraculous cures. He was elevated to sainthood on October 17, 2010, in recognition of the miracles that he performed during his lifetime. AP Images

"Andre Bessette has become the Rocket Richard of miracles."

Aside from walking on water, which for hockey players is not all that miraculous, there are stories of actual miracles performed by Maurice Richard as well. He once scored a goal with two opposing players draped over his shoulders from the blue line in. And then there was the young child in the hospital who said the last thing he wanted was to have Maurice Richard come and see him. Richard came and the journalist who tells this story said, 'I would almost like to get sick just to get a visit from Maurice Richard.' So that's the kind of passion he created." There are numerous anecdotal stories about miraculous healings through the touching of Maurice Richard's jersey.

The funeral of Maurice Richard was a significant milestone in Quebec history. As a religious metaphor, it represented a crossroads, a point of intersection for the Catholic Church and Les Canadiens. "It's very relevant," said Bauer. "Before the Rocket's death there were two very parallel paths—the Catholic Church and the Habs. Quebecers belonged to one and cheered for the other—and there was no real problem. The funeral of Maurice Richard was when the two paths crossed. From that time forward the two entities have become more separate than before. Now it may be very different because there is no need for both. There is no longer a correlation between the Catholic faith and being a Habs fan."

There are exceptions. Whether out of conviction or desperation, rabid fans still turn to God for the occasional assist. Bauer cites the example of Victoria, an 11-year-old Montrealer who felt that she was committing a sin if she missed a Canadiens game. Victoria sought to bring the 2009–10 Habs through the playoffs to a Stanley Cup by prayers to Frere Andre and by climbing the 283 steps to the St. Joseph Oratory on her knees.

The day before the April 15, 2010, Montreal playoff game with Washington, a Montreal radio station concocted a pilgrimage to Saint Joseph's Oratory. About 20 "pilgrims" dressed in Canadiens garb climbed the steep incline on their knees. Said Bauer, "There are still some crossing points—some tie-ins with the Catholic Church and Habs passion—some connections, especially in very critical times when you think that all the players' skills and gifts are not enough to win a game. People prayed all day to St. Joseph to help the Habs win that game."

The Catholic dogma became the Francophone Quebecers' dogma that is reflected in the Montreal Canadiens' dogma: "Through suffering, you shall win."

These incidents aside, have hockey and the Habs replaced the Catholic faith among Quebecers? Has participation in the Mass been replaced by attendance at games? "I think it's difficult to say something like that," Bauer cautioned. "On the contrary, people tell me that before—in the '50s or '60s, the Habs were a religion and now it is just a business. So it's open to interpretation. You can say that the Habs are replacing the Mass, but you can also say that there were more connections to religion when religion was at a high point in Quebec. I think you can defend both hypotheses.

"I think there is now a new way to practise religion that is more individual, more event by event. People go to big events like the Pope's visit and then nothing for three more years. In hockey you exist game to game while you are waiting for the playoffs. So it's the same for hockey and religion. Perhaps you were more faithful or had more fidelity before than you do now. For the players it is the same, like Jean Beliveau has this *seash de de tuat de Coeur*. He's a kind of image of the Montreal Canadiens. Now you have these players who are coming for one, two, three years and then going elsewhere— or the Habs sell them. In religion it is the same. You do not have the same fidelity to the church or you don't have the need or obligation to take part in every Mass, every Sunday."

Hockey has even trespassed into the once churchly domain of charity and public welfare. "I asked one of my students to write a paper about the Foundation of the Canadiens and it was very interesting to discover that the Habs took this traditionally church charity thing and they endorsed it and now maybe the people are more likely to give money to the Habs Foundation in order to do something good than to give it to any

church. It's a kind of Habs influence on the society because if you give money they organize things. They build arenas for skating. It's a new kind of influence for sure."

If the Montreal Canadiens are a religion, they are a very open and ecumenical one because they have welcomed Protestant players, Catholic players, Russian Orthodox players, and Jewish owners. "In that aspect it is very ecumenical," Bauer agreed. "In another way it is not very ecumenical at all because if you cheer for the Habs, you have to exclude, even hate, all the other teams: the Leafs, the Bruins, and every other team except maybe for some team in Florida that has a lot of Quebecois players. It's ecumenical in Montreal in the religious way but there is a lot of violence and tribalism involved as well.

"It's one of the critiques that I introduce to my students about this Habs religion. It's too much of a tribal religion for me and I think a religion should ideally bring some love and teach you to love your neighbour, not hate him. It's a criticism I address to the Canadiens de Montreal as a religion—maybe it's different as a sports team."

Where do the Toronto Maple Leafs stand in this new religion? Roch Carrier's book *The Hockey Sweater* once captured the sentiments of Quebecers in a simple yet profound way. The story is based on an incident from the author's own childhood in the rural village of Sainte-Justine-de-Dorchester, some 300 kilometres northeast of Montreal.

In a few short pages, the book manages to deliver a microcosm of Quebec with all its French-English-Church complexities through the experience of a 10-year-old boy. "As for church," he wrote, "we found there the tranquillity of God: there we forgot school and dreamed about the next hockey game. Through our daydreams it might happen that

"Before the Rocket's death there were two very parallel paths—the Catholic Church and the Habs. Quebecers belonged to one and cheered for the other—and there was no real problem. The funeral of Maurice Richard was when the two paths crossed. From that time forward the two entities have become more separate than before. Now it may be very different because there is no need for both. There is no longer a correlation between the Catholic faith and being a Habs fan."

—**Professor Olivier Bauer**

we would recite a prayer: we would ask God to help us play as well as Maurice Richard."

In Carrier's story, all players in the village wear Canadiens colours with Maurice Richard's No. 9 sewn on the backs. Except the storyteller. Due to a mixup with the T. Eaton's Company, another bastion of English culture that the French were forced to deal with, he receives a Toronto Maple Leaf jersey instead. "I wept," he said. Like mothers everywhere, his did not understand why a perfectly good sweater that fits beautifully should cause such behaviour. She refuses to return it. "Monsieur Eaton's an *Anglais;* he'll be insulted because he likes the Maple Leafs," she tells him.

The boy wears the jersey and is ostracized by young and old alike. When he becomes frustrated, the young vicar tells him, "My child, just because you're wearing a new Toronto Maple Leafs sweater unlike the others, it doesn't mean you're going to make the laws around here. A proper young man doesn't lose his temper. Now take off your skates and go to church and ask God to forgive you." As for the boy, he could only ask God "to send, as quickly as possible, moths that would eat up my Toronto Maple Leafs sweater."

Much has changed since those times and while the rivalry between Montreal and Toronto is still intense, it has lost some of its edge. "Some may call the Maple Leafs the

infidels, and maybe they were at one time but not now because they are not a problem," said Bauer. "They are too bad. The infidels would now be Pittsburgh and Boston. The Leafs need to be better to have a good rivalry. They are not so important or significant—you can lose to them and it doesn't matter." The idea of the Leafs being too bad to be evil is enough to make the most devoted Leafs fan question his or her faith.

"The very Protestant character of Toronto used to spark the rivalry," said Bauer. "Conn Smythe was very angry at the Catholics and Quebec players."

In his autobiography *Conn Smythe: If You Can't Beat Them in the Alley,* the Leafs owner confirmed his attitudes toward Catholics. The seeds of these attitudes were planted when the son of a Belfast Protestant was just a young boy. "We sincerely believed if we were captured by the priests, we'd never be seen alive again," he admitted. Later, his childhood fears hardened into outright intolerance toward Catholicism. It was an easy leap from distrust of Catholics to distrust of French Canadians. Speaking to a Montreal audience, he famously began: "Ladies, gentlemen, and Frenchmen."

For the ex-military man, religion was all tied up with patriotism, hard work, and sacrifice. His philosophy was that God helps those who help themselves. "I've always thought that Catholics have it pretty easy—do anything they like, then confess, and be forgiven," Smythe wrote. "It's the opposite of, 'as ye sow, so shall ye reap.' I know that there is no such thing as being forgiven." Originally known as the Toronto St. Patrick's, Smythe ditched the St. Patrick's name because it was too Catholic and named Toronto's team after a national symbol—the maple leaf—in hopes of branding them as Canada's team.

In *Putting a Roof on Winter*, author Michael McKinley writes: "Of course, Canada did have another team, something Conn Smythe knew all too well. Since his democratic bigotry also included French Quebec, the 'Canada's team' claim not-too-subtly suggests that those who worship at the altar of the Montreal Canadiens do so in treachery."

Smythe's Maple Leafs teams were constructed in his image, and the fact that his Maple Leaf Gardens was built on Church Street was more than appropriate.

Some English Canadians have been critical of Rocket Richard for compiling his scoring records while other young men were overseas fighting the Nazis. In actual fact, Richard had twice tried to enlist but was turned down due to injuries incurred in hockey battles. Strangely, Smythe—who served with distinction in both World Wars—was a big fan of the Rocket. "Richard was the only Catholic player he would have liked to have," said Bauer. In fact he liked him so much that he tried to make him a Maple Leaf, offering the Canadiens $25,000 for him. The offer was rejected.

With the exception of the Richard offer, any proselytizing that happened was done by Montreal and not Toronto. The bottom line was that Toronto almost never went after Quebec players. Meanwhile the Habs didn't have any qualms about choosing the best players available, be they English Protestants or French Catholics.

Meanwhile, at the Church of the Montreal Canadiens all are welcome. Professor Bauer's class has people talking and discussing religion, which was the point in the first place. As for the Catholic Church, they can only sit and wait and dream of the time when they were the dominant religion of the province. "I think there is some resentment from the church to the Canadiens' popularity," said Bauer. "From time to time the Bishop of Quebec is very nostalgic of the time when the church was publishing the rules of comportment and so on—so I think there is resentment or at least regret. It's mixed with some hope that it could come again, that it could be the same again. They wait for the situation to change."

Pierre Castonguay summed it all up in a poem in *Le Devoir*.

The Creed of the Canadiens

I believe in the Canadiens, the club almighty
Creator of Heaven, earth and the Holy Flannel
And in Maurice Richard, our Saviour
Who was conceived of sane mind
Born for the good of the homeland
Suffered under Clarence Campbell
Was crucified for a bad decision
That almost killed us
And ascended into Heaven
And is seated at the right hand of the great
    Referee
From thence he shall come to judge the good
    players and the cowards
I believe in the Holy NHL,
The Communion of old Canadiens heroes
The forgiveness of years without the Stanley
    Cup
The resurrection during the playoffs
And glory everlasting.
Amen.

A giant puppet of
Maurice Richard
is pulled along
at the 2009 Saint
Jean Baptiste
Day Parade in
Montreal.

AP Images

6

HOW HOCKEY EXPLAINS
TWO SOLITUDES

SOMETIMES IT TAKES an outsider to make you see things as they really are. Such was the case when southpaw Bill "Spaceman" Lee arrived in Montreal to pitch for the Montreal Expos. On his first visit to the Montreal Forum, baseball's foremost iconoclast witnessed the two solitudes that he had previously only read about. "The English fans sat down in the good seats," recalls Lee. "The further up you went the more French it got and the more raucous it got. Kind of like a Shakespearean play at the Globe Theatre. The people in the front rows sat on their hands and the peasants, they were the ones who laughed at the tragedies and cried at the comedies. They loved it when the mighty fell."

When Hugh MacLennan wrote *Two Solitudes*, he wasn't talking about hockey, but he could have been. Published in 1945, the novel centres on the tensions and mistrust that exist between French and English in Quebec and Canada. Through the intervening years, it has become a kind of shorthand for the alienation of the two cultures. The frictions are still being played out in many forums, including junior and professional hockey rinks. Exacerbated by the departure of the Quebec Nordiques for Colorado and the dearth of French players on the Montreal Canadiens, there has been a perception among Quebecers that their province is underrepresented in the NHL, and some think that English Canada is once again the villain in the piece. Segments of the radio, TV, and newspaper media feed the resentment on a daily basis and some politicians are only too happy to use hockey as a political football.

Montreal-born Mario Lemieux led the NHL in scoring six times and was awarded the Hart Trophy as the league's Most Valuable Player three times.

AP Images

Dick Irvin has little patience with those who attempt to ascribe linguistic motives to the Montreal Canadiens' front office decisions. Irvin thinks that most in his province have moved past such chauvinistic concerns. "I don't think people care about the number of French players in the lineup! If the 2009–10 edition of the Canadiens had gone on to win the Stanley Cup, they would have had the greatest parade in history. It's the media and the politicians who make an issue of this, in my opinion. When you go to a game and a Russian scores the winning goal with a Czech and a Swede getting the assists, they cheer just as loud as if it had been a French Canadian. The average guy who goes to a game—and there are 21,273 of them every single night—they don't care! It's still the Montreal Canadiens."

There was a time, Serge Savard recalls, when Montreal had a distinct advantage in assembling powerhouse teams. "I guess we had good management. We had people who put the best teams together—but the Montreal Canadiens had a big advantage for a while when they could put the first two French Canadians on the top of their list before the draft. That really helped them." Even when things changed, the Canadiens went to extraordinary lengths to secure Quebec players. "After that they made manoeuvres to draft Guy Lafleur—the best hockey player in the league for 10 years," Savard said. "Guys like me, Guy Lapointe, Rogie Vachon, and all those guys, we weren't drafted. There was no draft in my time. We were almost the last ones who weren't drafted. I was part of a sponsorship team and we simply joined the organization. We wanted to play for the Montreal Canadiens—and that was the end of an era."

Before Savard, there was a time when there was no question about what team young Quebec boys wanted to play for. "My dream as a young hockey player was to wear the Canadiens sweater," said Jean Beliveau. "That was always my dream. Still today in the QMJHL, I'm sure their dream is to become a member of the Montreal Canadiens."

Montrealers have always embraced their team, regardless of the backgrounds of players. Irvin points to the fact that throughout the rich history of the franchise, Les Canadiens always had their share of stars who were not French Canadians. "It was the same when guys like John Ferguson or Larry Robinson were here," he said. "It was great to have the French heroes, but Ken Dryden wasn't French, nor were Larry Robinson and Bob Gainey and Pete Mahovlich. These guys played on what I consider the best team that there ever was in hockey. Sure you had Guy Lafleur, Guy Lapointe, Savard, and Jacques Lemaire and that's fine. You always had that kind of a mix with this team."

There is a selective amnesia in Quebec, a memory that the Montreal Canadiens were once a French team. This collective hallucination conjures up a time when hockey, this important component of French culture, was performed by Quebecers for Quebecers on the ice of the old Montreal Forum. The distinctive French *joie de vivre*, the passion, the art that supports the craft of hockey were all there in these Flying Frenchmen. They were distinctive in style and content. Professor Bauer from the Universite of Montreal thinks that the arrival of radio and then television in the '50s helped to plant this false memory. "It was the beginning of the French identity of the team," he said. "There is a parallel between the passion for the Habs and the arrival of television. In the '50s few could go and see the Canadiens but TV brought the games into the living rooms of all Quebecers. From the '50s to the '80s the Habs were the most French team in the NHL and it was also the most success-

According to Dick Irvin, not all French Canadian players yearn to play in the hockey hotbed of Quebec. "Being a French player in this city is not easy," he said. "I used to say that Guy Lafleur would go to the bathroom and there'd be a French reporter following him because there might be another French reporter in the men's room and Lafleur might give him a story."

ful time for the Canadiens. There is a kind of mythology that originates in this time. Most people remember that the Canadiens were a French team with Maurice and Henri Richard and Jean Beliveau, and so on but it was not the case. It's still a very common perception here in Quebec. The French touch."

Professor Bauer thinks that the hockey club has always mirrored the city. "From the very beginning the team represented the multicultural and cosmopolitan nature of Montreal," said the theologian. "There has never been a time when Montreal has had only French players, not even at the beginning. There were always people from different parts of Canada...from Ontario and elsewhere. I was surprised when I discovered that Howie Morenz was the son of a Swiss immigrant—and a Protestant and Presbyterian too. And when he died, his funeral was held by the very reverend chief of the Presbyterian Church at the Montreal Forum. So the first big star was a Protestant and a Swiss immigrant. Auriel Joliat was the same. His parents were from Ottawa. So it was always very diverse, even then."

When the Montreal Forum was about to close its doors for good, Dick Irvin was chosen to co-host the ceremonies. He considers it one of the highlights of his 17-year career in the broadcast booth. The stars of Habs teams from the glory years were there: Richard, Beliveau, and the rest. But his biggest thrill was watching two great goalies. The position of goalie is as solitary as any in sport and the symbolism of these former greats, one English and one French, was impossible for him to avoid. "What really got to me was seeing Patrick Roy and Ken Dryden in uniform with goalie pads on. Dryden hadn't had pair of goal pads on since his last game in 1979. And there they were. Kenny wasn't too thrilled about them taking shots because he had his glasses on but Patrick was all set. He wanted to have a real shoot-out, a real warmup with guys shooting at him. I don't know why that got to me. I'd seen some of the others playing old-time hockey, but to see those two goalies out there and for what they meant to the team during their heyday there, it was a very special night."

As a Francophone, Savard scoffs at suggestions that there is any political consideration at play in the decreased number of French players on the Canadiens. "Some people are making it an issue, but it's not an issue. My best friend was an Anglophone, John Ferguson, and John and I did talk about it. We were a big family. It bothers a lot of people that it is not an issue. Actually, Mrs. Marois [PQ leader, Pauline Marois] claimed that the Montreal Canadiens were a big promoter of the federalist camp. I don't know why she would say that."

Ferguson was extremely popular with French Canadian fans. "He got tons of letters

Serge Savard played on eight Stanley Cup championship teams in 17 years with the Montreal Canadiens. After he retired, Savard was named the Canadiens' general manager.
(Melchior DiGiacomo/Getty Images)

from Francophones," Savard remembered. "John was known as big bad John and people loved him. He became very, very popular with French Canadians and he couldn't even speak French. He loved them and they loved him because he played with heart. They spoke the same language as far as hockey was concerned. He got a lot of requests to go and visit kids in hospitals and people in old folks homes."

Savard sees the Canadiens as a successful example of a bilingual Quebec organization. "I guess it bothers them because it works so well," he suggested. "She [Marois] said in the middle of the debate that the Montreal Canadiens didn't really draft in the Quebec League. She had an issue with that, but it had nothing to do with politics. It was just a decision of the Montreal Canadiens."

Nevertheless, Savard feels that the problem begins at home and that blame for the lack of French Canadians on the current Montreal roster rests with the organization. "That's their own fault," he said. "It's not that you *have* to draft a French Canadian but I mean it's their local product. My son and I have a team in the Maritimes, in PEI [The PEI Rocket of the QMJHL] and if we have a chance to draft a guy from PEI, a local kid, we will.

"When I was the manager in Montreal I had four or five full-time scouts in Quebec. Afterward they had one part-time scout in the province. That's their problem. They miss all the good kids, the good local kids. Why?"

"That kid [David] Perron for example, we knew a lot about him because he was in the Q [Lewiston Maineiacs] and my son told me a lot about him. Well, Montreal had two draft picks in 2007 before him in the first round [Nos. 12 and 22] and they let him go [Perron was drafted No. 26 and ended up with St. Louis]. Instead they took two high school kids from the States who never played [Ryan McDonagh and Max Pacioretty]. That kind of move would never happen when I was manager because I just wouldn't let him go. So that's their own fault—their chief scout is an American and they draft a lot in Europe and they didn't look very close—not only in the Quebec league but in Quebec in general."

Savard feels that conditions were right for the greatest crop of Francophone players in history to be harvested in Quebec, and yet their backyard garden wasn't properly tended. "Sure, the rest of the NHL teams are just as guilty, but if the other teams in the National Hockey League don't look at the Quebec League very closely, that should be a big advantage for you," he said. "If you look very closely there will always be good players coming out of there."

Dick Irvin suggests that media talk about percentages of French players has not damaged the team in the minds of Quebecers. "The passion for the Canadiens has not waned a bit. If anything it's more. It's gotten more intense. The PQ tried to stir things up here saying there weren't enough French players on the team, but you've got to remember where that's coming from."

Beliveau is pragmatic—if a bit wistful—about the lack of French players on the Canadiens in recent years. For a scrupulously apolitical guy, Beliveau chose the wrong province at the wrong period of history. It's a time that cries out for commentary and opinion and it's a place that thrives on it. He played in front of Duplessis, Levesque, Trudeau, Chretien, and other giants of the province. But Beliveau is himself such a giant in Quebec, such a hero, such a sportsman, such an icon to French and English alike, that he is truly above politics.

"First of all, when the NHL draft started in '67–68 things changed," Beliveau said. "Sometimes you wish to pick a certain player but all of a sudden you lose your pick. Before that, each NHL team had their own system of signing players. It was completely different but now with the rules surrounding the draft, things have changed. Sometimes you wish to pick a certain player but all of a sudden you lose it.... When your team is performing it doesn't matter. There's no doubt that the management of the Canadiens . . . they're not blind. They know that a big percentage of their supporters are French speaking, but what can they do?

"Take the [2010] draft, the first player that was picked up from the Quebec junior league was Brandon Gormley at No. 13 [Gormley went to Phoenix; Montreal picked 22nd and selected American Jarred Tinordi], so not only the Canadiens but also the management of many other teams pick players that they feel they need. You always try to take the best youngsters."

Savard thinks that political intrigue in hockey is a myth. "I don't think I ever felt pol-itics involved in hockey," he said. "It may look like that. The team used politics to get grants and things like that but I really don't think so. All the years I spent with the Montreal Canadiens, politics was off limits and I think it's the same thing in Quebec City. They just want a team back, which is normal. Nothing to do with politics.

"We had the Molsons as owners at three different times and now it's the Molson kids. This time those kids seem to want to be really involved. It's not the brewery anymore. In my time it started with Senator Hartland Molson, and those guys were fans, you know. The team was owned by the brewery and those guys were behind the bench. They wouldn't miss a game, but they'd never get involved. I was manager over 12 years and never would they interfere in one of your decisions, never would they suggest it. They gave you 100 percent leverage in what you're doing. They had faith in you and that's the way it was run— like a big Quebec family."

Dick Irvin Jr. is no stranger to the cultural cauldron that is Quebec. Not only was he the longtime mainstay of hockey broadcasts on *Hockey Night in Canada*, but his father coached the Canadiens to Stanley Cups. "When my dad was coaching back in the '40s and '50s he used to have a phrase for it. He used to say 'You have to play two tunes on your fiddle when you coach the Montreal Canadiens.' He meant the French and the English."

"I can remember in Quebec City and at the Forum, at the height of the separatist movement, there were a lot of people who wouldn't stand up for "Oh Canada" and some still don't but nothing like before. Now when I go to games I go to the press box and I look out over the cheap seats up top and everyone is standing. Still, it's there, there's no doubt about it. The Montreal-Quebec rivalry was really great—and Quebec had Dale

Hunter from Ontario and the Stastnys from Czechoslovakia. They were their best players along with Michel Goulet. They had a couple English players on that team over the years."

From an American perspective, Richard Johnson thinks that the Montreal Canadiens–Quebec Nordiques rivalry became a battle for the hearts of Quebecers. "Who's more Catholic than the Pope? That's basically what it was. We're going to be more Francophone than you, although the last time I checked, unless the Stastnys took a Berlitz course, they are not French. Marcel Abut [former president and CEO of the Nordiques] played the Francophone card time and again and when the Nordiques started, the Canadiens were owned by the Bronfmans and Irving Grundman who had taken over from Pollack was the GM—it's always been the case with the Canadiens—how French are we? That never was a problem when they won. When they won no one was worried that Doug Harvey wasn't first-language French—although he was from Montreal and probably spoke French as well as anybody. The fact is that the Nordiques played up on what had been the Canadiens' strength and subverted it a bit."

Irvin feels that people have moved on since those days. As a frequent visitor to the Bell Centre, the longtime observer is hard-pressed to see any change in the level of passion for the team. "You go to a game now and whether a Russian or an Englishman or whatever scores, no one cares. Sure, you get the radicals on the phone-in shows and there's a guy on radio here in Montreal apparently railing and ranting that we need more French players. My question is: Okay, you've got 15 French players on the team. Are you happy? Yeah, sure. But you finish last—30th in the league. They think that 20 French guys can rule the world?"

Johnson thinks that the Montreal Canadiens have often served the role of champions of the downtrodden. "Hockey was once a vehicle for Quebecers to exact revenge for past wrongs, real and perceived—slights imagined or experienced that this army of blue, blanc, and rouge would avenge for them. Another Coupe Stanley being lofted in the Forum."

Now that things have changed and Montreal no longer enjoys proprietary rights to players from the province, there is understandably an adjustment period. "They are a hostage to history," Johnson suggested. "The Canadiens' past can never be recaptured with a predominantly Quebec lineup because those rules have changed." In the end, he sees the distribution of French players throughout the NHL as a positive development for hockey and a source of pride for Quebec. "The fact is that a new generation of supporters has come forward so it doesn't really matter. The world now comes to Montreal and that's well and fine because the players that the city of Montreal and the province of Quebec continue to send to the world are extraordinary. There is no diminishing of great players from Quebec—they're just not wearing the CH on their shirts."

Johnson thinks that now that the French culture in Quebec has come into its own there is less need for such parochial considerations. "Now Quebec is spreading their culture and their goodwill across North America. There are French stars in virtually every NHL city. Ironically this may do more to promote and maintain the French culture in Quebec than a strong all-French Montreal Canadiens team."

Politics has been a blood sport ever since Quebec took it on the chin at the Plains of Abraham on September 13, 1759. They have been trying to even the score ever since. On that occasion, the predominant colour was the red of the British forces as they swarmed the hill and the French retreated in disorder. The entire battle took about 15 minutes, less than a period of hockey, or three five-minute majors for fighting. History was changed in those few minutes. They had to wait about a hundred years for hockey to be invented, but then they saw their chance and they took it.

On October 2, 2010, more than 60,000 Quebec hockey fans gathered on the Plains of Abraham for La Marche Bleue. This was about 50,000 more than actually fought on the opening day of the Battle of Quebec some 250 years earlier. On this occasion the only shots taken were with digital cameras and iPhones. Everyone was wearing Nordique blue and it resembled a giant pep rally with everyone in a festive mood. Emotion, nostalgia, and civic pride were in the air, and something else with a more pungent smell. Oh yes, politics. It was possibly the most political event on the Plains since Montcalm and Wolfe had their fundamental disagreement.

Montcalm and Wolfe were understandably absent this time around but among those present were Bloc Quebecois leader Gilles Duceppe, Parti Quebecois leader Pauline Marois, Quebec City Mayor Regis Labeaume, and assorted MPs of the PQ, Conservative, and Liberal stripe.

The issue at hand this time was not conquest, but money. Quebec was looking to the federal government to come up with roughly one-half of the funding—about $180 million—needed for a new hockey arena to entice an NHL franchise back to Quebec City. The whole episode was a microcosm, not only of Quebec vs. the ROC (Rest of Canada), and French vs. English, but of cosmopolitan Montreal vs. French-as-French-can-be Quebec City.

"I was interested in the colour of the Canadiens jersey, because it's red," said Bauer. "And red is for Canada and blue is for Quebec. That's why the [Quebec] Nordiques (fleur de lis) wore the blue jersey. No one calls the

Canadiens the red team. McGill University [an English school] teams are called the Redmen. The Canadiens uniform is "the tricoleur." It is clearly the red team but no one wants to call it that because it seems too Anglo, too Canada."

When the Nordiques were the second team in Quebec, they tried desperately to out-French the French. And although they failed, it seemed more acceptable to them to have Czechs rather than English Canadians on their roster. Professor Bauer thinks it was a good marketing strategy. "Because of the Canadiens de Montreal, the Quebec Nordiques probably did the smart thing in trying to become an all-French team. In French we call it a padre de niche—something that fits—maybe not for everybody in Canada, but it was more interesting for people in Quebec. It also helped in getting money from the Quebec government for broadcasting and so on. I think it was not possible to instill a rivalry with another multicultural and cosmopolitan team like in Montreal. It was the right card to play. French Quebecers identify with the blue colour of the sweater, with the fleur de lis. The fact that they were not all French players didn't matter. There were some English players and some foreigners but it was very *integrated* foreigners—like the Stastny brothers who learned French and were very happy to be in Quebec. I think the message was that you can come from outside but you have to integrate and become a Quebecer.

"Despite it all, the bottom line is still winning. When the Habs win the Stanley Cup everybody will be very happy with the team regardless. It's easier to cheer for the winner whatever the language they speak."

Beliveau draws on an Old-World comparison to describe the one-time rivalry between the Nordiques and Canadiens. "I have a good friend in Glasgow, Scotland," he said. "There are two franchises in the Scottish league in soccer—the Rangers who indirectly represent

Guy Lafleur starred for the Montreal Canadiens from 1971 to 1984. The Quebec native is the all-time leading scorer in Canadiens history, notching 1,246 points (518 goals and 728 assists) in his 14 years.

Focus on Sport/ Getty Images

the Protestant people, and the Celtics who represent the Catholics, and they each have their own stadium. Imagine that in the same city! I attended one of those games and I can assure you the stadium was full. So such rivalries are good for the sport. Rivalry is good as long as you don't go overboard with it."

"I think there is a lot of resentment to the fact that there are not many French Canadian players on the Canadiens and that even the captain [American Brian Gionta] can't speak French. There is a lot of discussion and perhaps the love, the passion for the Nordiques of Quebec of the Marche Blue is part of that also. Because everyone's thinking that it could be necessary to have a French-speaking team and I think they have given up on waiting for that in Montreal. The Habs are a team of Montreal. French fans see it as a business and they don't like some Anglo owner. They just want to get some money. First people are hoping for a French team in Quebec, with a French-speaking owner."

It's somewhat of a vicious circle. There are no French role models on recent Canadiens teams, therefore Quebec youth are drawn to other sports and activities. This ensures even fewer French Canadian stars in the future. "There are fewer people who are interested in ice hockey in Quebec," agreed Bauer. "Maybe it's because there are no French players on Montreal to watch and emulate anymore. It's not encouraging. Finding enough good French players would be a problem. What would be the level of skill of such a French team?"

Bob Sirois played 286 games of NHL hockey with the Philadelphia Flyers and the Washington Capitals from 1974–80. The 6′0″, 178-pound right winger scored 92 goals and added 120 assists in parts of six seasons before hanging up his skates. Now 57, the Montrealer is a successful businessman with strong feelings about the NHL and its attitudes toward Quebec players.

Sirois is author of *Discrimination in the NHL: Quebec Hockey Players Sidelined* (*Le Quebec mis en eche* or *Quebec Bodychecked* in the original French edition). Sirois' premise is that there is a systematic bias against French Quebecers by the NHL power base in English Canada. The cover of the French version of the book, which came out a year before the English edition, features a cartoon faceoff between a blue-clad frog and a much larger, red-uniformed bull.

The genesis of the Sirois book was an incident that occurred in a December 13, 2005, game between the Phoenix Coyotes and the Montreal Canadiens at the Bell Centre in Montreal. As coincidence would have it, all four game officials that night were French-speaking Quebecers. When Coyotes right winger Shane Doan was assessed a gross misconduct penalty during the game, it was reported that Doan had made ethnic slurs about the Francophone linesmen and referees. Denis Coderre, Quebec MP and former Secretary of State for Amateur Sport and the former the Minister responsible for *La Francophonie*, complained to Hockey Canada and suggested that Doan should not be eligible to represent Canada at the 2006 Olympics in Turin. An investigation by the NHL dismissed the allegations and he was allowed to play for Canada.

Doan subsequently sued Coderre for defamation, claiming that he had never uttered any such remarks. Coderre countersued. The matter was eventually settled out of court in 2010. Doan conceded that derogatory remarks had been uttered by the Coyotes during the game and agreed that it was unacceptable. He also allowed that Coderre had every right to condemn the incidents. However, he continued to deny that he was guilty, despite linesman Michel Cormier's report to the contrary. The incident left a bad taste in the mouths of Quebecers who saw this as another in a shameful litany of wrongs, going back to the Richard riot and beyond.

Bob Sirois was at the game. "When the incident happened, my business partner looked at me and said, 'Hey, Bob, is that still happening? Does the NHL of today excuse this kind of language?' I said 'That's English Canada. They do whatever they want. Quebecers, if you are not a superstar or a first rank player you are not going to last long in the NHL.'"

Sirois told his friend that since the 1970s he doubted if there were more than 60 French Quebecers who played more than three years in the NHL for teams other than the Canadiens and Quebec Nordiques—a period of about 40 years. When his friend voiced his skepticism, Sirois accepted the challenge and set out to prove his contention. The result of his research was his book *Discrimination in the NHL.* His research was vetted by the Department of Economic Science at Ottawa University.

"When I wrote that book I had two things in mind—proving my theory and creating a major reference book that would show which teams drafted a lot of Quebecers and what teams did not." His research confirmed that only 63 Quebec players played in the NHL without having worn either the Montreal Canadiens or Quebec Nordiques uniform during that 40-year period. And altogether there are only 176 Quebecers from 1970 to 2008–09 who played more than three seasons in the NHL. Out of that total almost 45 percent of them won NHL honours, trophies, or represented their team at the All-Star Game. In other words, only the most talented French-speaking Quebecers have NHL careers of more than 200 games.

"The NHL is the English Canadian league that *gives permission*—that *allows*—only the *best* players from all nations to play. Quebec,

Europe, even America—only the *best* players from these nations can make it to the NHL because when it comes time to equal talent they always take the good old Canadian boy." When Sirois expressed these views on TSN's *Off the Record*, host Michael Landsberg asked another guest, former NHLer Bobby Holik, if this could possibly be true. A native of Czechoslovakia, Holik said, "I agree 100 percent with Bob Sirois, because...I had to go through the same shit every year."

Sirois contends that 70 percent of hockey operations personnel—scouts, GMs, and coaches—on virtually every team in the NHL are English Canadian and suggests that this domination drives the draft selection process. "It's normal," he said. "When you're sitting at a table and the majority is from one region of the country, they will choose from their own backyard. When you're up to the third, fourth, or fifth round that usually happens."

But Sirois also hints at something darker than just picking hometown heroes, a belief that players from certain backgrounds play a certain way. "It's not racist, but they always find a fault, a problem with the way a Quebec player plays—or an American player or a European player. The real way of playing hockey is the way the good old Canadian boys play. We hear it all the time. They say that French players are not as tough, they don't know how to play defence, they are only one-way offensive players. They have great goalies and that's about it—and they only have great goalies because they are getting so many shots when they're juniors. The list is long. We've heard them all."

Sirois confesses to watching Don Cherry on *Coach's Corner*, not to "catch him" but because often he "makes sense" in his hockey analysis. However, Sirois points to Cherry as a big part of the perception problem regarding French Quebec players.

"He has been planting all those stereotypes in the rest of Canada for years. Everyone who listens to Don Cherry hears them. Kids who are 6 to 12 years old and growing up in Manitoba or Saskatchewan are listening to him. They're drinking in his words and they will think the same thing also. So he has created those stereotypes. I read a lot of blogs, especially since my book came out. Many say I'm a 'fucking idiot from Quebec,' but I read a lot of these people and they're talking the same way that Don Cherry's talking, so that's the sad part. That's the sad part. I don't know why he's such a hero with some politicians in Canada. He shouldn't be because he's not helping the country *at all*—not on the French side or the English side.

"Since he's been talking every time a guy dies or has a major injury in Afghanistan, whether he be French, Irish, Canadian, whatever—he's almost crying, or sometimes actually crying. I appreciate that of him and maybe that's the thing that's kind of mellowed him lately toward the French because there are a lot of French soldiers that have died also. It makes people realize that stereotypes and saying all kinds of unfounded things does not help the NHL—or the great country that Canada is, between the French and the English."

Ironically, some critics have accused Sirois of being little more than a French version of Cherry at his worst, with his own pro-French biases clouding his judgment. Others question his motives, suggesting that he has a political agenda and is using hockey as weapon to attack English Canada. His English book came out just months after controversial statements by Parti Quebecois Leader Pauline Marois in which she complained that there weren't enough French-speaking players on the Montreal Canadiens. Her party's language critic,

Pierre Curzi, had earlier hinted that there was a kind of federal conspiracy at play in the makeup of the Habs roster. The lack of Francophonie was "not by chance," he railed on the French-language show *Les Franc-tireurs*. The accusations received a lot of attention in the press both inside and outside Quebec. Most people agreed that the charges were absurd and irresponsible. And then along came Bob Sirois' book to add fuel to a fire that was all but extinguished. The timing of its publication suggested conspiracy to some English Canadians. Sirois laughs off the claim.

"My father is a French American, born and raised in the United States, in Maine. All my family, all my relatives on my father's side, all the Sirois—there were none who were Quebecers—they all live in the States. I'm the only one living here so that makes me an American French separatist. We're going to separate Maine from the rest of the States! My political view—I believe that there are two nations in this country just like everybody knows. But I don't think that just because we are two nations we cannot live together. I played hockey in Switzerland where it's a confederation of three different nations—French, Italian, and German—and they get along well. So I'm not that hard separatist who says, 'Hey, lets get our own country.' No, I fully understand what Canada is all about and there are two nations there and sure I would push for more power for Quebec in regard to immigration and different things, but I'm not the kind of separatist who wants to become a country with borders and all that. Far from it."

He does, however, feel that Quebec is a nation and as such should have their own team in the World Junior Hockey Championships. He cites the "contempt that Hockey Canada has for Quebec hockey players." Only when

there is a Junior Team Quebec will "we finally grasp what actually is the mysterious Quebec style of play that leading Canadian hockey analysts have attributed to Quebecers, often with contempt."

As for the comments from Marois and Curzi, Sirois attributes them to a failure to communicate, and seems almost embarrassed by the fuss. "They explained themselves really badly. What [Curzi] was saying—and I've talked to the gentlemen—was that it used to be that the Montreal Canadiens were always being called the Flying Frenchmen. It was a nice and clear indication of what Quebec was all about. Well, now it is no more the Flying Frenchmen because there's almost none left. That's about all he wanted to explain but he explained it very badly."

Sirois does not buy the argument that the QMJHL of recent years is too large and the talent pool too shallow. He also rejects the theory that the QMJHL is not preparing players for the rigours of NHL hockey. He dismisses these arguments as media hype from the English Canadian OHL and WHL.

"They've always said that," Sirois said. "The last 5 or 10 years or even my time when I played in the Quebec league they were saying the same thing. I remember when I arrived at my first training camp with the Flyers. I was looking at all these guys from the West and the Ontario league and I had heard so many things. Well, after playing a couple of shifts, a couple of games, I thought 'Holy geez, they're just like us.' There's no difference. A human being is a human being."

The other argument that he is quick to counter is the one that most teams use: they will always choose the best players available. "When Serge Savard was general manager of the Montreal Canadiens," Sirois said, "he said this a hundred times. 'If they have equal talent I will always choose the player from Quebec.'

And a few times he had it and some reporters asked him why and he said, 'In the rest of the NHL [if they] have equal talent they won't take a Quebec player.' So who is there to judge what is equal or not? We're talking about a real fine line there. When Bob Gainey was in Minnesota and Dallas for eight years, he drafted two Quebecers. Can you imagine if he had been general manager in Montreal in those years—the 1990s—and he had only drafted two Quebecers in eight years? They would have hanged him in a public square."

Sirois goes so far as to say that if you play at the midget level in Quebec you might want to assume an English surname. "If your family name is English you get one chance out of 334 to be drafted, but if you're French it's one out of 618," he claimed.

One of his most influential critics has been prolific hockey author Andrew Podnieks. When *Discrimination* (*LeQuebec mis en echec*) first came out in French, he wrote: 'Sirois' biggest statistical error is to consider NHLers in terms of ratio to the entire population of the country." Podnieks then provides the ratio of Quebec hockey players to Canadians in the rest of the country. "In 2005–06 there were 482,483 male registered players in Canada. Of that number, 83,215 (or 17.2 percent) were from Quebec. There were 518 Canadians in the NHL that year, and 91 from Quebec (or 17.6 percent). The percentage of Quebec-born players in the NHL is almost identical to the overall number of participants. Where's the racism here?"

"Podnieks never read the book," countered Sirois. "He assumed a lot of things that weren't in the book and after that he criticized whatever he *assumed* was there. When he says that I measured the population of the country, there is none of that in the book. And the chart that he's talking about—the real way to measure players by counting the number of registered hockey players in different countries, *it's in my book.* He never saw it! Everybody used his article to criticize my book. In the new English version I prove Podnieks wrong 100 percent and that's why he didn't say one word this time."

"In the NHL [in 2009–10] there were 400-some Canadian players from the rest of Canada and only 187 players from the US and yet over the last 10 years there are more kids playing minor hockey in the States than in Canada. But they do the same things with the Americans too. If they have equal talent they go for the good old Canadian boys. It's not Bob Sirois' opinion, those are the facts, those are the numbers.

"I start my book in 1970, the first time the Montreal Canadiens weren't allowed to draft the first two Quebecers. It was normal when you only had six teams in the NHL that one team was always picking the best players. Most of them were English Canadian. So sure, Montreal was the team of the French and the five other teams were the rest of Canada. That's what the league was and it stayed like that for a long time."

Sirois states that some teams have been much more accepting of French players than others. When the Philadelphia Flyers franchise entered the NHL in 1967 their farm team was the Quebec Aces. Keith Allen was the first Flyers coach and Marcel Pelletier the chief scout. "They knew one thing—if they wanted to have crowds in Quebec City then they'd better have a lot of Quebec players," said Sirois. Whatever the reasons, the decision to recruit French players to the Aces paid off in spades for the parent club. During their four years in Quebec City before moving to Richmond, the farm team sent no fewer than 14 Quebecers to the Philadelphia Flyers.

Sirois also cites Buffalo as a franchise whose faith in French players was rewarded.

Punch Imlach had been coach, general manager, vice president, and part owner of the Quebec Aces in the '40s and '50s and he knew something about French talent. One of his former Aces was the great Jean Beliveau. When Imlach became the first coach and general manager of the Buffalo Sabres in 1970, he turned to the province he knew so well. His first move was to pick Gilbert Perreault in the team's initial draft, hardly a shock to anyone, since as a junior Perreault had superstar written all over him. But Imlach didn't stop there. He built his team around French players. To Sirois the moral of the story is to have faith in the talent of Quebec players. "People who have something to do with Quebec like Philadelphia and Buffalo have drafted the most Quebecers since 1970. Philly and Buffalo have brought in an average of one Quebec player a year.... When you look at other teams it's one every six years or seven years. Since Carolina's been in the NHL only one Quebecer played more than one year with them. So there are major differences between teams."

The stand taken by Sirois begs the question as to whether this is some kind of vendetta based on personal experience. "I had no problems when I played. I saw incidents on the ice against other teams but inside our own team maybe three or four guys didn't like the frogs. But then again they didn't like the Jews, they didn't like this group, they didn't like that group. It's normal. It didn't bother me and most of the Quebecers who played in the NHL. In Washington there were three of us, Guy Charron, myself, and Bob Picard. We were the No. 1 and No. 2 scorers and defence on the team so guys couldn't bitch too much about us, I guess. My coaches were no problem, they played me 20, 25, 30 minutes a game."

He emphasizes that the problem lay with players who were not stars. "I could see what was going on," Sirois said. "Often they would

bring a kid from the minors and some of those were Quebec kids and they were pretty good but they couldn't make it to the first or second line so they were sent back to the minors. That's a reality—I saw it happen."

One product of the QMJHL who was not overlooked is Sidney Crosby, an Anglophone from Cole Harbour, Nova Scotia. "He is the No. 1 player in the NHL now. Sure, Ovechkin is there. But if you look at Crosby's determination, he's already won the Stanley Cup! He goes all out every shift, not off and on—he stays on all the time. One hundred percent! I love him. It's a lot of hard work but people often say, 'Well, he's got so much talent.' Well sure he's got talent but it's much bigger than talent—he's working hard, he's a grinder, he always gives the second effort, and that's why he's so good. Because if you're just talking about talent—talented guys like Mario Lemieux—he's nothing compared to Mario Lemieux but he will produce just as much as Mario has in his career." The success of stars like Crosby fails to placate Sirois. "The sad thing about the Quebec league

Playing 17 seasons for the Buffalo Sabres in the 1970s and 1980s, Gilbert Perreault retired with franchise records in games played, goals, assists, and points.

Melchior DiGiacomo/ Getty Images

81

Bob Sirois played in 286 NHL games from 1974–80. In 2010, he authored the book *Discrimination in the NHL: Quebec Hockey Players Sidelined.*

Bruce Bennett

○ ○ ○ ○

Hockey and beer go together like baseball and Cracker Jack. And the Molson name is almost as famous for one as it is the other. It was only natural then that when the Molson brothers—Geoff, Justin, and Andrew—acquired the Canadiens in 2009, many Quebecers were reassured by the move. The brothers are continuing a family tradition with the purchase. In 1957, Senator Donat Raymond sold the team to Senator Hartland Molson and his brother, Thomas. Seven years later, the brothers dealt the franchise to cousins Peter, David, and Bill who maintained control until 1971. After another seven-year hiatus, Molson Breweries acquired the team from Edward and Peter Bronfman in 1978.

The construction of the Molson Centre (now the Bell Centre), which debuted in 1996, was largely thanks to Eric Molson, the father of the three new owners. In 2001 when no Quebec buyers came forward, American George Gillett Jr. became the majority owner with a winning bid of $275 million.

The latest sale attracted several bidding groups, including famous Quebec names such as Stephen Bronfman, Serge Savard, Celine Dion, and Rene Angelil. The eventual success of the Molson bid was lauded by NHL commissioner Gary Bettman.

Geoff Molson feels that ownership of this cornerstone franchise comes with special responsibility. He is acutely aware of the tradition of the club and its cultural importance to Quebecers. Not only is it a dynamic organization that must establish and maintain a winning strategy, it's also part of the heritage of the predominant language group of the province. Balancing the two aspects of ownership presents problems in a place with such political and social complexities.

and the Maritimes players is that there are 10 teams in the NHL that don't even have a full-time scout in the Quebec league and it's not only the Quebec players that aren't being seen, it's the Maritimes players also. Scouts come to the Quebec league only to see the superstars. The others no one has even seen in some cases.

"Crosby's doing what a lot of Quebec players have done—he's saving a franchise. Marcel Dionne saved the L.A. franchise, Gilbert Perreault and the French Connection in Buffalo, Mario Lemieux in Pittsburgh, Lecavalier in Tampa, Gilbert and Ratelle with the New York Rangers—the list is long and if you look at these guys, they were all the franchise players and they were the guys that were drawing the crowds because there are a lot of teams that wouldn't even be in the NHL if it wasn't for all these guys who came from the Q."

Molson's hockey coming of age was typical of Quebec youth, French or English. "My parents did a basement renovation and they basically made it unbreakable," he recalled. "If you can picture a gymnasium floor and squash court walls made of wood that you couldn't put a hole in unless you were Sidney Crosby. We had cages over the lights and two nets and lines on the floor for the faceoff. We either played knee hockey or ball hockey or murder ball. It was just a great room for hockey. In knee hockey, we had the little mini sticks that are maybe 2 feet high and they come with a little spongy puck so we'd just get on our knees and shoot it back and forth. Murder ball is just torture. Each kid gets five balls and you just throw them at each other. We played road hockey all the time in the spring and fall. It taught you to stick-handle and keep your stick down.

"When I was growing up, we lived across the street from an outdoor hockey rink. Pretty much every day when I finished my homework and dinner I was allowed to go out there and skate for a couple of hours just like any other kid. Those sessions were right after breakfast until lunch, then have a quick sandwich, and then go right back and then home for dinner. It was just one of those things with three brothers growing up together. It was our winter pastime and it was a lot of fun. That's how I grew up playing hockey. I actually didn't play competitive hockey until I was probably 10 or 11 when I started playing in the city leagues in the Eastern Townships.

"Later I became a defenceman but at the time I was a left winger and I liked Steve Shutt. As a kid I chose Shutt as a favourite just because I was a big fan of goal scoring at the time—and he used to score *a lot* of goals. And he wasn't Guy Lafleur, he was Guy Lafleur's linemate, so you know I kind of felt like he needed my support. He was a left-hand shot

as well, which made a big difference because I was a left-hand shot. That was important to me at the time. St. Lawrence [University] was where I decided I wanted to go to university. I was a walk-on on the hockey team. I was sort of up and down, always the No. 7 or 8 defenceman. We had a great team. We got to the finals one year in Division 1 and Final Eight another year and Final Four. There were times when they sent me to play in the junior ranks in Brockville and I played a year in France as well during my college days. But as much as I would have loved to have been on the roster all the time, I was always on the cusp. I was very proud to be there though.

"The Molson family has always been part of hockey, part of the game's history. My great uncle and my grandfather bought the Canadiens club back in 1957. It's been in the hands of our family or our company pretty much ever since, except for a short period, so I grew up with it and was around it on a very regular basis. It's something that our family knows well in terms of its relationship with the community and the importance of this team to Quebec. And so if there's an owner that understands that importance the most— purely based on history, it's us. We've had three generations of attachment to it.

"When we first sold it in my lifetime, Molson sold 80 percent of it to George Gillett and we held on to that 20 percent for the reasons I just mentioned—its relationship to the community and the importance of this team in the province. We wanted to make sure that the new owner was a good one, and if not we knew what our rights were by holding 20 percent. Finally George decided that he needed to sell and at first we sort of observed for a while to see what was going on in the marketplace, hoping that the right people were going to buy it. I was on the board of the Canadiens at the time and as we went through the process, I started to

Geoff Molson speaks at a news conference in 2009 after NHL board of governors approved the sale of the Montreal Canadiens to a group of investors, headed by Molson and his brothers Andrew and Justin.

understand that this move was possible for our family. As soon as I came to that realization and talked to my family about it, it was pretty much instantaneous interest. It was just a natural fit for us. And so we decided to go after it. We're happy we won. We still feel that obligation to the province and to the community with this team. That's the foundation of our belief and why we bought it.

"I don't think there's any huge difference between the way English and French Quebecers think of the Canadiens. I think the passion comes from all backgrounds. Being a great ethnic city, Montreal has people from all backgrounds. If I'm driving home listening to talk radio, which I do, I listen to the French station and the English station and I hear the same things being discussed. The attachment is pretty universal.

"As an owner, you have to feel pressure but it needs to be healthy pressure. The way that I approach these things is that if you're committed to winning and you build an organization around you that's committed to winning, your chances for success are greater. That's the best you can do. There are times when things will go well and there are times when things won't go well. My goal is to have a great organization that's well supported by its ownership all the way down to the players. I get gray hairs and nervous when I don't think we're at that stage, and there's always opportunity for growth.

"I try my best to turn all that pressure into positives. Over the years I've had a fair amount of exposure to the media but never anything close to this. That has pressure associated with it too, but if I'm true to the fans and if I'm true to the team, that's a very positive thing—the fact that you can stand in front of 8 million Quebecers and express yourself positively about your team. I try and interpret it as good pressure. The minute it becomes bad pressure, it's probably a good time to take a little holiday.

"In a city like Montreal, the Canadiens are so well covered that the media is desperate for new content. As a team and as an organization the content that we want to provide is: *tonight's the game and here's our lineup and we're excited about the players*—but that's not enough because there's too much coverage to say the same thing all the time. The pressure is on the players as a result. I wouldn't say it's because the media is negative, I'd say there's so much *more* of it now—everywhere. They have to watch everything they say and do. It could be anything from going to a bar where someone with a camera is taking a picture that can be put on Facebook within seconds, to walking out of the dressing room and saying something that they probably shouldn't have said. It's tough, it's tough on the players—way tougher than it's ever been before because technology makes everything so instantaneous.

"I made an announcement along with the bank that we refinanced part of our loan and it took 15 minutes from the minute it left our PR guy's computer to be on air and in the news; it took no time and that's the same with our hockey players. I watch these guys because I travel with them and they're always on their computers typing in their blogs, typing in their information. It's interesting.

"The media is always watching and there's the French-English thing. It was a hot topic last August because a few of our players who were French Canadian left the team and were replaced with players who weren't. I will always say the same thing and I believe it to be true. I'm committed to having the best possible team we can have on the ice and we're not in the game of politics. If we have a chance to have a local player who is going to be contributing to our success, that's icing on the cake. That's great! But we're not going to sacrifice winning, nor are we going to get involved in a political debate about language or party associations.

"I don't think I can analyze what has changed in Quebec society. I think the passion and the desire is still there. Quebec-born players are still in the NHL even though there are fewer of them. If you look back 30 years or less you'll find that there were very few Russians, very few Czechs, or Finns or Swedes or Americans. Now all of a sudden all of those countries—and then some—are participating, and it truly is an international sport if you compare it with basketball, football, or even baseball. The league has a good

8 to 12 countries represented. This idea of *picking* the nationality of the players on your team—it's very hard to do now because there are good players everywhere. If a great French Canadian player comes up through the system, there are 30 teams that want him and *none of them are thinking about local content*! So it's an added pressure that we put on ourselves.

"We want as many fans as we can get and we're aware that in Toronto and all across the country we have fans. From a marketing perspective, we want to be talking to them outside of Quebec as well—and that can be through television, that can be through the Internet. I wouldn't say that our objective is to steal fans from Toronto. I would say our objective it to maintain and build our own fan base. Kids will decide who they want to root for.

"The other interesting thing that's going on in the league right now is that kids, including my own, love their local team but they also love individual players, and I think that's really interesting. One of my kids may love Alexander Ovechkin but hate the Washington Capitals. I think it's healthy.

"I look at the great rivalries in sports and Canadiens-Leafs is probably similar to the Boston Red Sox and New York Yankees. Bostonians love to hate New York City and vice versa and I think it's driven by the sport more than anything. So you take that up here to Canada and since the beginning of hockey history the two most storied franchises have been battling against each other. Montreal is the smaller city with a different language. There's a bit of an underdog element. When you compare it with Boston and New York—Montreal is the Boston and Toronto is the New York. I think it's the sport that really contributes to that rivalry but I believe that it's also cultural. Quebec is a different world."

HOW HOCKEY EXPLAINS THE COLD WAR

IS IT POSSIBLE that Team Canada, and not Ronald Reagan, won the Cold War? Is it conceivable that it was Alan Eagleson's diplomacy and not Henry Kissinger's that helped to part the Iron Curtain? Was it a well-placed slash from a hired assassin named Bobby Clarke, and not the threat of nuclear annihilation that brought the mighty Soviets to their knees? Did Paul Henderson's dramatic 1972 Summit Series goal lead to Gorbachev tearing down that wall some 17 years later? Probably not. It was, after all, just a bunch of hockey games.

The fact is that the Summit Series changed Canada much more than it changed the Soviet Union. "We as a country are so divided—politically, language-wise, even geographically by regions," Henderson said. "There are so many dividing lines in terms of us being a country. We've really got five countries within the one country. Even when it comes to hockey, if Toronto is playing Montreal, I mean it's one country against another. That's just the way it is. But with Team Canada '72, there was none of that. We were all Canadian. That was the commonality. It was the first time—and maybe the only time—except in war—that we all got together and all the other stuff was cast aside. We were Team Canada and all of Canada was cheering for us."

No series of hockey games in Canadian history says as much about Canada, Canadian hockey, and Canadian character as the Summit Series of 1972. The eight-game competition serves as a microcosm of all that is good—and bad—about our country and our game.

Team Canada celebrates on the ice after Paul Henderson's game-winning goal in Game 8 to clinch the 1972 Summit Series.

Melchior DiGiacomo/ Getty Images

Alan Eagleson remembers his first foray into international hockey diplomacy. In 1966, then–Prime Minister Pierre Trudeau's government had formed a task force on amateur sport from which concerns were raised about the failure of Canada's international hockey teams abroad. The result was the formation of Hockey Canada in 1967. Eagleson was named to the first board of the fledgling organization and was sent to the 1969 World Hockey Championships in Sweden to meet with international hockey powers. "Everyone agreed to meet me except the Russians," said Eagleson. "I told Ambassador Arthur Andrew that we were making no headway. They kept saying they wanted to talk to [NHL president] Clarence Campbell and not me."

Eagleson decided to use one of the Russians' own weapons to secure the meeting. "Andrew had warned me that whatever was sent to our embassy the Russians were intercepting," he said. "By then I was running the NHL Players' Association so we concocted an idea. I sent a memo saying 'I would like to meet the hockey federation but I've been told that they will only meet Mr. Campbell. Mr. Campbell is the president of the league and he is the employee of the Capitalist owners and I run the Players' Association which is really a union so I am the union head.' And I mean literally within a day the meeting was set up for April 8, 1969, and that was the start of what became the '72 Summit Series."

Brian Conacher, a player with both international and NHL experience, remembers Eagleson as the right man at the right time for Canada. "Eagleson was a Nikita Kruschev kind of guy—belligerent, bully loudmouth kind of thing. But Eagleson was the man of the time really. He stood up to the Russians in the committee rooms where the rest of the Canadians hadn't. Eagleson could bang his shoe on the podium just as easily as the Russians could. That's what was needed, so because of Alan the team felt that they weren't going to be pushed around. If the Soviets were going to play games with them, they had at least somebody at the top level that was going to stand up for them."

Canada's role in the Cold War may not have featured the nuclear brinkmanship seen in the Cuban Missile Crisis, or the propagandistic power of the Space Race, but it did not lack intrigue or drama. The 1950s, '60s, and '70s were a time when new words and phrases entered our consciousness and our vocabulary; among them were "détente," "mutually-assured destruction," "peaceful coexistence," "nuclear deterrence," "spheres of influence," "tactical nuclear weapons," "embargoes," "blockades," "draft dodgers," "SALT I and SALT II," the "Red Button," "fallout shelters," and "antiballistic missiles." They were used regularly on the 6:00 news and in newspaper headlines.

The early '70s were still a time of espionage, propaganda, and mistrust. In January 1972, US president Richard Nixon gave the go-ahead for a space shuttle program. In February, Nixon visited Beijing and on a return visit in May had reached a rapprochement with Chinese leader Mao Zedong. These events made the Soviets even more nervous than usual. Late May brought a glimmer of hope as the United States and USSR signed the SALT I agreement and the Anti-Ballistic Missile Treaty in Moscow, but tensions remained high.

Canada's official stance during this time was markedly different from that of the United States. Under the leadership of Prime Minister Pierre Trudeau (elected in 1968), Canada was phasing out its nuclear arsenal and replacing it with conventional weaponry in preparation for the role of peacemaker and peacekeeper. Nevertheless, Canada remained closely tied to the United States in its foreign policy. A major producer of uranium, Canada was very much part of the arms race whether we liked it or not. As a NATO member we were a significant player on the international scene, and the more the Cold War heated up ideologically and militarily, the closer we were drawn to the United States.

As for the Soviets, their curtain was still made of iron and their resolve of steel. They were using every propaganda weapon at their disposal to illustrate the superiority of their system of government. One of those weapons was sport, and one of those sports was hockey. In 1971, Soviet Premier Alexei Kosygin and Canadian Prime Minister Pierre Trudeau had discussed "hockey diplomacy" during a state visit to Moscow.

On the surface, the 1972 Summit Series between the USSR and Canada was simply an opportunity for both countries to showcase their finest athletes. Trudeau also saw it as a way for the peoples of Canada and the USSR to put political differences aside and connect on a human level, through a common passion for hockey. His other, unstated, agenda was to help repair the damage done to national unity after the divisive October Crisis in Quebec two years earlier. With a team that included players from across the country—and notably a half-dozen Francophone Quebecers—it seemed a sound strategy.

The eight-game tournament was originally promoted as the "Friendship Series." As things unwound, it became perhaps the biggest misnomer since World War I was dubbed "the war to end all wars." "A friendship series?" chuckled Eagleson. "That's what someone in Foreign Affairs suggested. I didn't comment at the time and haven't since I never looked upon it as *anything* but a competitive series. My discussions with the Russians were always on the basis of, *Listen, you have proved that you have the best amateur hockey players in the world even though I don't agree with your definition. I feel that Canada has got the best professional hockey players in the world but we can't play in the world championships because we're playing in the NHL Stanley Cup Playoffs. So let's play each other and then we'll have the bragging rights—either you'll be right or we'll be right.* Long before the series, probably in 1970, [former Soviet coach] Anatoli Tarasov had announced that his players—his team— were the best hockey team in the world. That got our dander up."

For both nations, this competition was a struggle of ideologies, national pride, and personal pride and, oh yes, hockey supremacy. "It was not only a Cold War in those days, it was a frigid war," said Eagleson. "My wife and I went to Moscow and we were followed everywhere. I mean it was so obvious! Everywhere we went there were two guys in black fedoras and long great coats. It was like something out of a John le Carre novel."

Team Canada's Ron Ellis agreed that there was much more to the games than hockey. "It was as close to war as I'll experience. It was one way of life against another. Canada believed that we were the birthplace of the game and they were trying to take something that was ours away from us. And of course the politics. We knew that if they beat us they would use this to a big extent as propaganda. *We beat the Canadians so our system must be good.*"

For Bobby Clarke, the politics were secondary to the hockey. "I think it was more hatred of an opponent than ideological," Clarke said. "I hated them when I played against them but in '86 they came to Canada and I had Tretiak out to my house. Took him shopping and got him a whole bunch of leather clothing and all that shit that he couldn't get in Russia. Over the years I found that as soon as you got away from the game they were no different from us really, they were just hockey players. They

Team Canada head coach Harry Sinden (centre) steps onto the ice at the 1972 Summit Series. Sinden's international experience extended back to the 1950s.

Melchior DiGiacomo/ Getty Images

weren't politicians. They could have cared less about politics just like the rest of us."

Thus, for Canada it really was to be a Cold War—ice cold to be exact. The game of brinksmanship that Canada played would involve being behind by two goals to the Soviets after two periods in Game 8, the biggest game in Canadian hockey history. Canada's strategic blockade consisted of 11 defencemen and 3 goalies. The provocateur/assassin turned out to be Clarke and the Secret Weapon was Paul Henderson. The Strategic Command consisted of head coach Harry Sinden, assistant John Ferguson, and mastermind Alan Eagleson.

Canadian coach Harry Sinden was a battle-tested Cold Warrior, his experience extending all the way back to the late '50s. In 1957 Sputnik 1 had successfully been launched into orbit around the earth and the space race was officially on. That same year Canada and the United States had refused to participate in the Hockey World Championships because of the Soviet's invasion of Hungary. The tournament, held in Moscow, was won by Sweden. In 1956, Canada had lost the Olympics to the USSR, which meant that they hadn't captured a world title since the Penticton Vees beat the USSR 5–0 in the final game in 1955. "There were three years in which our hockey supremacy internationally had a pretty big void in it," said Sinden. "Now in '58 we were going to participate again."

The whole country was primed for redemption. Representing Canada in '58 was the 1957 Allan Cup champion Whitby Dunlops of the OHA senior A league. In addition to Sinden, who captained the squad, the team featured former Toronto Maple Leafs captain Sid Smith as player-coach. The Soviet team came to Canada for the first time to play a series of exhibition games in preparation for the championships in Oslo, Norway. North America was rife with anti-Communist hysteria. "The Cold War was in full flight," recalled Sinden. "The country was pumped and when they came it stirred interest unbelievably of Canadian hockey fans." Like today, amateur hockey usually got little attention or respect. But Canadians were anxious to regain their hockey credibility, and superiority, in an international showcase.

"Everybody knew about it but it didn't get the exposure of the NHL, but all of a sudden it goes right to the top of the interest level with this mysterious Soviet hockey team that had won the Olympics," Sinden said. The two teams were to play one game in Toronto followed by a few others across the country. "The opening game at Maple Leaf Gardens was a big, big event—for the country and for Toronto in particular," Sinden continued. "That, along with the fact that it was the middle of the Cold War and we'd lost or hadn't participated in the championship the prior two years—put the '58 championship on everybody's mind. It really was, as far as the fans were concerned and in the press, like the Stanley Cup final. Diefenbaker was the Prime Minister and we got telegrams from him. We got thousands and thousands of signatures or names wishing us well while we were in Oslo."

It was these exhibition tilts that helped to seal Canada's international hockey reputation for skill, for ability—and for thuggery. "Our reputation amongst international teams was that we had very, very aggressive players; very, very physical players; dirty players—all of whom were prepared to fight at any time." It was a reputation that was to precede them to Europe and set the stage for more of the same. "Some of it came off the game in Toronto," recalled Sinden. "We won 7–2 but they scored the first two goals and then we changed our tactics and became very physical with them and ended up winning the game by quite a margin." Far from being ashamed of the aggressive label, the Canadians went to great lengths to promote and even exaggerate it. "We carried on that image as best we could," Sinden remembered, "even faking it in pretournament games so that we would go into the World Championships hopefully with everyone a little intimidated. The Europeans didn't admire that at all."

Whatever the reasons, the Canadians cruised to victory in Oslo, winning all seven games to reestablish world dominance. They outscored the opposition 82–6, the closest contest the final game, a 4–2 win over the Soviets.

In 1959 Canada won it again. Belleville represented the country and they repeated the physical tactics and intimidation employed in 1958. Says Sinden: "We had used those physical tactics [successfully] in '55 too with the Trail Smoke Eaters. Our tactics had a lot to do with our victories [back then]."

By the time the Winter Olympics rolled around in 1960, the Canadians had new management and different coaches. The games were played in Squaw Valley, California, scarcely a hockey hotbed. The Olympics possessed a prestige factor that made it unlike any other sporting event in the world and the Canadians adjusted their play accordingly. "Just what the Olympics stood for tempered the Canadian team," admitted Sinden. "It had a different air to it than the Worlds. I don't recall it [violence] being nearly the issue that it was in 1958. It was played in North America, and the Americans were closer to the European philosophy, a college type of thinking. They were all college kids on the US team, not the Junior A, pro style that the Canadian national team had in those days."

The United States went on to win their first hockey gold medal with Canada capturing silver and the Soviet Union settling for bronze. "Politics were there," said Sinden, "but hockey didn't get attention in the US until after they won. Had it been a clash of basketball teams, the political significance would have been much greater." Canada's team, the Trail Smoke Eaters, won the Worlds again in 1961. That was to be it for the next 11 years.

By the time the 1972 Summit Series arrived, everything had changed. During the intervening years from 1960, the Canadian teams had not fared well against the world. Olympic rules forbade professionals from competing; however the Soviet Union found a clever way to get around this restriction. There was no doubt that hockey was their full-time profession, but these elite athletes were given other job descriptions, most notably as soldiers in the Central Red Army. This put Canada at a distinct disadvantage in international competition, since Canada's best players were playing for money in the NHL and other North American pro leagues. Canadian teams had returned home as also-rans since 1961. Olympic glory was equally elusive with two paltry bronze medals to show from 1956 to 1972. Meanwhile, the USSR had monopolized the World Hockey Championship since 1962, winning nine straight before finishing in second behind the Czechs in Prague in 1972. The Soviets had also brought home gold in the three previous Olympics. In protest of the unfairness inherent in the amateur ruling, Canada boycotted both the IIHF World Championships and the Olympics from 1969 onward. The '72 World Ice Hockey marked the first time that two tournaments were held during an Olympic year. Prior to this, the Olympics winner had automatically been designated world champion.

Canadians saw the Summit Series as a chance to put Canada back where it belonged, on top of the hockey ladder. The series would feature four games on Canadian soil followed by four in Moscow.

One of the key members of Sinden's Team Canada in the Summit Series was Montreal Canadiens defenceman Serge Savard. With five full NHL seasons under his belt, plus a Conn Smythe Trophy as MVP in the '68–69 Stanley Cup playoffs, Savard was an established star when he joined the team. By the time he finally hung up his skates after 17 seasons, he would have won seven Stanley Cups in 14 seasons as a player in Montreal. Despite the NHL success, the '72 series holds a special place in his heart.

"For me it was probably the biggest thrill of my sports career," Savard said. "I put that ahead of any Stanley Cup I won. I don't think an athlete could have elevated himself as high as we did in '72 if he didn't feel that way. It meant a lot more to us. We represented our country. But it was more than that because we got caught in the middle of a war. There were two systems that were comparing themselves. The Russians were trying to show the world that the Communist system was the best system in the world. And they were trying to show the world through their athletes that the best athletes were formed in the best system! We were caught in the middle of that whether we wanted it or not, and we had to prove it's not true."

Brian Conacher thinks that the political tenor of the times was at the forefront of most people's thoughts. "The Cold War and all that went with it was weighing on people hugely," he suggested. "It became them against us. We represented our way of life and our political system and it was Capitalism against Communism and Socialism and stuff like this. That was very much a part of it and I think that's why at the end of the series there has not been a Canadian sports event that more unified the country for a short period of time than that series. It took a long period of time for the Canadian public because there was a certain apathy toward the series initially because we always felt that *yeah, they might be good but we've got the NHL* and only a handful of people in the country really recognized how good not only the Soviets were but also the Czechs and Finns and all of those countries."

The opening game in Montreal provided Canada with its most public gut check since an inebriated John A. MacDonald vomited on stage during an 1867 election debate. Unfortunately Canada's spies, also known as scouts, were rather ineffective and failed to secure the vital information that might have prepared the team for the Game 1 missile attack launched by the Soviets.

Less than 10 minutes into the series, with Canada leading 2–0, the line of Ron Ellis, Bobby Clarke, and Paul Henderson came off the ice. Ellis recalls a conversation with Henderson. "Paul and I are sitting there huffing and puffing and Paul looked at me and said, 'Ron, this is going to be a long series.' We knew at the 2:00 mark. We were huffing and puffing and my chest was burning and my legs were burning and the Russians were dancing."

Paul Henderson noted that it took a while for a group of players from different NHL teams to gel. "The problem we had was that we had 35 players—the best players in Canada," Henderson said. "There are 17 of us that can get on the ice so you've got 18 guys that are totally pissed off, especially when you're not winning. Everybody felt they should be in the lineup, which is a recipe for disaster. When you're a superstar and you're handed the role of being cheerleader, that is very, very difficult. Finally we got to the point where, *this has got to be the team*. I mean there were no changes for the last three games. When you know these are the guys you're going to go to war with, it's a lot easier to come together as a team. When you put another guy into the lineup it just changes the chemistry all the time. It was difficult for the coaching, and it must have been very difficult for some of the Hall of Famers who couldn't get Clarke, Ellis, and Henderson out of the lineup."

If the Russians were to make their own movie version of the series, it would no doubt start with a bunch of smirking, overfed Canadian players sitting in the stands watching Russian players practicing. Snide remarks about their inferior equipment and strange practice routines would pass between them. Meanwhile the Russians would go about their business.

"They were drinking and womanizing and to them it was just a laugh," said former *Hockey Night in Canada* producer Ralph Mellanby, who was a consulting producer for television coverage of the Summit Series. "They thought *we're going to kill these guys*, but the scouting reports were bad, the players were misled. And they didn't have any goaltending..." The final score of Game 1 was a devastating 7–2 in favour of the Soviets.

"We had never seen that," said Mellanby. "We didn't realize that they had invented a new way of playing hockey. We had never seen that before that first game. In our day, you picked up your man. I remember Esposito walking up to me after Game 5. He said, 'Where does Alexander Yakushev play? He lines up at centre then I can't find him. I'm trying to find him to check him.' That wasn't the way [the Canadians] played. They played in zones. I said, 'He goes wherever he wants. It's like soccer.' Once our coaches got on to that—and I give John Ferguson even more credit than

Tony Esposito tended goal for the Chicago Blackhawks for 14 seasons. A key member of the 1972 Summit Series team, Esposito played in goal in four of the eight Series games, winning Games 2 and 7.

Bruce Bennett Studios/Getty Images

Harry for that—once we learned how to break down their system, the coaching won it for us."

Coach Sinden and his staff had done their best to purge the team of such overconfidence. "They called Game 1 a wakeup call," Sinden said. "I'll be honest with you. I was awake all the time. I think the rest of them were sleeping. They were cocky, although they were careful not to let it show too much, publicly or otherwise. But it was definitely there." Sinden knew that between 1960 and 1972 a different group of people had taken over the international hockey program and their influence had resulted in changes that continued to evolve over the next 10 years. "It was now more of a gentleman's approach to the contest for Canada," said Sinden, who saw a connection between this evolution in style of play and Canada's dearth of championships.

"I tried to impress upon them that intimidation would not be a factor against the Soviets in this series," Sinden added. "Those tactics weren't going to win in '72. I was convinced of that. We were going to have to match them in ability and skill. And it wasn't long—one game to be exact—before our team realized that. We did change. The Soviets were now expecting us to be pretty rugged because it was a professional team they were going to play, not the Canadian National Team. I knew how skillful these players were. And I knew from '58 and little bit from '60, they were on the same level—they improved a lot in the 10 years. They were on the same level as the NHL players."

With few exceptions, the Canadian players came to the series out of shape, flabby from a summer of inactivity and too many sports banquets. Their plan was to play themselves into shape. Meanwhile the Soviets, using methods that were revolutionary by North American standards, arrived in tip-top shape. "They had fantastic condition-

ing," said Sinden. "They did a lot more weight training than we did in those days. They had a big emphasis on what they called dry land training. I'd say they trained 50 percent off the ice and 50 percent on, where we were about 95 on and 5 percent off."

Serge Savard, who ended up playing in five games (of which Canada won four and tied one) knew immediately that after a summer of golf, banquets, and barbeques, Team Canada lacked the conditioning of the Soviets. "There is no doubt that they were in better shape," said Savard. "They trained 11 months a year in those days. But you know, we came back right away. We won the second game."

In Game 2 at Maple Leaf Gardens, Tony Esposito replaced a shaky Ken Dryden in net and the Canucks overcame the shellshock of the previous game to prevail 4–1.

While Sinden admits that the Russians were in better shape, he defends the preparations that Team Canada made for the international encounter. "I'll tell you this: I've run a lot of training camps and ours was second to none for me," he said. "I knew what we were going to be up against. Our workouts were as difficult as I could make them. I had the team and I was their boss, but I wasn't their employer. They were volunteers and you can't have exactly the same control over them in that situation as you do if you control their jobs . . . and their income.

"The Russians probably were ahead of us in conditioning to the point that even three or four weeks of really hard skating by us wouldn't allow us to catch up to a team that had probably trained for six months. But we weren't bad. We weren't bad at all."

Sinden also introduced some exercise regimens that left veteran NHL players and skeptical media shaking their heads. "I introduced a stretching program prior to every practice for this team out in the hallways of the arena—

before practice, before they even got their equipment on," he said. "Most people were shocked that we were doing this, you know? And this wasn't weight training, this was just a big stretching program, sit-ups and push-ups and things like that. That stuff was usually left up to the player himself in those days. So again the Soviets had a major impact. It changed everything. They changed our thinking big time. From 1960 on we understood and started believing that, but Canadian amateur teams started to do it before the NHL."

The Commies vs. The Capitalists road show moved west to Winnipeg for Game 3, and the Canadian team squandered leads of 3–1 and 4–2 before settling for a 4–4 tie.

In Vancouver for Game 4, Team Canada had yet another loud wakeup call. This one came in the form of boos. The team played poorly and left the ice at the end of a 5–3 loss with the jeers of Canadian fans assaulting their ears. The cockiness that prevailed in training camp was now completely gone and suddenly a sense of desperation permeated the team.

After the humiliation, a shaken Phil Esposito went on TV to express the feelings of his team. Using words such as "disheartened," "disillusioned," and "disappointed" to describe the mood in the dressing room, he assured fans across the country that they were giving it "our 150 percent." He went on to say that they were playing only, "because we love our country, and not for any other reason.... We came because we love Canada." His final sentence sounded at once chiding and hurt. "I don't think it's fair that we should be booed," he said.

Eagleson sees the booing as a double-edged sword. It was shocking, but it also served to rally Canadians around their beleaguered team. "We get to Game 5 and Espo's big speech in Vancouver was a major factor in getting the country behind us," he recalled. "Who knows what would have happened if

they had not gotten behind us? But Espo's interview with [CTV's] Johnny Esaw certainly was one of the turning points of the series."

Coach Sinden admits he was surprised to hear the boos. "I was as upset as the players over it," he said. "We didn't expect any of it. I guess that's why it seemed worse than it was. We had played a poor game, a very poor game and it was there. Our reaction to it, including my own, was embarrassment that we had performed poorly. In some ways we magnified it to cast part of the blame on the crowd."

Ever the pragmatist, Bobby Clarke felt the team got what they deserved, that the fans were just reacting to a poor performance by the team. He thinks that most of his teammates understood that. "I think everybody was mad," he said. "They were mad that we got booed, but they were mad at themselves, not the fans. I can speak only for myself, but there was anger at the way I'd played and the way we as a group had played. It wasn't the fans. We deserved what we got."

Eagleson isn't as willing to forgive and forget. "The booing in Vancouver was so bad that I vowed publicly that I'd never play another game there if I had anything to do with a Canadian team," he said. "I finally reneged and reluctantly agreed to play once more at the '84 Canada Cup. We stunk the joint out. Once again I vowed, 'That's it. I'm never ever going to go there again.'"

Clarke, one of the few Canadian players who arrived in good physical shape, feels that the team simply ran out of gas on the last leg of the Canadian half of the series. "We started off in such poor condition," he said. "We won a game and tied a game mostly on emotion. In Vancouver we had nothing left to give."

Entire books have been written about it, but Alan Eagleson manages to summarize the first four games of the Summit Series in very concise fashion. "It started out in Montreal with a major deflation," he said. "Then we get to Toronto and it's elation. We get to Winnipeg, we're up 4–2 and we end up tying them, instead of being happy—deflation. We get to Vancouver—total deflation."

The two teams had a two-week break before hostilities resumed in Moscow. With a bitterness fed equally by a critical media and sky-high fan expectations, the Canadian players practised and stewed.... It was now clear that many of them hated the Russians and all they stood for.

En route to Moscow, the team made a stop in Sweden for an exhibition. Coach Sinden points to one workout that might have been a turning point for the Canadians.

"In retrospect you look at it and say it was," he said, "but at the time we didn't have that in mind. There were 35 players on the team and it was too unwieldy to have one practice for 35 players so we split them and had two workouts. John [Ferguson] would run one workout and I'd run the other. But this particular day—the day we were about to leave Sweden and go to Moscow—I had them all come on the ice at the same time. And they all got out there and there were three goalies: Dryden, Tony Esposito, and Eddie Johnston and they were just skating around, waiting for the practice to begin when John and I came out and told the goalies to go back in and take their equipment off—we wouldn't be needing them. That was a bad sign for the players.

"I began and I put them through conditioning drills, skating drills, every possible one I'd ever done in my career until I couldn't think of any more to do...and the longer we went, the more determined they became—I'll never forget it, and finally they had probably had enough, but I was worse than them, I had had enough. Peter Mahovlich turned to me and he said, 'Is that all you've got?' To

me, it was symbolic that the team was determined to do whatever it would take. When I look back upon it—it's easy now because you've won the thing—but it was symbolic that these players were prepared to do what it would take in Moscow."

"I agree with Harry," said Clarke. "When we got into Sweden we started getting stronger physically, better conditioned, and better prepared to play at the level that was required to win."

Eagleson agrees that the stopover in Sweden was crucial to the coming together of the team. "We got rid of the sores within the team," he said. "It boiled to the surface in Moscow but it was stewing in Sweden, and that's where the team came together as a team. I can remember 9 or 10 players coming to my room before we played the first game, and one of them said, 'Oh, I just don't think we're going to win another game.' I just listened to them and I said, 'Hey guys, if that's the way you feel you should just go home.' They were saying, 'Harry and Fergie aren't this and they're not that, and they're not disciplined.'... Shit! Just a bunch of bellyachin' and I couldn't afford to alienate them. Because we could afford to lose five or six but we couldn't afford to lose 9 or 10."

In order to stem the mutiny and create a cohesive unit, Coach Sinden was forced to make some hard decisions for the overall good of the team. Back in August, when players were asked to volunteer for the series, Sinden had promised to play everyone in at least one game. Now he was forced to renege on this commitment. "I wasn't able to manage that and so I had broken a promise to them after seeing what we were up against in Montreal," he said. "Most of them understood what we were up against. Most, but not all. That probably prevailed all the way through to Moscow. These were all National Hockey League stars, and they were not used to not dressing for every game and when they did dress they were used to playing a lot of minutes. The team we were up against was so good that we had to try and manage it with our best players against these particular opponents."

Bob Clarke thinks that the Team Canada brain trust deserves most of the credit for turning the series around. He singles out one man for most of the praise. "Harry Sinden," Clarke said. "It was the best coaching job ever done in hockey. He's coaching 35 guys all of whom think they're stars, somewhat stars, or kinda stars—all premier players on their own team. We came out of Canada having been beaten and we had players who wanted to quit. [Frank] Mahovlich doesn't come to Sweden and doesn't show up until Moscow. We get to Russia and players leave the team. Then the Russians decide the wives can't come. We went through more messes on that team than you go through in five years in the NHL—in dealing with high-ego people. Not all of them, but if you're a good player, you've got some ego. Everyone thinks they should play. That's the best coaching job in hockey that Canada's ever had."

After the exhibition games in Sweden, a team meeting was held in advance of the trip to Moscow. Many issues were discussed and seemed to be resolved. Once in Moscow the mutiny that they thought they had averted began. "[Vic] Hadfield changed his mind and once he did [Buffalo coach] Punch Imlach didn't have any difficulty persuading Gilbert Perreault and Rick Martin and Jocelyn Guevremont to go as well," recalled Eagleson. "Imlach was certainly persuading Martin and Perreault. His argument wasn't a bad argument, but it wasn't the time or place for it. Imlach's argument to the press—to George Gross back in Canada—was, 'Well, they're not playing over there so they may as well be over here where we pay their salary.' Remember these kids were young. Martin I think was about 20 and Perreault 21. But Perreault scored a goal for us in that first game over there and he would have been a major asset. Martin wasn't going to play anyway. Guevremont wasn't going to play and I don't think Hadfield was going to play. So the others we didn't lose but certainly we'd have liked to have Perreault stick around."

Once in Moscow, the Canadians were inside the jaws of the Russian bear and as significant as this series was back home, it was equally important in the heart of the Communist world. A few days prior to the series, on September 1, the Soviets had suffered a propaganda setback when American Bobby Fischer defeated Boris Spassky to claim supremacy in chess. But that was chess, the game of the elite. Hockey was the game of the proletariat, the sport of the people.

"It was the biggest event in Soviet sports history," said Sinden. "I get my hair cut here in Boston—I live in a town called Winchester—and my barber is a Russian who lived in Moscow and was a wrestler on the Red Army team at the time. He's a little younger than those players would be but he's in his sixties now. He'd have been around 20 years old then. He knew a lot of the players—he knew [Vladimir Petrov] very well—and he has told me what the mood was in Russia then. Not everybody had televisions and the quality wasn't very good. In most apartments if a guy had a television you couldn't get through the front door for people. They were all there to watch this thing on his television. He said it was an absolutely unforgettable, unforgettable series. He was very impressed by the whole thing. Oh sure they knew we were *the* hockey country. They absolutely knew all about us. Their purpose was to show that it was a myth, that we were not any better than they were."

The stories of intrigue and espionage that North Americans had read about or seen in movies suddenly became real for some. Frank Mahovlich was convinced he was being spied on. Mellanby remembers the impact it had on the big right winger.

"It affected Frank. He went nuts over there," Mellanby said. "They finally had to bench him and that's why. He was of Ukrainian descent and Stalin killed all the Ukrainians in a mass murder during the Second World War. He was afraid that someone was going to kill him. He had a very bad time and they had a hell of a time trying to settle him down because he was a nervous wreck. Meanwhile his brother Peter didn't give a shit. He just kept playing."

"I would say that Frank Mahovlich's value to the team in Russia was zero," Eagleson said. "It wasn't his fault. He started going downhill prior to the game in Vancouver—totally out of character. I've never seen Frank act like it before or since. He jumped on top of Tretiak and then just stayed on top of him for 30 seconds. And then before we went to Moscow he wanted to have a meeting with me and Fergie and Harry. He wanted us to get tents and put the tents up in Red Square and I said, 'Frank, we can't do that!' He'd had difficulties in the past emotionally and I'm sure the pressure of this series was getting to him, which was too bad because he's a great guy and a great hockey player and it was sad to see that happen. He and Pete were night and day, but they always were from the time they grew up."

Some players refuse to blame off-ice cloak and dagger events for anything, taking a more pragmatic approach to it all. "Frank saw espionage everywhere," Savard said. "He didn't have to be in Moscow to see espionage. I didn't experience anything while I was there. Obviously things were not like that in Canada in those days. We were in a Communist country with army people at the doors of the hotels. Their own people were not allowed to get in the hotels to see how people lived in the Western world. That's the way it was. Later on I became the owner of a hotel in a communist country [Cuba] and it was the same thing. There was nothing wrong, what happened there, and the proof is going on the big surface and losing the first game and winning the last three."

Clarke is another Canadian who dismisses stories of off-ice espionage and intimidation. "There were no incidents," he contended. "None. Talk about being safe. You're a bunch of Canadian hockey players playing Russian hockey players in Moscow! There's not much danger involved there. Sure there were soldiers with guns outside and in the rink but so what."

Clarke prefers to remember the ties that many Team Canada players established with the Russian people. "It was really neat. We had bags of gum and candy and we had pantyhose that we gave to the young people. There were always kids around us and we kept things in our pockets for them. There was never a moment that anyone was in danger. Why would they be tapping our phones? That's a lot of paranoia."

Mellanby disagrees. "Our hotel rooms were bugged and the players knew it," he said. "All the guys were very upset. I was the one who blew the whistle finally—I told them they were being bugged through the telephone. They said their telephones went off at 3 in the morning. I said that's when they bug you—through the mic in the telephone. Stay away from the telephones and they won't hear anything. You have to remember that I had a lot of experience in international stuff. I was the one who went to John [Ferguson] about it. I found that out from a friend of mine who was in the Soviet KGB. I said, 'How do you bug the rooms?' He said, 'Through the phones.' Once they knew that, a lot of the guys just ripped the phones out of the walls."

"We brought steaks over from Canada and they were confiscated, but not until we won a game," Eagleson said with a laugh. "We were fine until we won a game, which goes to show how the heat was turned up as the series went on. We won the Sunday game and Ken Dryden had a great game. We won 3–2 after having lost the first 5–4 in Moscow. We got there in a roundabout way, but they confiscated our steaks. At that point the Russians thought, *Geez, maybe this is not a shoe-in.* They still thought they'd win but they made life miserable, starting right then. They cut in on our ice time. We went out to practice the next day and they had probably 700 or 800 kids skating around on our ice. We solved that. I had Rod Gilbert and Brad Park go out and hit some slap shots and that got rid of them. Pete Mahovlich did it with a flourish. He pretended he was going to line the kids up against the boards and hit them with the puck, and they scattered very quickly.

"They used high-handed techniques and they tried anything they could to upset us— and we couldn't do much about it. That was the difference. If this happened in the United States you'd go to the police but there was no one to talk to. I would talk to my counterpart [Alexander Gresko] and he'd say, 'I can't help you. I don't own the rink.' He wouldn't take responsibility for anything.

"That was typical of our RCMP. Here was a guy that they had not been able to find out about—although it would have been easy if they'd looked it up. He was a high level KGB officer who'd been kicked out of England for spying for the Russians from the USSR embassy in London. And in 1972 here he was representing the Russians, and he and I were in Trudeau's office! It was incredible.

"Again, we were neophytes in all of that. Because Canada was small by comparison, I think we thought, *Oh, the KGB would never be interested in us.* We soon found out differently."

Mellanby swears that one of the most colourful and bizarre stories to emerge from the Summit really happened. Some Canadian players found what they thought was a listening bug concealed under the carpet of their room. When they tried to remove it, a chandelier crashed into the lobby one floor below them. "The chandelier story is true," he said. "Espo was one guy who was involved. The chandelier came crashing down in the hotel lobby."

Eagleson, who should know, questions the accuracy of the account. "I think the story is apocryphal," he suggested. "There was lots of bugging, but that was a story that was concocted. It certainly never happened to me and was never reported to me and it was never billed to me. I know one thing—if it had happened the Russians would have been all over me to play the bill for the chandelier!"

The first game in Moscow featured a collapse of major proportions. With 3,000 Canadian fans in attendance, Canada ran up a 4–1 lead in the third period only to cough it up. After the bitter taste of Vancouver, Eagleson feared the reaction of the fans. "We had already taken terrible, terrible hits in the press. Oh, they slaughtered us! Oh, awful. And then to get to Russia, lose the first game like that. When we came off the ice after having blown a 4–1 lead, I thought, *Holy shit, if we get booed here, our guys are going to be very upset.* And instead of that the 3,000 fans stood up and cheered them off the ice."

Because there were no fax machines and telegrams cost $10 each, the Canadian players really had little idea of what was going on back home. After all, they had boarded their

Team Canada is introduced before one of the Summit Series games at the Luzhniki Ice Palace in Moscow.

Melchior DiGiacomo/ Getty Images

plane in Vancouver with the sound of boos still echoing in their ears. It was then that the Canadian team got a much needed boost. "What was happening back home hit us in waves," recalled Eagleson. "On the morning after the loss, at about 4 someone was pounding on my door. I go outside and there was a green garbage bag—a big bag filled to the brim. I open it up; telegram Team Canada, telegram Team Canada, telegram Team Canada, Team Canada—from all over Canada. We took them to the rink early, got a couple of guys and sorted them province by province. And we did them from every province so that every player who was from that province could take a look and see what the people of Flin Flon were sending and what the people from Okotoks in Alberta and Smithers, British Columbia or wherever. We just walked into the rink and for a hundred yards as you walked down to our dress-

ing room, the players had an extra five million fans with them, all the way down that corridor. By the time that week was over I bet we had a hundred-thousand bucks worth of telegrams at ten bucks a pop."

One thing was for certain, the arrogance of training camp had dissipated, gone like the pipe dream of an eight-game sweep. It was replaced by a kind of resolve that touched on desperation in Game 6 when Bobby Clarke applied a vicious two-handed slash to the ankle of 5'8", 165-pound Russian star Valeri Kharlamov. With two goals, Kharlamov had been named MVP in the first game in Montreal and had used his explosive speed and agility to get around the Canadian defence. The ultimate in cheap shots knocked him out of the seventh game and rendered him ineffective in Game 8. The Russian press called Clarke's actions a "crime," and even many Canadians were outraged. Kharlamov had won over many Canadian fans with his brilliant play. "There's no stopping the admiration for good hockey players in Canada, no matter who they are," said Sinden.

Brian Conacher saw the play from the broadcast booth. "The retrospective of it, looking back 35 years later, it's the only aspect of the whole series that still leaves a bad taste in my mouth. No matter the fighting or the spearing or the slashing, a lot of that is reflex, but that was blatant, intentional, and with the intent to hurt, and when we got that desperate I thought that was the low point to me, not only in the series but in Canadian hockey."

Reports soon surfaced, not denied by Ferguson, that the assistant coach had "whispered in Clarke's ear" that he should disable the crafty little left winger. The very suggestion that Ferguson ordered the slash causes Serge Savard to bristle. The late Ferguson was Serge Savard's best friend. "Everybody mentions that John Ferguson told Bobby to do that," Savard said. "He never told him to do that! That's the bad part about Fergie. He

took pride if people said, 'Oh, Fergie ordered that.' Fergie didn't say it that way.... Fergie did not say 'Bobby Clarke go and do that.' He said, 'Do something,' like a lot of coaches would say. 'Something' could mean a lot of different things. But for Bobby Clarke 'do something' meant doing what he was doing in the National Hockey League. And he did the same thing that he would do on me. If you look at film from those years, he got me in the ankle a few times. That's how Bobby Clarke played and they [the NHL] let him do that. If you look at pictures you can see me with ankle guards in those years because that's the way he was doing things."

"Clarke only played the way he was playing in the NHL. That series was going to be played under the NHL rules—they made the rules, and that's just the way it was then. Bobby Clarke did not do anything different than he was doing in the NHL, which was wrong!"

Eagleson doesn't buy the story that Ferguson told Clarke to injure Kharlamov. "It's a little bit like the chandelier story," he suggested. "There's no doubt that Fergie said, 'This guy is killing us. Somebody get him out of here.' The kind of thing you would say. But it's now gone to the extreme where now it's 'Go break his ankle!', or 'Go break his leg!' or 'Take him out of the game!' I just don't believe it was as simple as that. Knowing Fergie it was 'Jesus Christ, this fucking guy is getting so many chances! Someone get to him and teach him a lesson.' I don't think he ever said to Bobby Clarke, 'Go break his leg.' As much as Bobby Clarke is a good friend—never a client but a wonderful friend and a great NHLPA president—I can only point to his entire career and say that he was not that type of player.

Assistant coach John Ferguson watches from the bench during Game 6 of the Summit Series. Ferguson was accused of ordering Bobby Clarke to apply a two-handed slash to the ankle of Russian star Valeri Kharlamov in that game.

Melchior DiGiacomo/Getty Images

"He was a tough player and he gave it everything and he lost his teeth to prove it. But he was not considered to be a malicious, dirty player by anyone. He commanded the respect of his teammates. Paul [Henderson], who is also a great friend and a client, made the mistake of getting caught off guard by a press guy and said, 'Oh well, I'll have a tough time explaining [Clarke's hit] to my grandchildren.' So of course that got Clarkie upset with Henderson. But Clarkie handled it well. I thought he had the best line. He said, 'Hey, Paul Henderson had no complaint at the time and he was my linemate. If it was that bad why wasn't he over giving me shit?' which is the best answer. That happens once in about every 10 games on an NHL club today! He was always tapping guys on the ankle and some guys still do that today if you watch."

As a foe who faced Clarke regularly in the NHL wars, Savard isn't ready to let his former teammate off so lightly. "I like Bobby—I became friends with Bobby Clarke—but that doesn't mean that I agreed with what he was doing. The best thing that ever happened to hockey was when we beat [Clarke's Flyers] in four straight [in 1976 Stanley Cup Finals]. Skill always triumphs—if you have the skill. We were probably physically stronger than them, but we never used it the same way that they did."

As for Clarke himself, he has no problem recalling the incident and does not sugarcoat the facts. "There are lots of things that have been said about it but it's pretty uncomplicated," Clarke said. "We went up the ice going into our end and he turned off one way and I turned off the other and his stick kind of came up and nicked me in the face. It didn't cut me or nothing, just nicked me, so it gave me an excuse I guess. So I hunted him down and took a wild swing with my stick across

Bobby Clarke keeps an eye on the goal during one of the early Summit Series games in Canada. The line of Clarke, Ron Ellis, and Paul Henderson proved to be Canada's most effective.

Melchior DiGiacomo/
Getty Images

his ankle. I did it. I'm responsible for it. I don't feel bad for it. It never bothered me. I don't brag about it, I don't talk about it. I just did it. I didn't try to break his ankle. I just wanted to make sure I whacked him some place that wasn't covered with equipment."

When asked if Ferguson had told him what to do, Clarke steadfastly refuses to pass the buck. "I don't recall that happening," Clarke said. "I think John would certainly be capable of telling me but he'd also be capable of *saying* he told me to take some heat off of me. I think John was just protecting me. That's what teammates do. You're all in it together, eh? Everyone will tell you that John Ferguson was a great teammate. I didn't play with him but . . . he said that to take the heat off of me. When we got back home, I didn't get very much criticism. Most Canadians that I ran into said they were glad I did it. It may have been a turning point."

Clarke's linemate, Ron Ellis, smiles about an incident when he and his Team Canada teammates returned to the NHL. It happened the first time that Ellis' Maple Leafs and Clarke's Flyers faced off. "Clarke speared me," he said. "We had just become very close—but that's Bobby Clarke."

After Game 1, Sinden had assigned Ellis the role of checking Kharlamov. He feels partially responsible for the Clarke slash. "Maybe I was partly at fault here," Ellis said. "Maybe I wasn't doing a good enough job and Ferguson wanted him slowed down a bit to give me a break. Fergie knew which guy to ask. If he'd asked Paul or me it wouldn't have happened. Bobby was a young guy with a lot of respect for John."

"I hated what they were doing to us," said Henderson. "They were embarrassing us. I hated their system. I hated Communism. Their system was so abusive—trying to take over the world. I mean they were ruthless.

And trying to put themselves off as amateurs. I mean it was a joke! You just had no respect for that. Unfortunately we took it out on the players and they were just pawns of the system—and turned out to be really, really nice people."

Kharlamov, the centre of the controversy, was killed in a car accident in 1981 at the age of 33. When Savard saw a chance to honour the Russian star, he embraced the opportunity. "I'm the one who promoted Kharlamov to the Hockey Hall of Fame because I'm on the voting committee. I presented him and he got in. I thought he was their best player."

Savard's biggest regret is that the incident has been overblown, diverting attention away from the skill it took for Team Canada to come out on top and leaving the impression that it was intimidation and dirty play that triumphed. "The movie they did about '72 was a terrible movie. They spent 20 minutes on that incident. That's not all that happened. Why didn't they promote Henderson? Why don't you promote Cournoyer, who had a hell of a series? You need more skills on a bigger surface, so it's not the goons or the tough guys who won the last three games on the big surface; it's the skilled players who won that series."

Sinden, for one, does give credit to Savard and other skilled players. "Savard played in five and we won four and tied one," Sinden said. "As soon as he got going we were fine. I agree with Savard absolutely that it was skill that won that series and not intimidation. Two things contributed to us realizing that's what we had to do to win. One was that things had changed in the 10 or 12 years from '58, '59, even '60, and the second was that opening loss in Montreal. That made all the difference in the world. They were just too good; they were actually as good as we were, no question about it. We knew that we'd have to find other ways to win the series—and as you know, we just did do it."

After Canada emerged triumphant in Games 6 and 7, the Summit Series had come down to the final game, with everything riding on the outcome. It was the culmination of an odyssey, with all the twists and turns, detours, and drama that go with it.

The Canadians had faced questionable and often terrible refereeing throughout the series, especially when the teams reached Moscow. "Eagleson was such a hero there," said Mellanby. "The two refs that did the fifth game were Franz Baader and Josef Kompalla, but Eagleson used to call them 'Badder and Worser.'"

Eagleson remembers the intense battles to get fair refereeing for the ultimate game. It was here that he assumed the role of Captain Canada, defending Canada's rights against the Evil Empire. "There was Rudi Bata, the Czech, and there was Franz Baader, the East German," Eagleson explained. "And there was Josef Kompalla, another East German. So we had Bata and Baader and Worser—and the Worser was Kompalla."

"They had insisted that no referee be permitted to referee unless he was an International Ice Hockey Federation referee," said Eagleson. "That ruled out all of the best referees in the world because the best ones were the pros who covered the NHL."

The original agreement had been to alternate the choice of refs throughout the competition, and overall it had worked well. When the assignments for Game 8 were made, however, all hell broke loose. "The Russians said, 'No, the man you picked, Uve Dahlberg, is sick.' So I phoned Dahlberg and he said, 'Hell, I'm not sick. I've just been told by Starovoitov [head of the International Ice Hockey Federation referees] that I will never referee another IIHF game if I'm not sick!'

"They were going to give us both the East Germans. We finally said, 'well, if we can't get Dahlberg, we want Rudi Bata.' I knew Bata, being from Czechoslovakia, didn't like the Russians any more than I did and he wasn't too bad. Then we got stuck with Kompalla and he made a mockery of the whole thing. The most miraculous thing about that last game, with the exception of Henderson's goal, was the fact that we were even still in contention despite all the penalties."

The game itself had so many moments of high drama that it's hard to believe it could all be contained within the strictures of a regulation three-period hockey game. After the first period, the game was knotted at two goals apiece, but the Russians came out flying in the second frame, scoring at the 0:21 mark and adding two others to give them a 5–3 margin heading into the final period.

As the minutes ticked by and the drama continued to unfold, Eagleson was suddenly drawn into the on-ice action.

"We were down 5–3 at the 2:00 mark or thereabouts. Pete Mahovlich in on a line with Esposito and Cournoyer—two centremen. Pete goes into the corner and pushes two guys off and throws the puck out and I can see it to this day—'cause I was looking right over Espo's shoulder. He sends it right out to Espo. Espo swings and kind of whiffs and then—it's still there—and he bangs it in. So that makes it 5–4. Not bad."

When Eagleson looked at the puck in the net, he was annoyed to see that the goal judge had not put the red light on. "When he finally did it was for about one one-hundredth of a second," he recalled. "It was a great big bulb—like a globe on a pedestal or a disco ball—a massive big thing with a diameter of a foot. Whenever the Russians scored they left it on for a full minute. When we scored the light went on and off—Bing! Bing!—before you could say Jack Robinson. What I knew and most people in the rink didn't know was that the Russian goal judge was Victor Dombrowski who was the head Russian referee on the international ice hockey circuit. So he wasn't giving us any breaks at all, not that it mattered."

As play resumed, the Russians pressured the Canadian zone but goalie Ken Dryden stood tall against the onslaught. At the 12:00 mark, the teams shifted ends as was the practice throughout the tournament. Eagleson was surprised to see the goal judges shift ends as well. "Now Dombrowski's down at the other end," said Eagleson. At the 12:56 mark, Yvon Cournoyer scored on a slick hookup with series star Phil Esposito. The game was tied, or so you would think. "This time Dombrowski doesn't put the light on at all!" said Eagleson, still outraged after all these years. "I see the referee Rudi Bata pointing that the puck is in the net, but there's no light! We've got 3,000 Canadian fans there wondering what the hell was going on. I got out of my seat which is 10 feet from the scorer's box to go and tell the announcer to announce the goal because I was afraid there would be a riot.

"Suddenly there was a whole line of cops in front of me. All I want to do is tell the announcer to announce that it's a goal so everybody's going to at least know we're not being cheated. Well, before I could do that, the cops grabbed me. I always said up to then my favourite hockey player was Bobby Orr, but after being in the hands of the police and being dragged and pummelled all the way down to the exit, Peter Mahovlich became my favourite player. Pete was the one who was tall enough and he just jumped over the boards in one leap and hit one of the soldiers with his stick and then another one and then all the players followed—and then they counted the goal. They were soldiers in the big armed coats and most of them had guns. They weren't ordinary security people. I was

rescued and watched the rest of the game from the Team Canada bench."

The final sequence seemed to happen in a haze. Henderson was on the ice and made the most of his opportunity. Eagleson recalls the seconds leading up to the biggest goal in Canadian hockey history. "Paul was at the other end of the bench where I was and I guess maybe he had an 8- or 10-foot jump and bingo he was flying and Cournoyer fired the pass off to him and Paul kind of whiffed on that shot and then went flying headfirst into the boards—of his own volition. Nobody pushed him there, he just slid. He was down and as he was getting up the two Russian defencemen were there and all they had to do was flip the puck out and the game would have been over and it would have been 5–5 and that was it. But for whatever reason they hesitated and Espo poke-checked and shot. By then Henderson's up and he gets the rebound and Tretiak stops it and he either had two or three shots, he certainly had two and maybe three before it went in."

What followed was patriotic pandemonium. Ron Ellis remembers the elation when the puck went in the net.

"There was so much going on when he scored," Ellis said. "The emotions, fighting back to tie the game and the Russians sending someone around to tell us that if the game remained tied they were going to declare victory because of more goals scored. It happened just after we tied it 5-all. What a stupid thing for them to do! What a great motivator for us, because I was almost to the point that if this game ends up tied, the series is tied and everyone goes home happy. But that just spurred us on and when Paul scored that goal, I was one of the first guys over the boards. We were all huddled together. We started chanting, 'We did it, we did it...' but we still had 34 seconds to kill off. I was actually very honoured. Harry

Ron Ellis was one of only seven players to play in all eight Summit Series games.

Melchior DiGiacomo/ Getty Images

Sinden sent Pete Mahovlich and myself and Phil Esposito on to kill off that final 34 seconds. I remember Paul saying to me when the game was over, 'That guy wasn't going to go anywhere.' I had him so wrapped up! For me, for myself, I was pleased that Harry had enough confidence in me because a lot can happen in 34 seconds."

"I always said that's the reason Paul became religious," said Alan Eagleson. "Was there divine intervention in that goal? I don't know if there was divine intervention or not but I know that Paul certainly intervened, for whatever reason. Mind you, he had been one of our best players and you always want your best players on the ice in the last couple of minutes."

Mellanby remembers confronting Henderson just minutes after the dramatic conclusion to the series. Canada's newly minted hero was in a trancelike state. "I'll always remember I went down to the dress-

ing room after the final game and saw Paul," Mellanby said. "He looked like a truck had run over him. He was sitting there stunned and I talked to him and he didn't even hear me. He was so stunned."

Ever since the red light flashed to signal Henderson's game- and series-winning goal, the Summit Series has been dissected, analyzed, and scrutinized. It has also been romanticized, politicized, memorialized, and idealized. Some say that it was Canada's coming out party, proof that the country could meet a challenge and overcome it. Others say it was a victory of "our" system over "theirs," an ideological win by a democratic country over a totalitarian state.

Harry Sinden, who was the mastermind behind it all, puts it in perspective. "What did the Summit Series say about Team Canada? As much as anything it defines the Canadian attitude and the North American attitude as opposed to what I perceived to be the European attitude," Sinden said. "We were losing in that game by two goals and came back to win it. That is something that most of those Canadian players grew up with. By that I mean you're never out of it. You always should keep playing to the end. It's a trait of the North American athlete—particularly in hockey. We all did it through our junior careers and our youth careers and to me it was the big difference. If the Soviet team had been behind by two goals going into the third period, I don't think they would have ever caught us like we caught them. Not at that time. They did not have…it's not so much that they didn't have it as individuals, but their ability to draw from something—their experiences and their training—to come from behind. I truly believed that at the time that if you got ahead of these people they couldn't come back and beat you."

But what about patriotism? What about national pride and the beaver and the Bluenose, and fields of golden Canadian wheat, and the Rockies, and Peggy's Cove and Niagara Falls and the Mounties? Didn't that make you want to destroy the Hammer and Sickle and send a message to a repressive regime? Surely that was the inspiration. "No, I wouldn't want to say that," said Sinden. "I don't think that had anything to do with our team. I don't know what it had to do with theirs, it might have. But it didn't have anything to do with our team, and frankly, I don't think we were playing for Canada, or any of our fans, or the press, or anybody else in that series.

"They were playing on the instincts that they had grown up with in the game of hockey, the pride of being so-called the best players in the world from the NHL. Upholding their own personal reputations as the greatest hockey players in the world had much, much more to do with it. I've told this

to people before and it's not something that they want to know or to hear. I'm not saying that national pride wasn't there. It certainly was there. They were all proud to be Canadians and they loved it and all that but it was not, in my opinion, the motivating factor."

Mellanby, who as executive director of *Hockey Night in Canada* had seen the NHL game and its greatest players up close, thinks the Series transformed Canadian hockey.

"The Russians literally changed the way we played the game," he said. "I went to dinner with Jean-Paul Parise and John Ferguson after the first game in Russia, which we lost. I said, 'What now?' Fergie said, 'You mean outside of shooting the refs?' Then he told me what he and Harry had come up with. This is where good coaching won that series, because on the big ice the Russians constantly used what we now call the one-, two-, or three-man fore-check, but they called it flooding zones. They kept trapping our defencemen and Harry had asked John what he thought. 'We're going to fire the puck around the board and try to outman them on the breakout.' I thought, *You can't miss. You're gonna trap them with one, two, and three guys in all the time.*

"It may not have worked in Maple Leaf Gardens but in Luzhniki Arena, because of the big ice surface, it did. You break a guy out on the other side and it's going to be two-on-one or three-on-two, and that's exactly what happened."

"But being there, even though there were 3,000 Canadians there and a bunch of Americans, you never got the feeling of what it meant to the country until you got home. You really didn't know. You know what it meant to us? That series was the first time I ever saw the Canadian press unified! The great writers were there: Jim Hunt, Red Fisher, Jim

Paul Henderson skates in front of the Russian goal. Henderson scored the winning goal in the last three games of the 1972 Summit Series.

Melchior DiGiacomo/ Getty Images

Coleman, Trent Frayne; they were all there. Every Canadian was against the Russians—even the press."

Mellanby sees the series as a completely unique event that can never be repeated because of the context of the time. "It was a moment in history and it will always be *the* moment in Canadian hockey history. There isn't the same feeling now. It's great to win the [2010 Vancouver] Olympics but you can't compare it to '72. We don't hate those people anymore. Like Esposito said, 'I wanted to kill those bastards. I hated them.' You'd never get that feeling again because now you're playing with them all the time. You're never going to get that feeling about Ovechkin when you're on his team and then you're playing against him for Canada. They all know one another. There's a bigger rivalry now between the US and Canada."

Did the Summit Series achieve its desired result for either country? Certainly the Canadians were not the smiling ambassadors that Trudeau had envisioned. And although the Russians had shaken Canada's hockey establishment to the bone, they did in the end fail to show their superiority. The truth is that both countries gained from the series: hockey knowledge, certainly, but something more.

Constructing a democracy from the philosophical rubble of a totalitarian state is a daunting task. During his diplomatic career, Jeremy Kinsman served as Canadian ambassador to several countries before assuming the position in Moscow in 1992. It was like walking into a house that's being constructed without the aid of a blueprint or a skilled carpenter. The Russian reformers needed help and Canada was more than willing to show them the way to free speech, voting, and home ownership. With the best of intentions, Canada provided experts in law, banking, and democratic governance. "Even by the time I arrived...it was clear that neither teacher nor pupil could get inside the other's head," Kinsman wrote. "For 100 years, Marxist theorists had composed treatises and charters on how to transform capitalism into socialism. But no one had a blueprint for travelling in the opposite direction.

"I remember making coffee in our Moscow kitchen and hearing the minister in charge of economic reform, Anatoly Chubais, say on the radio that they were going to do privatization 'Canadian style.' Spilling the coffee, I asked myself what in God's name was he talking about?

"I soon asked him in person. 'It's a hockey thing,' he said. 'Remember the Canada-Soviet series? Our guys would try to keep control of the puck until they could get an ideal shot on goal. Your guys would throw it down to our end and pile in afterward and see what came out of the chaos. Your guys won.

"'Tell me,' he went on. 'How do we decontrol in a controlled way?'"

The Russian minister had summed up Canada and Canadian hockey perfectly. We had decontrolled in a controlled way and had made order out of chaos by our willingness and ability to adapt and change. Canada played with passion and allowed talented individuals to improvise and freewheel, but always within a team framework. The Soviet system was highly scripted and businesslike; some have said robotic. The hockey part changed quickly, with both countries incorporating aspects from the other's playbook. By 1989, Sergei Priakin had become the first Soviet to play in the NHL when he suited up for the Calgary Flames. It wouldn't be long before the NHL would have scores of Russian

superstars skating on the same lines with Canadian stars.

Thus did the Summit Series make a profound and lasting impact on two countries. Did Team Canada play a role in ending the Cold War? Although words like *glasnost* and *perestroika* were not in the hearts—or even the vocabularies—of Canadian players, our passion for hockey and for winning had made an impression. The Russians saw us at our best and our worst. Despite losing and despite some of the cheap physical and verbal shots taken by both sides, the lasting impression of Canada had been a positive one. As Serge Savard put it, "Canada was on top of their list. They didn't like the US then, but Canada was seen as a great country."

Canada's Greatest Goal?

Paul Henderson is asked to compare his 1972 goal against the Soviets with Sid Crosby's overtime winner in the 2010 gold-medal Olympic contest. "In my mind what goal was bigger is incidental," he says. "They are two goals that need to be celebrated and remembered. I think Crosby's is an identifying marker for this generation. For my generation—and I get it every day—it was the same thing. 'Don't worry, Paul, your goal was still the goal!' Whether his is bigger than mine or mine is bigger than his is the wrong question. Hockey defines us. When we win on the ice every Canadian feels they won."

Henderson is less reticent when it comes to which goal was better. "I had to watch Crosby's goal twice," he says. "With Crosby the puck was in the net before you even knew it. I mean I couldn't even score on the first try—it took me two shots to get it in there! There is no question who is the better hockey player. You're comparing apples and oranges. The difference between the quality of hockey players then and now is amazing. In terms of the impact of the goal...mine was certainly felt across the country. A couple of people told me that they had their noses broken when buddies jumped up from their chairs and elbowed them right in the nose in the excitement. One guy had to go to the hospital to have it set."

8

HOW HOCKEY EXPLAINS ALAN EAGLESON

THE LAST FOUR DIGITS of Alan Eagleson's phone number are 1972. Lest you think that's just a cool coincidence, the same four digits are part of his email address and are featured on his car's license plate. Eagleson fervently hopes that the significance of those numbers will serve as his lasting legacy.

There is little doubt that the 1972 Summit Series between Canada and the Soviet Union represented Eagleson's finest hour. Sadly, there are other numbers and other dates. Like 1994, in Boston when a federal grand jury indicted Eagleson on various counts of embezzlement, fraud, and racketeering. Or 1996, when the RCMP charged him with four counts of fraud and theft in his dealings with Hockey Canada, the NHL Players Association, and the NHL. Or 1998, when he pleaded guilty in the U.S. and Canada, was sentenced to 18 months in Toronto's Mimico Correctional Institute near his family home, had his Order of Canada removed, and resigned in disgrace from the Hockey Hall of Fame.

How did Alan Eagleson go from being the most powerful figure in hockey and one of the most influential men in Canada to disgrace and virtual exile from the hockey world? How did the man who once conferred with Trudeau, Mulroney, and Turner—not to mention Orr, Howe, and Hull—become a pariah and by some estimates the most hated man in hockey? It's a sordid tale of greed, betrayal, and shame.

Love him or hate him, no one can deny that Eagleson changed Canadian hockey forever. He burst onto the scene as a crusading young

Alan Eagleson leaves Mimico Correctional Centre, located west of Toronto, in 1998 after serving six months of an 18-month sentence for fraud.

AP Images

lawyer called in to settle a player-management dispute in Springfield, Massachusetts. The legendary Eddie Shore was owner of the AHL's Springfield Indians and ruled with an iron fist, ironically a charge that would later be levelled against Eagleson. The most recent incident involved Shore's suspension of three players without pay for dubious reasons. Finally the players refused to play for the man who treated them with disrespect bordering on contempt. Reputations are not made in battles with lesser men but with giants, and Shore was not only the team owner, but he was also manager and coach. It was an ideal opportunity for the ambitious Eagleson to show his stuff, the defender of the downtrodden vs. the tyrant.

After months of negotiations, Shore turned over the direct operation of the team to others and eventually sold the team to the L.A. Kings to serve as their farm club. Eagleson had ridden into town and emerged victorious in his showdown with the Hall of Fame defenceman. Eagleson was looked on in awe by players in the AHL and word soon reached the NHL about this gutsy young lawyer. From that case, Eagleson became a formidable powerbroker. His successful intervention would serve as the genesis of the NHL Players Association, which today benefits players past and present. Eagleson's contributions to international hockey are huge. The success of the 1972 Summit Series not only showcased the game to the world, but it also changed the way we play the game. He followed that up with the Canada Cup, which built on the patriotic fervour of '72.

Not unlike Conrad Black, Eagleson, the "Hockey Czar," suffered a humiliating fall from power. The difference lies in the fact that unlike Black, Eagleson was not was born into extreme wealth and privilege. Eagleson, the son of a factory worker, fought and clawed

his way to the top using whatever methods were at his disposal.

When the fall from grace came it was socially ostracizing and emotionally devastating. The phone still rings at the Eagleson household but the players who once were his closest friends are seldom on the other end. He is no longer on their call list. Black had voluntarily given up his Canadian citizenship in order to become Baron Black of Crossharbour. It was a price that he voluntarily paid and is still paying. Alan Eagleson was stripped of his Order of Canada medallion and forced to resign his membership in the Hockey Hall of Fame. The first honour recognized what he had done for his country, the second what he had done for Canadian hockey. It's a tossup as to which meant the most to him. The bottom line is that both Black and Eagleson both have effectively been banished, one by choice and one decidedly not.

With his reputation in tatters, there is little wonder that Eagleson points to 1972 as his greatest achievement. The date is pretty much unsullied. It was a more innocent time, when the most important issue he had to face was winning hockey games against the Evil Empire. He may have become overzealous, even caused minor international embarrassment, but he was one of us at that time. He was fighting for Canada, and we were darn glad to have him on our side. There is no question that Alan Eagleson was the major author of his own demise, but the final chapters were written by former Maple Leaf defenceman Carl Brewer and Massachusetts newspaper reporter Russ Conway. With Brewer's assistance, Conway brought to light a sordid story of corruption and deceit, a story of scandal that Canadian media all but ignored.

Eagleson had started out as a hero, a champion of players' rights and a pioneer who created the first lasting player's union. An earlier attempt to organize, headed up by Doug Harvey and Ted Lindsay in the late '50s, was quickly broken by the all-powerful owners.

Ironically, it was Brewer who helped to bring Eagleson to prominence when he hired him as his agent in the '60s. Their relationship grew from there and was mutually advantageous until Brewer's retirement. It was only then that the three-time Stanley Cup winner began to examine, and eventually question, Eagleson's business practices.

By then he was known as "the Eagle," and was virtually unassailable. His reputation as an agent had been built on his most famous client, Bobby Orr, to whom he had delivered a record contract with the Boston Bruins. He was also head of the players' union and wielded great power in international hockey circles. In 1972, he added the Summit Series to his list of accomplishments and soon after that the 1976 Canada Cup. Along the way he had helped the retired Brewer reestablish his amateur status so that he could play for Canada internationally.

Nonetheless, for Brewer, something wasn't right. The pension funds were woefully inadequate. Legendary players like Howe and Hull who had helped to make the NHL rich and successful were receiving embarrassing pensions. Brewer was as tenacious as a dog with a bone. Because Eagleson's clientele included players and management, many saw his role in the Players Association as a conflict of interest. A 1989 investigation uncovered "shocking...sweetheart agreements with the NHL." The author of the report, Ed Garvey, went so far as to call the union-management relationship a "charade." There were real doubts about who Eagleson was working for and which side he was on. A pattern of secrecy and distrust only served to keep players in the dark. In an effort to defuse

an explosive situation, in 1992 Eagleson left his position as head of the NHLPA and was replaced by Bob Goodenow.

The matter continued to fester with no result. Allegations were taken to the RCMP but no actions resulted. Finally Brewer had had enough. He took the case to Conway at the tiny *Lawrence Eagle-Tribune*, a small newspaper in the Boston area. In 1991, Conway used Brewer's information, in addition to his contacts with the Bruins, and other investigative research to tell the story that no big Canadian daily dared touch. Conway's work was later the basis for his book *Game Misconduct: Alan Eagleson and the Corruption of Hockey*.

The house of cards began to tumble as players, former players, and even Eagleson associates fed damaging information to Conway. As charges continued to mount, the Eagleson camp struck back with accusations that retired players were trying to raid the coffers of current NHLers. Finally other newspapers were forced to enter the fray.

Meanwhile, the wheels of justice continued to turn, albeit slowly. In 1992, a Canadian court determined that more than $20 million of back pension was owed to 1,300 former NHL players. Then came Eagleson's US indictment in '94 followed by a similar proceeding in Canada in '96.

Eagleson finally admitted his guilt in 1998. As outlined by the FBI, the litany of charges against him ran from the pedestrian, fraud involving the conversion of airline travel passes at Canada Cup tournaments, to the Dickensian, a fraudulent scheme to deprive disabled players of insurance money that was rightfully theirs.

It was Eagleson's treatment of his most famous client that drew the most attention to the case. Bobby Orr was viewed by the public as a quiet, unassuming superstar, a man who had single-handedly redefined the role of a defenceman. Canadians loved the modest superstar who courageously continued to play the game despite badly damaged knees. When fans learned that Orr was all but bankrupt at the conclusion of his career, they were shocked.

Shock turned to outrage when details began to emerge. When Orr signed a contract with the Chicago Black Hawks in 1976, fans assumed that the Bruins had been outbid in their attempts to keep the icon in Boston for the remainder of his career. Amazingly, Bobby Orr had the same assumption. It turned out that Eagleson had not informed his client about the full extent of the Bruins offer, a rather significant omission since it involved 18.5 percent ownership of the team.

What kind of a man would do this to a man like Bobby Orr? How did the man who NHL players once cheered as their "great emancipator" become vilified and scorned as a traitor and villain. When Eagleson was sentenced there was scarcely a wet eye to be found. Today, some 13 years later, Eagleson talks about the glory days of his past and opines about the fleeting nature of fame.

"I had a great run for 30 years," he said philosophically. "I formed the NHLPA single-handedly. I masterminded the '72 series. I created the first 'Team Canada' name and now the phrase is used for sports and government business promotions around the world. I created the Canada Cup Tournament and made it the World Cup of Hockey. My successor, an American, scrapped it, and replaced it with a tournament that has been played twice in the 20 years since the last Canada Cup in '91.

"I convinced the major junior teams to form a Junior Team Canada and created the Junior Canada Cup in 1978. It was held in four Quebec cities and proved that it had great appeal. My concept in '78 has now become an annual major sports attraction for all Canadian hockey fans."

The list of achievements reads like a résumé from a fallen angel looking for a place in hockey heaven. But those particular pearly gates have slammed shut.

"I was born on April 24, 1933," Eagleson explained. "My parents used to tell me that on April 4 they stayed up all night because of me and Kenny Doraty. Doraty scored an overtime goal for the Leafs in the longest game in Maple Leaf Gardens history. [Doraty scored at the 4:46 mark of the sixth overtime period to give the Leafs a 1–0 victory over Boston in the fifth game of the Stanley Cup semifinals. The goal came at 1:48 A.M.] I never heard of Kenny Doraty before or since.

"I was an ordinary kid playing local hockey but I was a pretty good lacrosse player. One of my lacrosse opponents was Bob Pulford. He and I became very close friends. I went on to law school and he went on to the Leafs. He carried on his high school education and got his B.A. some years after I did. I eventually helped tutor him to keep him through, so he got his B.A. in about '59 or '60. I was out by then.

"All through high school I was just a squirt at about 5′4″ or 5′3″ and about 100 pounds. Then in grade 13 I put on some height, about 8 inches, and gained about 40 pounds. By the time I got to university I was a normal size, 5′11″ and 170 pounds, and I've stayed at that ever since. Today I play tennis—picked it up after my lacrosse career was over."

Bobby Clarke is emphatic in his belief that Eagleson has earned the right to be in the Hall of Fame. Moreover, he thinks the pressure to expel him was unfair and unworthy of hockey's greatest players. "Eagleson was in the Hall of Fame for what he did for the good of hockey," Clarke said. "That's why he deserves to be in the Hall of Fame, and he still should be! You can't judge. Look at the list of Hall of Famers, look at Clarence Campbell. He's there. There are lots of people in the Hall who've broken laws."

Eagleson's voice softens when asked if he attends reunions of the 1972 Team Canada squad. At that moment it's hard to remember that people once trembled when he entered a room and that even grisled veterans could be intimidated by his domineering personality.

"This is what I laugh at— Vic Hadfield goes but I don't," Eagleson said of Hadfield, who left the team before the conclusion of the series. "But what I do is [go out to dinner with] Harry and Fergie and Serge and Dale Tallon and Marcel Dionne and 8 or 10 others. Each year a couple of more guys come, which makes it nice for me.

"I've got a picture of Team Canada '72 right in my office. It sits there and beside it is my career in politics at Queens Park, the graduation picture in 1967. As my son said when all of this stuff happened: 'Dad, you know what? You'd better keep an eye on that picture. I think they're trying to white-out your photo.'

"It [the Summit Series] was the defining moment not only in my hockey life but in my entire life, other than family aspects. Nothing will ever touch '72. I mean the '87 Canada Cup was wonderful—the big win there and '84—all of those were great, great things but nothing will ever touch that.

"One of the nicest things I got and I have it up on my wall in my den is a letter from Ambassador Ford in December '72 saying, 'Dear Alan, I've read some of the criticisms about you and the team but I want to tell you

Alan Eagleson presents the Canada Cup to Team Canada's Wayne Gretzky (left) and Larry Robinson after Canada defeated Sweden in the finals of the tournament in September 1984.

Bruce Bennett Studios/Getty Images

that you and Team Canada did a great thing for Canada in [Russia]. You had 50 million or 100 million people or whatever it was watching Canada excel and you and your team did more to sell Canada to the average Russian than anyone ever imagined, including myself.' Let's put it this way: before the '72 series Canada was famous for two exports, hockey and wheat. And now we're not as famous for wheat.

"Both of them are dead now, but the other man who was a tremendous, tremendous supporter was Ed Ritchie—the deputy minister of foreign affairs. Some of the federal members were concerned that because I was a Tory I was going to do something untoward that would hurt them. Remember we were right in the middle of an election in '72. But Ed Ritchie stuck right with me and John Munroe was another one. They did everything they could to help us.

"Trudeau was terrific. When we landed in Montreal he was there to greet us coming off the plane. He was just absolutely wonderful. He invited me up to 22 Sussex after that and he couldn't have been better. He was a fan on top of all that. He was a sportsman.

"Marvin Miller is a good friend to this day. I laughed because they're talking about a new constitution for the Players Association, which they changed from the one I had when I ran the association for 25 years. It was word for word the copy of the constitution of the Major League Baseball Players Association that I got from Marvin Miller. He's a great guy and should be in the Baseball Hall of Fame, should have been there long before this.

"Donald Fehr is now running the [NHLPA]. Don doesn't need any advice from me. He's been a friend for many, many years. There were two that were in before him and after Marvin. I worked with Don for about 12 years while he was running the baseball players' association and he's a good man. I'm happy to see it run finally by someone who is of some consequence. I wasn't a fan of Bob Goodenow nor Ted Saskin and I certainly wasn't a fan of Paul Kelly.

"In the circumstances, I think that anyone who can corral 30 owners—former NHL president John Ziegler only had to corral 21— Bettman's got a better deal. He only has to get two-thirds to win the battle. Bettman on some things only needs to get 50 percent plus one. But Bettman cannot be dumped unless it's an overwhelming majority. Ownership in the NHL has totally changed. There are only a couple of personal owners now. Pretty well everyone else is corporate owned. Big difference. Of course, in the original six it was just a little fiefdom because the Norris family owned two of the six franchises. Sounds like the CFL.

"Today [the NHLPA] may look like it was nothing, but in those days it was a big, big,

big step. As much as the '72 Series was the most exciting thing, I think the most important thing I ever did was forming the union. That was Bob Pulford and I and I went to see Marvin Miller and sought his advice and I went to talk to a fellow in London who'd set up a union for their professional football [soccer] players. It was tough because in those days I think one of the biggest reasons I succeeded was because of Eddie Shore. When Springfield went on strike and Bill White called me in December of '66, I became a friend with Brian Kilrea and we're friends to this day. And Bill White was one of the first guys to call me to see if I wanted to go down and meet with him. Everyone told me, 'Milt Dunnell, this guy is going to have you for lunch.' Other than that I was coming off a couple of winners. I had Bobby Orr beating the Bruins on the contract in August of '66 and I had Carl Brewer beating the NHL by getting his release in October of '66 and this happened on December 15 of '66. Within a month I had the biggest defenceman of all time up to Orr out of the game. I consider one of my greatest successes getting rid of Shore. It showed how if you band together, you can win."

○ ○ ○ ○

"I'll answer the question in this fashion," Eagleson said when asked if being out of hockey is painful. "It hurts, but only for a second or two because I had wonderful times and there's no sense at my age having any regrets. I've got a lot less time ahead of me than I have behind me. I've got lots of friends. The nice thing is that no matter who I call in hockey, I get a warm response. So if I'm going to Raleigh, North Carolina, and I need some tickets for the game I call and whoever answers, responds. Now in some cases they only know me by name but no one has ever hung up saying, 'Up yours!'

"I'm quite happy in my life and I've survived. Things have gone well for me after all the bad times. When I think back, I was 58 when it all started in December 1991 and from then until July 1999 it was just eight years of constant pummelling. And then it was like taking a dose of salts to get things out of your system. It was tough to swallow but I did it and I didn't look back. I just went on with my life and the reason I was able to because of some friends in particular, the late Justice Estey, the late Justice Supinka, John Turner, Bill Davis, and several hockey players—many of them all-stars. I can remember one of the reporters called Brian Greenspan and he said, 'Well, what do you think of this player or that player and what they said about Eagleson?' And he said, 'Well, let me give you our list of players who are with him. I like our all-star team against your journeymen.'

"I had a call the other day out of the blue from Gary Unger. Hadn't heard from him for many years. Just to see how I was doing. Those are things that pick you up.

"Bobby Clarke, I'm in constant touch with him and Marcel Dionne. And [Serge] Savard. Whenever I need something in Montreal, I just call Serge and he solves the problem, whether it's a hotel room or tickets to a game or tickets to a racetrack. And Harry too. I always send Paul [Henderson] a note on the 28th of September for obvious reasons."

How Hockey Explains Fame in Canada

"My license plate is TC-72 but this is an indication of how time goes by," Eagleson said. "My gas station is an Esso dealer in town. So he has a young guy working the pumps here in Collingwood. So he comes out and he's talking to me while this young guy pumps gas—he's about 18 or 19—and he says to the kid:

'You know who this is?'
'No.'
'It's Mr. Eagleson.'
'Oh.'
'You see that license plate?'
'Yeah.'
'You know what that is?'
'No'
'Well it's TC 72, Team Canada '72!'
'What's that?'
So there you are. It's like: 'Didn't you used to be Alan Eagleson'
'Yeah, and I still am.'"

○ ○ ○ ○

What does the Eagle do in retirement? Does he still follow the game he once all but controlled? "My interest in hockey is still high," he said, "but the games I enjoy most are the ones my grandson and my neighbour's sons play. I have kept many friendships in hockey, including many ex-players, coaches, managers, and media types."

"I have been successful in real estate development since I retired to Collingwood. I enjoy my life with my wife, my son and his family, and my daughter and her family. My joy is my three grandchildren—two boys, ages 18 and 2, and one girl, age 15. I play tennis two or three times a week with 50- and 60-year-olds and hold my own. I ski downhill and cross-country three or four times a week. I kayak daily on Georgian Bay from April to November.

"I don't owe any money to anyone. My wife and I travel to Europe two or three times a year and to New York City and Palm Beach for opera and sun respectively. We celebrated our 50th wedding anniversary in 2010.

"I have no complaints. I fought through the adversity which came my way and am enjoying every moment of every day with my family and my friends."

9

HOW HOCKEY EXPLAINS FEMINISM

IF YOU HAD ASKED teenage girls of the 1930s and '40s to name five famous Canadian females, you might have heard the names Marie, Yvonne, Emilie, Annette, and Cecile, known collectively as the Dionne Quintuplets. Well, we've come a long way babies! If the same question were asked today, a large number of girls and women would include the names of Team Canada members who brought home gold at the 2010 Vancouver Olympics.

Of course, today Canadian women shine on the world stage in almost every imaginable field, including entertainment, the arts, and literature. Along with the Shania Twains, Norah Joneses, Ellen Pages, Karen Kanes, and Margaret Atwoods, we now see names like Hayley Wickenheiser, Shannon Szabados, and Marie-Philip Poulin. Perhaps the names don't yet have the household resonance of Crosby, Iginla, and Toews, but give them time.

Now that Canadian women have excelled in every previously male domain, save perhaps spittin' and scratchin', the sky's the limit. And as astronaut Roberta Bondar proved, the sky isn't all that limiting either.

Hours after the Canadian women had won the gold medal with a 2–0 win over the USA, they celebrated on the ice of the all-but-deserted Canada Hockey Place by smoking cigars and drinking champagne and Molson Canadian. Predictably, they received some criticism for this. They were, after all, women and some men still can't accept that such goings on are ladylike. One suspects, however, that Nellie McClung, a Manitoba force of nature who was instrumental in gaining women the right to vote, would have been proud. Nellie's credo was: "Never retract, never explain, never

Hayley Wickenheiser celebrates with the Canadian flag after the women's ice hockey team defeated the USA to win the gold medal at the 2010 Winter Olympics in Vancouver.

AP Images

119

Marie-Philip Poulin has been referred to as the Sidney Crosby of women's hockey. The Beauceville, Quebec, native contributed to Canada's 2010 Olympic gold medal team.

Bruce Bennett Studios/Getty Images

apologize—just get the job done and let them howl."

Hockey Canada saw fit to issue an apology for their impromptu celebration. Marie-Philip Poulin, at 18 officially too young to consume alcohol, also offered an apology. "We just wanted to enjoy the moment and that's just what happened," she explained. "And it won't happen again."

The veteran Wickenheiser, captain and undisputed on-ice leader of the women, was somewhat less contrite. She suggested that a double standard was at play in media coverage of the incident and that if the men's team had held a similar celebration, there would have been no outcry.

"It's celebrating," she said. "It's hockey, it's a tradition we do. When we see a Stanley Cup winner, we see them spraying champagne all over the dressing room. You see 18-year-old kids there and nobody says a thing."

It took Canadian IOC member Dick Pound to put things in perspective. He told CBC's Peter Mansbridge, "I think it's kind of like killing a mouse with an elephant gun. These kids have worked like dogs for years and months, and the pressure is off. They had a huge game and a great win. Hey, let them have some fun."

The gold-medal final victory was the 15th straight Olympic victory for the Canucks. The only loss was a tough one, coming in the 1998 gold-medal final at the hands of the archrival Americans.

The women's game has detractors, of course, and former NHL macho man Tiger Williams is one of them. "I'm not a fan of women's hockey," he admitted. "As a game of hockey, great. The more people you get out playing the game the better, but as an Olympic sport, no. You only have two countries that can compete and that doesn't fly with me."

Tiger has a point. To reach the semifinal round, Canada easily swept by Slovakia 18–0,

Switzerland 10–1, and Sweden 13-1. They handily defeated the Finns 5–0 to earn a place in the final. The Americans' route to the final was also a rout. They defeated China 12–1, Russia 13–0, and Finland 6–0 before knocking off Sweden 9–1 to reach the final. Together the powerhouse Canadian and American squads outscored the rest of the field 86–4 in the opening round and semifinals.

Howie Meeker also remains unconvinced that the women's game is even a legitimate sport. He's especially critical of the lack of competition at the highest levels of the game. "There are only two teams in the world!" he argued. "Canada and the United States. They could play a man short—or a lady short—the whole game and win by 10 against anybody else! The local media and the hockey people have built it up, saying that it's really something. It's not! It's not hockey! And anyone who plays it knows it's not hockey."

"It should never be an Olympic sport with only two viable teams. It's Canada and the US. They both have teams that go for gold and one's going to get gold and the other's going to get silver for sure! The game they play is not under hockey rules. I'd make it a special division or something else and specify that the two games are different."

Former Montreal goalie Dryden agrees that there is a dearth of elite teams outside of North America. "There is a point to be made about women's hockey teams as part of the Olympics—on the basis that very few countries participate, and that really there are two at the top who are significantly better than the others in the competition. Canada and the US are a whole lot better than Finland and Sweden and anybody else who plays. Part of the consideration for the Olympics is that if you're going to be offering medals you've got to have a competition, and if the competition is just between two countries then that may not make it a valid Olympic sport. That's one side of it."

Former Team Canada player Brian Conacher draws a parallel with the Canadian men's teams of the '50s. "The women's dominance today is exactly the same scenario as it was for our Canadian men in the early going. You'd go over and beat Finland 12–1 or 16–2 or 29–whatever—ridiculous scores that don't do anyone any good. It's a bit like the analogy of ladies' hockey today—or women's—they aren't necessarily ladies. There's only two women's teams today in the world that are competitive and that's Canada and the US and those games are very competitive, usually down to literally one goal either way in most games. Canada's men's teams were like that originally and in the long run that doesn't necessarily argue well for the sport. What the women's game needs is to get better teams from Sweden and better teams from Finland and from Japan and the sooner the better, so they are going through the same scenario that we once did."

One defence of women's hockey comes from what many might consider a surprising source. "I believe women's hockey should stay in the Olympics," said former Philadelphia Flyers captain Bob Clarke. "I see no reason why it shouldn't be. These other teams are going to get better. Unless they have the Olympics to play in, how do you know when they are better? Let them play. Someone's going to win a bronze and that's pretty good. The Americans were always behind the Canadians 10 years ago, and now they're right there with them. Don't kid yourself—the Swedes and Finns are going to get better."

Clarke feels that the women could teach the men a lot about how the game should be played, and he's not just talking about skills. The former Broad Street Bully thinks that gratuitous hitting has gotten out of control in the NHL. "Many of today's NHLers are *only* trying to hit somebody—and when you do that you're going to hurt them," he said. "That's one of the reasons why we're getting so many injuries."

"I think women's hockey is actually ahead of the men in some ways. I mean let's face it, we like contact and we like body-checking but in women's hockey, they play a game that the NHL could learn from. When they go to check somebody, they are going to get the puck. If they're getting the puck and they collide with somebody, that's okay. Well, that's what men should be doing. Men should be trying to get the puck when they're hitting somebody. You can hit somebody who's got the puck as long as you're trying to get the puck. Many of today's NHLers are *only* trying to hurt somebody—and when you do that you're going to hurt them. That's one of the reasons we're getting so many injuries."

Alan Eagleson is a man who knows a lot about international hockey. The mastermind behind the '72 Summit Series and the Canada Cup, he followed the exploits of Canada's men's teams long before that. A hockey historian, he can not only rhyme off names of players from his youth, but also harken back to the early days when Canada's dominance was almost embarrassing. He thinks that people should look to the history of men's hockey and wait for the rest of the world to catch up.

"I am in favour of women's hockey being an Olympic event," he said. "In men's Olympic Games hockey in the old days, Canada won games by 43–0, and there were only three or four competitive teams. Today there are 12 to 16 decent teams."

Concern about the lack of international competition is not limited to the public. In the midst of the competition at the 2010 Games, International Olympic Committee president Jacques Rogge issued a thinly veiled threat. If the competitiveness of women's hockey did not improve, the sport might be dropped from the Olympics. "There is a discrepancy," he said. "Everyone agrees with that. This may be the investment period for women's ice hockey." He went on to say, "I would personally give them more time to grow, but there must be a period of improvement. We cannot continue without improvement."

Wickenheiser reacted to the remarks with a combination of resignation and frustration. "When you just pay attention to the game every four years, that's what you see. It would be nice for people like that to really get involved in other countries and push for the game to develop."

When the Canadian men were winning lopsided victories in the early days of international competition, other countries learned and built their own teams around the Canadian model. Wickenheiser sees the success of the Canadian and US programs as something other countries can shoot for. "I

think we're right at the edge of moving to the next level," she has said. "I think we're in good shape and Canada and the US will push the rest of the world."

Improvement across the hockey-playing world won't happen without hard work and commitment at all levels. "I think that's up to the rest of the world to put some resources into their federations. We've demonstrated that women can play hockey at a very high level and there's no reason it should be taken out of the Games. We commit, we train, we have a lot of passion, we're full-time athletes. So it's up the rest of the world to catch up. It's not as easy as it looks, trust me."

Within weeks of Rogge's comments about a woeful lack of parity in international women's hockey, the IOC president was roundly criticized by former Canadian Governor General Adrienne Clarkson. Speaking through an open letter to the *Globe and Mail*, Clarkson called Rogge's comments "a slap in the face" to women. "Women have been playing hockey in Canada since the early 1900s, and they began playing in leagues at least 70 years ago. By 1975, with a lot of hard work and very little help, we had a network for women's hockey that worked toward a world tournament."

Clarkson told the *Globe and Mail,* "I was mad. I wanted to immediately say to him, 'Did not men's hockey need to improve in the 1920s?'" The newspaper referenced the 1924 Winter Games, in which Canada outscored the rest of the field 122–3.

Clarkson went on to tell the *Globe and Mail* that only through continuity and commitment can other nations hope to become competitive. The goal of playing in the Olympics is the greatest motivator of all. "They can get better, but they can only get better with encouragement," she continued. "That means women need to know there will be future World Championships and an Olympics every four

Members of Canada's 2010 Olympic gold-medal team pose on the ice after receiving their medals.

AP Images

years. We have to make sure we're at Sochi in four years and make enough noise."

In spite of his acknowledgement that the game is currently top heavy with North American talent, Dryden has no doubts on the subject of the sport's worth. "Is it a valid sport? The answer is absolutely! It's a terrific sport and the way in which women play hockey is great and it's getting better and better and better and better all the time. The only reason why the rest of the world is not doing very well in it is that the rest of the world has many fewer resources, many fewer rinks, and ice time. So they have to make choices of who's going to get the ice. Is the ice going to go to the men or is it going to go to the women? So in those countries the ice time goes to the men, and the women have had far less chance to develop their game than they have in Canada. There's no other country that, even remotely, has nearly as many rinks per capita as Canada. This is a time in Canada when there are fewer young boys who are playing hockey and all of these rinks need to fill their ice time, and so they are desperate for old timers' hockey to grow and for women's hockey to grow."

On November 8, 2010, two women were admitted to a previously exclusive male club. The two women in question were Canada's Angela James and Cammi Granato of the United States. NHL commissioner Gary Bettman was on hand for the historic occasion. "I think it's a historic night and I think it's great for hockey at all levels," he said. "Both Angela and Cammi are inspirational. They're pioneers once again. What they've done in the game to this point has been terrific and I think they're great role models for other girls and women looking to devote themselves to this game." Howie Meeker vehemently disagrees. A recent recipient of

Angela James (left) and Cammi Granato admire their Honoured Members rings during the 2010 Hockey Hall of Fame induction ceremonies. James and Granato were the first female players inducted into the Hall of Fame.

AP Images

the Order of Canada and a member of the Hockey Hall of Fame in the builder category, Meeker taught generations of young males the skills of the game. He is not ready to accept that women's hockey is even hockey. "If I was a member of the Hockey Hall of Fame as a player," he said, "I would seriously consider withdrawing my name. I mean women don't play hockey!"

Meeker's opinions are extreme but certainly not unique. Women have been forced on the defensive ever since the game was embraced by the Canadian public.

Granato attacked the subject at her induction ceremony. "It just comes with the territory because we're used to doing that, we're used to defending ourselves," she said. "I had to defend myself from the time when I was in a rink when I was a little kid and people wondered, *Why is she playing?* We just have to keep repeating ourselves over and

over.... But this helps, I tell you, being here. Having this committee and this Hall accept us really helps."

Being pioneers in any sport is never easy, as Jackie Robinson could attest, but James and Granato have paved the way for other young women to follow. Meeker makes it clear that his objections are based not on gender, but on maintaining the integrity of the game.

"Women, in every other sport that men participate in, play with men's rules and regulations. The only difference is in golf where I think they move them up a little bit to tee off. The thinking there is, okay, you hit the ball as well as we do with every club, you putt as good as we do, but you can't hit it as far because you're not as strong. But every other sport—the wrestlers, the boxers, the football players, the basketball players—same rules. The greatest thing about the game of hockey—the greatest thing is that you can perform the skills under the threat of being hit. But women don't want to be hit! To play the game of hockey without being hit—well, that's not hockey!"

Dryden, former Minister of Social Development in Prime Minister Paul Martin's cabinet, disagrees with that way of thinking. Dryden bristles at the notion that women's hockey is "by definition" not real hockey because it lacks the element of violence. "The fact that someone said that doesn't make it interesting or worthy. There is no such thing as a game by definition having an element of this or that. People create their own game and play those games in lots of different ways and it is not *by definition* anything. I mean at one time by definition you could not pass the puck forward in hockey. You had to pass backward as in rugby. At one time by definition in football you could not pass the ball forward, you had to pass it backward as in rugby so the fact that someone said something does not give it any validity whatsoever."

Meeker's position seems somewhat at odds with his fervent belief that hockey is foremost a game of skills. Ironically, the author of the iconic *Howie Meeker's Hockey Basics*, seems to be arguing the case of his nemesis, Don Cherry, a promoter of rock 'em, sock 'em hockey who nevertheless has openly embraced the women's game. Although he is almost certainly on the wrong side of hockey history on this one, Meeker claims to be defending the feats of Hall of Famers who excelled despite the ever-present chance of body checks and physical intimidation. "Those guys that made it into the Hockey Hall of Fame made it under duress," he said. "There wasn't a game they played that there wasn't someone looking for them. You drop your head and you make the wrong play and you put yourself into position where you are going to get hit legally—*then you're going to get hit*! *And you're going to get hurt*. When you watch the women, they just skate by a checker. They make no attempt to make bodily contact with that checker. Even I could star at that game! I could. I could have been a hell of a hockey player without the threat of being hit!"

Meeker uses his own NHL experience to make his case. "It took me a long time to understand why on a team of ten players, five or six fall into the 8 to 10 category while the rest are fours, fives, and sixes. We [the Toronto Maple Leafs] had one of the best bodycheckers within the rules to ever play the game—'Wild' Bill Ezinicki. In my six or seven years in Toronto, I saw him hit guys 30 or 40 pounds heavier than he was and hurt them. I mean really hurt them—I thought he killed them, you know, and all legal. He never got a penalty for hitting illegally."

Himself a Hall of Famer, Dryden would be proud to have qualified women join him in hockey's ultimate place of honour. "The fact is that I was on the board of the Hockey Hall of Fame for five or six years at a time when there started to be some voices talking about whether there should be women in the Hockey Hall of Fame. My point was always: Of course! This is not the NHL Hall of Fame. This is not the Canadian Hall of Fame. This is not the Men's Hall of Fame. This is the Hockey Hall of Fame! What you are supposed to do with a Hockey Hall of Fame is to reward all of those who have been important to hockey—and that is anywhere in the world, male and female. If you are a legit Hall of Fame you, of course, consider the possibility. Not only the possibility, but at some point, of course, inducting women into the Hall of Fame."

In her November 8, 2010, column, the *Toronto Star's* controversial Rosie DiManno wrote about the historic induction of two women into the previously all-male enclave. Referring to James and Granato as "estrogen trailblazers," she called the move to enshrine them, "a socially engineered exercise in smashing gender barriers." A more fitting candidate for the Hall of Fame, she suggested, was Marguerite Norris, the first woman to have her name on the Stanley Cup with the 1954 Detroit Red Wings. Norris was president of the Detroit club, having inherited the title from her father James Norris. She presided over two Stanley Cup wins in two years. DiManno suggests that the boardroom is the only place in the hockey arena where men and women can be judged equally. Those who wish to be judged by male athletic standards are "crossing over as freakish iconoclasts in male leagues or breaching the ramparts of male Halls."

DiManno feels that based on statistical evidence there were lots of male hockey players more deserving of such an honour. "What's being acknowledged here, I assume, is the pioneering spirit and grit of these particular ladies, and the extent to which they popularized hockey as a sport for girls," she wrote. "There's nothing wrong with that, in its proper context, which is more cultural than intrinsically athletic—achievements normally assessed by Hall numbers. Otherwise, Paul Henderson would be in there too, strictly on the basis of 1972. But he doesn't get an individual plaque for saving Canada's ass at the Summit Series."

"My daughter saw the article and she emailed me," Paul Henderson said. "She said, 'Dad I know what I'm going to get you for Christmas. I'm going to get you a plaque that says 'Henderson Saves Canada's Ass in 1972!'" Henderson believes that the women's game has taken giant steps in recent years. "The skill level of these girls now is incredible, and it's fun to watch," he said. "I'm amazed at the skill level of these girls. You watch our national team and they can fire the puck and skate and pass. It's finally getting an audience."

While women's hockey goes back to the early 1900s and beyond, the first national championship wasn't until 1982. In 1987, Toronto played host to an international invitational tournament featuring six countries. This served as the impetus for the International Ice Hockey Federation to sanction the first women's World Championship. In that initial championship, the Canadian women peppered East Germany and Sweden with a total of 119 shots, outscoring them 32–1. The Swedes managed only 3 shots on goal and the East Germans 12. Nevertheless, it was the beginning of a very profitable and mutually advantageous partnership for the Canadian women and TSN, which televised the games. More importantly, the profile of the game had been established and the ground had been laid for the acceptance of women's hockey at the Olympics.

Dryden has watched the evolution of the women's game and was present for the first world championship. "Our daughter-in-law, our son's wife, played on the Canadian women's Olympic team in Salt Lake in 2002 and so we watched a fair number of women's hockey games. I remember in 1990 the world championship was in Ottawa and I was invited down to drop the puck for the final game. I think it was the first time there had been national television coverage of it. The Ottawa Civic Centre was filled."

The Canadian women wore what *Maclean's* magazine described as "garish pink-and-white uniforms bearing stylized maple leafs." Dryden was struck by the passion that players and spectators brought to the event. "There were 9,000 there but the Canadian women's team at that time wore hot pink and it was unbelievable, the Canada jerseys instead of red being pink. The pants being pink and the socks pink and then probably out of the 9,000 people in the arena, 7,000 were wearing pink. It was an unbelievable sight, but the women are playing hockey really well now and 10 years from now they'll be playing it even better."

Women's ice hockey finally became an Olympic sport at the 1998 Nagano Olympics. Unfortunately, the heavily favoured Canadians finished second to the United States in that historic event. To say that it was an upset is an understatement. The Canadians had captured every single World Cup title since its inception in 1990. The seeds of one of the great Olympic rivalries were planted.

Angela James checks a German player during the 1990 Women's World Hockey Championships in Ottawa. Considered the first superstar of modern women's hockey, James scored 11 goals in five games to lead Canada to the gold medal.

AP Images

When they met again at the 2002 Salt Lake City Olympics, it was the Americans who were the favourites, and with good reason. Canada had gone 0–8 in pre-Olympic play with the US. The Canadian women exacted sweet revenge in Salt Lake in 2002, defeating the US 3–2 in the gold-medal final. They played with a zeal fuelled by patriotism since rumours had reached them to the effect that the US players had desecrated the Canadian flag in their dressing room.

In all, Canada has won three of the four Olympic women's hockey gold medals. In the process they have become heroes to a whole generation of Canadian women. Like men's teams of years past they are also the gold standard for young hockey players around the world. If history repeats itself, it's just a matter of time before women's hockey silences the critics for good. When that happens, we will look back at this time with some level of amazement. Former Ottawa mayor Charlotte Whitton once said, "Whatever women do, they must do twice as well as men to be thought half as good... fortunately, this isn't difficult."

The difficulty comes in being given the chance to compete.

CANADA
1867 1967
DOMINION
PENALTY
PERIOD
PENALTY
3
TORONTO
MONTREAL
2
18:04
5
ALL STAR WRESTLING
SUNDAY 7:30 PM.

HOW HOCKEY EXPLAINS TORONTO

IT HAS BEEN SAID that the one thing that binds Canada and Canadians together is a mutual hatred of Toronto. According to this shaky bit of folk wisdom, the West hates the city for its political clout and liberal ways while the Atlantic Provinces despise its condescension and resent it for usurping the benefits of Confederation. Both regions deplore the brain drain of young people gravitating to its bright lights and opportunity. Meanwhile, Quebec sees the Queen City as the embodiment of English Canada, with the countless injustices that go with that.

It's a good line but it's not true if it ever was. Sure the West has been ignored and disrespected. Certainly the East is often treated like the poor cousin with the quaint ways and funny accents. As for Quebec, entire books could be written on the complexities that exist between Montreal and Toronto alone. But hatred? No way.

Beneath it all, most Canadians have a grudging respect, a feeling of pride and ownership, and even a fondness for the place. The fact is that most Canadians have spent at least some time in Canada's largest metropolis, have friends and/or relatives living there, and have enjoyed its many diversions—culinary, cultural, and otherwise. Toronto is the home of the dreaded Head Office for many Canadians. For others it's a great place to get away for some shopping and soak up some Culture with a capital C. Since we lack a New York, it is also our version of that place where, "If you can make it there, you can make it anywhere."

Love it or hate it, Toronto is the financial heart of Canada, the media

A view of the Maple Leaf Gardens ice from the stands in the 1960s.

Frank Prazak/Hockey Hall of Fame

Conn Smythe (right) celebrates with Maple Leafs coach Hap Day (left) and star Syl Apps after Toronto defeated the Detroit Red Wings to win the 1948 Stanley Cup. Smythe was the principal owner of the Maple Leafs from 1927 to 1961.

Bruce Bennett Studios/Getty Images

capital, the centre of higher education, and the corporate engine that drives our economy. For these and other reasons it's also our most ethnically diverse city and according to UNESCO, the most ethnically diverse city in the world. It is a magnet for new immigrants. An astonishing 50 percent of the city's residents were not born in Canada.

Toronto is also our nation's bastion of culture. Among the artistic institutions based there are the Toronto Symphony Orchestra, the Canadian Stage Company, the Canadian Opera Company, the National Ballet of Canada, and the dear old CBC. In addition to ballet, opera, dance, classical music, and Rex Murphy, Toronto is also hub of the magazine and book publishing industries and the self-appointed arbiter of literary and fashion tastes and trends.

In the world of sports, Toronto is blessed with franchises in five major professional

sports: Major League Baseball, the National Basketball Association, Major League Soccer, the Canadian Football League, and the National Hockey League. It also beat out several other North American cities—including Montreal and New York—to become the permanent home of the Hockey Hall of Fame.

With due respect to all those dancers, singers, actors, musicians, investors, hitters, dribblers, kickers, and passers, the Toronto Maple Leafs are the institution that makes Toronto human, that blunts much of the jealousy and criticism aimed at it from the hinterland. You see, Toronto has what can only be described as an obsession with being world class. On the surface that's an admirable goal. What city would not want to be compared with Paris, London, Rome, or New York? Unfortunately Toronto has often managed to turn this noble quest into something truly cringe-worthy. "A place to live, a place to grow, Ontari-ari-ari-o," goes the song. Toronto's biggest erection, the CN Tower, is symbolic of this bigger-is-better attitude. Disguised beneath a mask of false bravado, it is just the same old Canadian inferiority complex writ large. Instead of waiting for others to notice their greatness, Torontonians feel obliged to point it out in great detail at every turn.

That's why we should all be happy that the Toronto Maple Leafs call this city home. The Leafs keep Torontonians humble, no small feat as most Canadians can attest. With all that the Ontario capital has to offer the country and the world, the Leafs are the one thing that makes Toronto human, vulnerable—almost lovable. The Maple Leafs have long since eclipsed Newfies as the subject of jokes most often told over medium double-doubles at the local Tim Hortons. The fact that Horton himself was a Leaf from the glory days makes the setting double-double ironic. In a country where Newfoundland is now listed among the "haves" while Ontario recently dipped to "have-not" status, the Leafs are perennials in the "have-not" column—as in *have not* won a Stanley Cup since Stephen Harper was an eight-year-old Torontonian with Liberal leanings.

To their everlasting credit, the people of this great city continue to embrace and support their Leafs despite their shortcomings, despite their world class deficit of talent, despite the fact that they haven't won a Stanley Cup since 1967. Despite all that, the Maple Leafs are still the defining team of Toronto. Hell, maybe even its defining institution, the Toronto Stock Exchange notwithstanding.

Of course mediocrity and Maple Leafs weren't always side by side in the thesaurus. In fact, until 1967, they used to be one of those Toronto entities that really *was* world class. There was a time when young Canadian boys from coast to coast dreamed of playing hockey for the Toronto Maple Leafs. Their heads were

full of images planted there by Foster Hewitt and other chroniclers of their heroics and their heroes. Back in the days of the original six, there were only two Canadian teams to root for. Montreal certainly had a huge following outside of Quebec, especially in the Maritimes, but thanks to Foster and a glorious Stanley Cup history, the Maple Leafs were still viewed as Canada's team. It's still true today. Even behind enemy lines, at NHL arenas in Vancouver, Calgary, Edmonton, and Ottawa, and yes, Montreal, the classic Maple Leaf jerseys are always on display in great numbers.

The Leafs wear the symbol of Canada on their chests, an inspired move by uber-patriot and uber-Torontonian Conn Smythe. Thanks to Hewitt and the Toronto media machine, the Leafs are the default team of choice for Canadians with no franchise.

Following are the experiences of several former Toronto Maple Leafs players. Like many Canadians throughout our history, they came to Toronto looking for work and discovered a city that was welcoming, demanding, appreciative, and invasive. Some came from other parts of Canada, some from within the province, and some from the city itself. Their stories say a lot about the proud traditions of this once-great franchise, not to mention the heart and soul that it takes to succeed there. These are some of the players who made Toronto the Mecca of hockey in English Canada. They represented the city well, despite the obstacles that were placed before them. There is little big-city braggadocio, only a pure and simple love of hockey and the city where they played the game. These players exemplify the tradition, the pride, the class, the connectivity, the lineage of great Maple Leafs players extending back to Ace Bailey and beyond. They help to explain the seemingly inexplicable loyalty and devotion that Toronto fans still have for Canada's team.

RON ELLIS was one of the most popular players for the Toronto Maple Leafs teams of the '60s and '70s. Born just north of Toronto in Lindsay, Ontario, his is the classic Maple Leafs story. Before graduating to the parent NHL club, he played his junior hockey with the Toronto Marlboros of the Ontario Hockey Association, where his 46 goals and 38 assists helped lead the 1963-64 Marlies to the Memorial Cup. With the Leafs, the 5'9", 195-pound right winger was initially inserted on a line with Bob Pulford and centre Dave Keon and was later matched with Paul Henderson and Normie Ulman to create a superb forechecking unit with an explosive scoring punch. Ellis was a member of the 1966–67 Leafs team that won Toronto's last Stanley Cup. His goal against Montreal in the Game 6 playoff clincher got the ball rolling for the eventual champions. He strung together nine straight 20-goal seasons but mysteriously retired after the 1974-75 season, a campaign in which he potted 32 goals, his second-highest season total. He returned to play four more seasons in Toronto before hanging up his skates for good. His career numbers include 332 goals, 308 assists, and a miniscule 207 penalty minutes in 16 NHL seasons. At the 1972 Summit Series with the Soviet Union, he was a key member of Team Canada, playing on a line with Paul Henderson and Bobby Clarke.

When his professional career was over, Ellis confronted a much tougher opponent than even the NHL had to offer—clinical depression. He faced it head on and came out on top. Typical of the unselfish style he displayed on ice, Ellis has assisted countless Canadians in their own struggles with this insidious mental disorder. An eloquent and informed speaker, he uses his hockey fame to emphasize the importance of recognizing the symptoms and seeking help. His book *Over the Boards: The Ron Ellis Story* (written with Kevin Shea) helped to remove some of the stigma that surrounds the illness. Ellis is now director of public affairs with the Hockey Hall of Fame in Toronto.

"My father was a very good hockey player and actually had a walk-on tryout with the Toronto Marlboros which Harold Ballard owned in the '40s during the war. Dad made the team and Harold actually became very fond of him. Of course Harold went on to own the Leafs and my father joined the air force as soon as he turned 18. After the war, with only the six NHL teams, it was very hard to break in so he ended up playing professional hockey in the States, in the American Hockey League. So I was a hockey kid, if you like, born and bred. I certainly had the game in my family, and in my blood. When I started to play, Dad became very much involved in the teams I played with. In fact, he coached most of my minor hockey teams.

"I was a Maple Leafs fan partly because of their affiliation with the Marlies, but we were like every other Canadian family in that regard. Most people had a little soft spot for the Leafs. Every Wednesday and Saturday night without fail we'd watch the games and, of course, listen to Foster.

"After Dad's professional hockey career he went back into the air force. They needed pilots so he rejoined and was stationed in Ottawa, so that's where I played my minor hockey. When the Leafs' scouts approached my family, I was about 14 years old. Punch Imlach and King Clancy actually came to my home in Ottawa and talked to my parents. The following year I became a Toronto Marlboro.

"At the time, being a Marlie was a really big thing, and as soon as I became a Marlie,

Ron Ellis played 16 seasons for the Maple Leafs, including scoring 22 goals for Toronto's last Stanley Cup team in 1967.

Melchior DiGiacomo/ Getty Images

I was Leafs property. The Leafs were one of only six NHL franchises and at the time they owned the Toronto Marlboros and Toronto St. Michael's. They were two powerhouses in the junior leagues and many players made the jump straight from the Marlies or St. Mike's to the Leafs. That's where they got virtually all of their players. If you look at the Marlies alumni, it included future Leafs mainstays like Bobby Pulford, Bobby Baun, and Billy Harris. St. Mike's was just as impressive. They sent guys like Frank Mahovlich and Davey Keon to the parent club. In addition to the junior pipeline, they also had a minor league system anchored by a pretty strong American Hockey League team in Rochester. I was fortunate enough to be one of those guys who made the jump directly from the junior ranks to the NHL. I was one of the last to take that route because after 1967 they introduced the draft.

"Toronto's last Stanley Cup win was in 1967. That's a long time ago and we could talk about the ups and downs of the Leafs for a long time. Suffice it to say that a lot of mistakes have been made during those years. Despite the lack of on-ice successes, there is no question that this city is the hockey Mecca, that hockey is the psyche of Toronto. That's why the Hockey Hall of Fame, where I work, is located here. The old Hockey Hall of Fame was at the CNE grounds. Before they selected Toronto to remain the home of the Hall a lot of other places were considered. They looked carefully at Montreal, New York, and Detroit, but the NHL and the powers that be said this is where it should be. That says something about Toronto and its hockey heritage.

"The very first All-Star Game was played here for Ace Bailey. Ace Bailey gave me my greatest honour when he brought his number out of retirement and asked me to wear it. It's a wonderful story. Ace had gotten hit from behind by Eddie Shore and his career was cut really short, so the first All-Star Game was held here in Toronto to raise money for him and his family and it went on from there. When I turned pro I certainly knew who Ace Bailey was, and at that time he was also the timekeeper at the Gardens and had been for many years.

"Unbeknownst to me he was watching me pretty closely and the year after we won the Cup in '67, he went to Ballard and said, 'I'd like to bring my sweater out of retirement and I'd like Ron Ellis to wear it.' I had no idea this was going on and then one day when I walked into the arena I could see Ace coming up the hallway. We hadn't really spoken before that. He said, 'Ron I'd like to speak to you a minute.' I had no idea what was coming. He said, 'I'd like for you to wear my sweater.' After I picked myself up off the floor, I said, 'Absolutely.' I was very proud to wear his sweater and we became very good friends after that. I remember saying to him when I was invited to tryout for Team Canada in '72, 'Ace, if I make the team I'm going to ask for No. 6 in your honour.' So that all worked out well. What makes it even nicer is that when I retired he said that he wanted his No. 6 retired again and he didn't want anyone else to wear it. Perfect. It was a great honour.

"Now they're moving the All-Star Game around but I think one of the most successful All-Star Games they've ever had was the last time it was here in Toronto. It was the 50th anniversary of the first one. Toronto is just such a hockey hotbed and you may well ask how it can remain a hockey hotbed when the team hasn't performed? The answer, I think, is that it's just been ingrained in a generation and has been passed on to the young people of today. That's all I can think of. In my dad's generation if I wasn't a Leafs fan he probably would have asked me to leave. It was passed along like a family heirloom. Today's Leafs fans live on hope. They've heard the stories from their parents and grandparents and they know that if Toronto ever wins again, the city will go nuts. They don't want to bail out. They are willing to hang in there because when the Leafs do win they're going to have to close the city. They're going to have to shut down the 401 and everything!

"In Toronto, when you're playing, particularly back in my era, everyone knew you. I think now it's a little harder to recognize the guys when everyone's wearing the helmets and visors. When my wife and I went to dinner people were very kind, saying hello and good luck to the Leafs and all that. But when we weren't winning, when things weren't going well, you didn't go out to dinner. You stayed home. It just wasn't worth the effort. People would come up and ask, 'What's wrong with the Leafs?' And they all had solutions. That's the thing about Toronto. Today, with all the people with cameras on their phones, players today have to be so careful even when they're out having a beer.

"Because Toronto is Canada's media centre, they are on top of everything. There's a lot of competition between radio and television stations and newspapers. The atmosphere has changed big time. During my playing days, the media were always with us, they travelled with us, they were on the bus with us, they were on the plane with us, they stayed at the same hotels with us, they ate meals with us. They became friends. The media would not drag someone through the mud. In fact they would almost protect some guys because they respected them as players. George Gross became a very good friend and when I retired I phoned him said, 'George I want you to handle the story. I want you to break it.' That's how close we became. You could actually talk off the record with these

guys and it wouldn't get printed. Now it's just completely opposite.

"When I was a young guy, Toronto was where I wanted to play and I sacrificed opportunities in order to play here. When the World Hockey Association came along, I had an opportunity to go to another team and double my salary overnight. That wasn't my dream. My dream was to be a Leaf, and my dream— and I was very fortunate to have it come true— was to play my whole career in Toronto.

"Today there's a different mind set—*I don't care where I play, just pay me.* A lot of these guys are content to be in Florida or Columbus out of the scrutiny of the entire nation. They face a lot less pressure than you do in Toronto.

"I always felt a bit of a freedom on the ice, away from everything. When I retired the first time, I had just finished my best year. I was in great shape and I worked hard all summer but I just felt very, very strongly that I couldn't play, and being a team guy I didn't want to be the kind of player who was in the lineup and out of the lineup. That's one of the main reasons I decided to retire. I retired for two years from hockey and even then didn't know what was wrong. I just knew that something wasn't right. I got away from the game and got my strength back and made a comeback.

"It was after my hockey career that I had my worst episode with depression. When you're younger your reserves are there. You're a little stronger and you can fight off things a little better. I discussed things with doctors, and finally identified it as depression.

"Your manly pride prevents you from talking to anyone. The most shocked person was my roommate Brian Glennie. I roomed with for eight years and when I told him I was retiring, he almost fell over because I had never given him any idea of how I was feeling. I went to the Leafs—Red Kelly was

coaching—and basically said there's something going on here. I don't really think I can play. They let me go. Without even saying 'Gee can you sit down with our team doctor?' Of course I left, and I didn't go to a doctor. That was 1975 so we've come a long way."

DARRYL SITTLER'S *story is a classic Canadian saga. I said classic, not idyllic. It was not all positive. In fact, far from it. He was with the Leafs at a time when the relationship between players and ownership was undergoing a fundamental change. His involvement in the players' union caused friction with Harold Ballard and Punch Imlach. Decisions were made that had nothing to do with building a winner. Sittler's story shows the perseverance that it takes to succeed in Canada's toughest town. The fact that he remained true to himself and his teammates says a lot about Sittler, a lot about Toronto, a lot about hockey, and a lot about being Canadian.*

"Believe it or not, as a kid I was a Montreal Canadiens fan, and Jean Beliveau was my idol. Despite that, I was honoured to be drafted by the Leafs in 1970. The nice thing for me was that Toronto is only about 60 or 70 miles from my hometown of St. Jacob's, just outside of Kitchener-Waterloo, so I didn't have to move away too far.

"The first time I came to training camp, Jim Gregory, our general manger at the time, walked me to the dressing room and said, 'You'll be sitting over there.' I looked and there was a number 27 over the stall! I certainly knew the significance of number 27: the great Frank Mahovlich. I was a first-round pick and that showed what they expected of me. That was pretty special.

"All you want to do as a kid is to make the hockey club and stay in the National Hockey League. Things just kind of worked out naturally for me. Within a few years the World Hockey Association came on the scene and some teammates left to join it. That gave me an opportunity to get more ice time. Then Dave Keon left and they were looking for a captain. Ronnie Ellis was the senior statesman of the team at that time and they asked him. He said, 'No, Darryl should be our captain.' It was an honour for me to be asked to be captain and to have the support of a guy like Ronnie. It was pretty darn good.

"So I was the captain under coach Red Kelly and then Roger Neilson. Jim Gregory was the general manager and I had a lot of respect for Jim and still do. But then as Harold Ballard got a little older, he started to make changes. Everything was erratic at times, because of Harold's personality. I think his age probably had something to do with that. He was diabetic and some days he got up and maybe was a little more miserable than others. It was a mixture of his personality and his health. Having said that, because the Leafs are such a high-profile team with such great tradition, anything that Harold did—or that a player did—was scrutinized and magnified.

"When you become captain of the Leafs you follow the tradition of guys like Syl Apps and George Armstrong and Teeder Kennedy. I knew the significance of that and realized there was a responsibility that came with it. I represented the Leafs, not only as player on the ice but as a spokesperson and member of the community off the ice. I took that very seriously.

"When Harold hired Punch Imlach, I can honestly say that I had a lot of respect for Imlach. In his previous stint as coach, he had won four Stanley Cups for the Leafs, but a number of years had gone by and things had changed. We now had a players' union and

Darryl Sittler played for the Maple Leafs from 1970 to 1982. On February 7, 1976, he set the NHL record for most points scored in one game with 10 against the Boston Bruins.

Melchior DiGiacomo/ Getty Images

Sittler's Scoring Record

Darryl Sittler recalls the events of February 7, 1976.

"It was an original six team playing in Maple Leaf Gardens on a Saturday night. That in itself creates excitement for the team and for city—and the country, I guess. The Canadiens were on the road so the game was broadcast coast to coast that night. I'd been in a bit of a slump before that. Ballard made some sort of comment in the paper about, 'Well, if he could find a good centreman to play with Lanny McDonald and Errol Thompson...' obviously giving me a shot. Then I went out that night and everything was falling into place. Sometimes you have no idea why it's happening but it's happening. At the end of the second period I had seven points and the statistician, Stan Obodiac, came down from the press box between periods and said, 'Darryl, I don't know if you know it, but the record of eight points is held by Rocket Richard. If you get another point, you'll tie him.'

"That's the first I knew there was a record of eight points, so I went into the third period knowing that there was a possibility of tying Rocket's record. I got a goal within the first three or four minutes and the building was electrified. Then I scored two after the fact and the last one was from behind the net. I threw it out front to make a pass to Errol Thompson, who was in the slot. Brad Park stuck his leg out to block the pass and redirected it between Dave Reece's legs. I threw my hands up in the air and shook my head and thought, *Holy Moses, this is unbelievable.*

"Did I think the record would become as significant as it is? When you go through it, you don't realize. It survived through the '80s with guys like Wayne Gretzky and Mario Lemieux. Wayne was scoring 200 to 240 points a year and I'm thinking, *Ok, there's probably a guy like him or Mario that's going to get nine or ten some night.* They both had eight a couple times but no one's got nine or ten so it's still a record today, 35 years later. On the 30th anniversary of the game, TSN flew Dave Reece into Toronto. It was the first time I'd met him and talked to him so that was kind of cool. That particular game, Gerry Cheevers was coming back to the Bruins from the World Hockey Association. They wanted him to make his debut back at Boston so he was on the bench watching. It was a good night; 1976 was my year."

I was the vice president of the players' association. I was captain of the team and I had a no-trade contract. Right away Punch wanted to challenge me on a bunch of issues and I had to make a decision whether to stand up for what I believed was right, or back down. All I wanted to do was win and be the best captain I could be.

"I gave a very emotional speech before we went to the ice to tell my teammates what I was doing and they were very supportive. Punch wanted some other player to put the 'C' on but nobody would wear it. They said Darryl's our captain and he's our guy and whether he has the 'C' on or not, he's our leader.

"Most of our fans at that time knew exactly what we were dealing with. There were so many issues written about on the front page of the papers the three or four months previous to that.

"Why was I a Montreal fan? As a kid, why do we choose our teams? I grew up in a household where there were six boys and my dad. For some reason, I just loved the way the Montreal Canadiens played the game—the speed of it. Jean Beliveau stood out. He was the captain at the time and he seemed so classy. I was a centreman, he was a centreman.

"I'm 20 and I get drafted and I'm playing in the Montreal Forum and it's Beliveau's last season, so I had the opportunity to face off against him. I remember looking up and kind of gathering my thoughts to put it together. I mean here's your childhood hero, the guy you dreamed of being someday and there you are playing against him. I'm wearing a Leafs uniform but it was pretty special.

"He retired after that and I went on to have a successful career and was inducted into the Hockey Hall of Fame in 1989. I got to know Jean through a number of Hall of Fame events and stuff like that. My wife Wendy passed away from cancer. She died in 2003 and the morning of her funeral I remember distinctly and with great pride that the phone rang that morning and it was Jean Beliveau. He said 'Darryl, I just want you to know I'm thinking about you today. I hope

you get through it.' I'll always remember that moment. He's such a distinguished person still today. He was and is a great ambassador for the Canadiens and for the game.

"Playing hockey for the Leafs is a great honour. I turned 60 in September 2010 and I think you understand and appreciate it more as you're further way from your playing days. I haven't played since 1985 so it's 25 years and people still feel like they know you. They want to shake you hand or get an autograph or get a picture with you and have nice things to say. So it's nice that you've touched some people's lives along the way.

"When Cliff Fletcher was named general manager and president of the Maple Leafs in 1991, one of the first calls he made was to me. He said, 'Darryl, I'd like for you to be part of

Longtime Maple Leafs coach Punch Imlach holds an ice cream cone in one hand as he shakes hands with defenceman Allan Stanley in September 1967. Dave Keon looks on. Imlach coached the Maple Leafs to the Stanley Cup championship in 1962, 1963, 1964, and 1967. Imlach's return to Toronto as general manager in 1979 was not as successful.
Bruce Bennett Studios/Getty Images

On the Roads and Rinks

"I played road hockey all the time," Darryl Sittler said. "Every day after school I probably did a few hours. It was very big in developing my skills. You learned how to stickhandle, shoot the puck, and develop the slap shot. We used to make our own nets. We'd take the two-by-fours and cut them up make a four-by-six net, get some Mennonite potato sacks, use the potato sacks as mesh and take shots on goal. One kid would play goal and we'd work on our skills there. I grew up in a very strong Mennonite area and the Mennonites weren't allowed to play organized recreational hockey, so they would make their own rinks outside. My brothers and I helped them. We'd play on an outdoor rink all winter long.

"In Canada, it's there for you to develop your skills—just the fact that you're out there on the ice. I was always conscientious to work on the things that I couldn't do well. I could deal with them when I was on the ice by myself. If I couldn't turn one way, couldn't shoot the puck on the backhand, I would practise those things to become a better player day in and day out. Not just at the regular, organized practices in indoor rinks. I'd do it on my own on the outdoor rinks."

our organization,' and offered me a position. It was wonderful. Believe it or not, Ballard never wanted to recognize players from the past. Cliff formed the alumni. The ownership had changed. Steve Stavro had taken over and hired Cliff and Cliff brought the class of the Montreal Canadiens with him.

"It's tough to pinpoint what it is about Toronto fans that make them so loyal and so passionate. The Leafs have had such a great history and tradition. We haven't won a championship, but we've had some pretty good teams that fans felt good about. I think people like that blue and white colour. It's a great sweater and logo and it *is* Toronto. It's like the New York Yankees. It's got history and tradition. We'd like nothing better than to have a good team here and give the fans what they all want, which is a championship.

The reality of it is, it's not easy to get there. There are 30 teams and it's not like it was back in the six team league.

"It's pretty clear that hockey is part of Canadian culture. For most families throughout Canada, it's become part of their social life. In our day it was *Hockey Night in Canada* on Saturday night, turning on the TV, and the family getting together. You have your bath and maybe get a treat and then watch the Leafs and Canadiens. Obviously the game has changed a lot in that there are more teams and more coverage than ever before. With the cable and satellite, most nights you can watch a game during the season. At the same time the reason it's changed is because there is so much more interest now than there was back then.

"I think one of the things is that Canada is a multi-cultural community and you're seeing some kids where maybe the families have come from other countries but they end up playing hockey—like Nazem Kadri with the Leafs. He's a Muslim and he loves the game and his family loves the game and why can't he be good at hockey if he plays the game and develops his skills? I think you're going to see more of that than ever before. I have two girls, both of whom played on teams. It's because first of all it's such a fun and healthy game to play."

JOHNNY BOWER *was one of those players who came east from small-town Saskatchewan to play in Toronto. In this age of agents and draft picks and scientifically measured skills, his journey to the NHL sounds like an odyssey of ancient Greek legend. Once he made it the Maple Leafs he was determined to stay. Bower is part of a vanishing breed of players who learned the game on outdoor rinks and had to improvise sticks, nets, pads, and even pucks.*

Maple Leafs goaltender Johnny Bower looks to make the save against the Rangers at Madison Square Garden in February 1967. The Hall of Famer starred in goal for Toronto's four Stanley Cup teams in the 1960s. Bruce Bennett Studios/Getty Images

"Tim Horton was opening up one of these Tim Hortons doughnut places on Dundas here in Toronto and asked about six of the Leafs if they wanted to come down and sign autographs for a couple of hours right after practice. He said everyone was going to get $25. I said to myself, "Twenty five bucks!" And I put my hand right up and [Allan] Stanley put his hand up and Bobby Baun put his hand up.

"We got down there and there must have been 200 kids lined up and we're sitting there waiting and waiting. At last the time's up. Now Tim gets up and he reaches in his pocket and he gives all the players the $25 each. Finally he comes to me and he says, 'John, I'm really short of cash.' I said, 'What are you talking about? The cash register's full.' He said, 'I can't take money out of there, you know that.' I told him to take $25 out of there and put a note that you took $25 out, but he wouldn't do it. Finally he says, 'I'll give it to you tomorrow in practice camp, okay?' I said, 'Okay, fine.'

"So anyway I go there a little bit early and I turned around and he'd paid me off in 18 boxes of donuts! Can you believe that? They were probably donuts that he couldn't sell. I don't know. By geez, I never did get my $25. And I had to get the donuts out of the dressing room real quick because if Punch ever saw 18 boxes of donuts beside me there, he'd go nuts. I got the maintenance guy to take them away and told him to give them to his crew—I don't care what you do with them—just get them out of here quick.

"Tim [Horton] was a great defenceman, a great stickhandler with a great shot. He was a tough guy but a good clean player. Not a good fighter but when he gave you the bear hug—boy he squeezed until you turned purple. He was strong. When he played with Allan Stanley, a lot of guys would go down Allan Stanley's side rather than Horton's. After a while they got wise and didn't want anything to do with Timmy because in the corners, I tell you, he just hit you the way you should be hit.

"I always had great defencemen. I had Bobby Baun, Carl Brewer, Horton, Stanley. Punch told me, 'I know how old you are.' I played against him when he coached for Springfield and we beat Springfield out. I had a great series against him which was one big factor that kept me in Toronto. He told me, 'You know I want to get a good, solid defence for you and you just do your job and you'll be okay. As long as I'm here in Toronto,' he says, 'we're going to win the Stanley Cup.' I said 'Well, I hope so.' That's the way it all started. Punch was very, very, strict—very demanding. Do this and do that. You practised like you were actually in a game. If you wanted to fool around after, okay. He was a good manager and a good coach. A lot of people think he was a little too tough on the younger guys like Pulford

and Keon and the others, but hey they had those young legs! We used to tell those guys, 'Hey, us older guys will carry you to Christmas time, but boy, you guys better get those feet going after Christmas.'

"I can only speak about the way the man [Imlach] treated me and he treated me great. He gave me heck a lot of times because I was falling down too much and all of that but that was hockey and I could take it then and I had to listen to him. He's the one who paid me so what am I going to do?

"The fans were great in Toronto. They deserve success. They're so patient. Right now they've waited 43 years since they last won the Stanley Cup. Boy oh boy! They can only sit on the hot seat for so long and that's it. They're starting to get impatient. If you're not playing well, they *know* you're not playing well. You'd better not go doggin' it or anything. They demand a lot of you. They're paying an awful lot of money to come and see you. If you don't play well, you're going to get some boos there. That's part of hockey too—in a sense. Someone likes you, someone doesn't like you.

"Toronto fans know hockey. They are very knowledgeable fans, I think. No matter where I go, what functions I attend, they can go way back—and they are smart too. They might say, 'Hey John do you remember that hat trick that Rocket Richard scored against you?' I say, 'Yeah please! Why did you bring that up once again?' I'd forgotten all about it and he brings it up. I don't speak anymore at functions—it's all questions and answers. Some of the questions go way back—even a little before my time—and you have to be sharp.

"In Toronto it's not only hockey—baseball draws pretty well, football's down a little bit, basketball's going good. It was the city of champions at one time and once you are the city of champions they expect you to be champions.

"They are loyal fans. Sure you'll get booed occasionally but I got booed a few times too for letting in bad goals and then you just pull up your socks.

"The rivalry between Toronto and Montreal was just fantastic. Apparently Montreal won more Stanley Cups than Toronto and Conn Smythe didn't like that so that's probably why the rivalry was there. When we used to play against Montreal, we all thought 'Hey we just played against the best guys in the world, you know?' I had a lot of respect for those guys and I have a very, very dear friend in Mr. Beliveau. I went out on card shows with him and he was a prince of a guy off the ice. You just couldn't beat him! He was a gentleman all the way and a great guy. It was always 'Allo Johnee' in French and if I stayed with him much longer I'd learn to speak French. He was great. And I talked to Rocket Richard and I remember the Rocket once got the hat trick on me. The season's all over and we're signing autographs there for the kids and I sat beside him and Gump Worsley was on the other side and he said to me, 'Johneeee, do you remember that hat trick I got on you.' I said 'Why did you have to bring that up? I had forgot all about that actually.' He said 'I just thought I'd remind you.' I said 'You don't have to remind me, I know. Thanks a lot!' He was dynamite. That guy would drive me up a wall, honest to God! I went to church, I lit candles. He must have been behind me and blew them out or something because he'd still get two goals on me the next night. I stopped him a few times but boy he drove me up the wall. Rocket Richard was the best I faced. My friend Gordie Howe gave me trouble too. We weren't friends on the ice. In fact I had trouble with everybody. They all loved me because I kept them all in the league.

"My eyesight wasn't great. I was failing on long shots. I remember one time we were playing against St. Louis and Alf Picard— I'll never forget him—he had a good low shot and I knew that but I don't know why but I didn't cut the angle off properly and the puck went right in the far corner of the net. I think that we had been tied 1–1 and he made it 2–1 and when the period was over I got heck from Punch. He said, 'What are you doing? What are you looking at? That was a routine skate save for you. You don't let those in. If you don't start playing well John, I'll out you at the end of the bench.' I said, 'I was screened.' He says, 'Screened? There was no one in front of you.'

"I didn't know what to do; I didn't want to tell him I didn't see it. So finally he tells me that I better go and get my eyes examined. On long shots I had a little trouble but my defencemen knew that and they blocked shots for me from quite a way out. But no one would block a shot from Dennis Hull or Bobby Hull! I couldn't see the puck around my feet. My defencemen had to come and tell me, 'Don't move, don't move,' because I couldn't see guys on the side. I miss the goal posts—my best friends.

"I did eventually wear a mask, but I didn't wear one for a long time. I told Punch, 'I can't see anything with that mask,' and Imlach said 'You can't see anyway so it shouldn't make any difference.' He was funny sometimes. That's why I got along so well with Punch. I had my problems with the mask so I took it off. In fact this is where you really incur your injuries—that's where they really happen because all of a sudden you relax a little bit and all of a sudden you get a deflection—bam—right over the eye. I had over 200 stitches over my face, but the wrinkles cover everything now!"

BOBBY BAUN, *another native son of Saskatchewan, was the epitome of toughness. Heroic toughness. He will forever be remembered for scoring the winning goal for Toronto on a broken leg. It's one of those events that becomes part of the legacy of a franchise, like Franco Harris' immaculate reception or Ted Williams' home run in his last major league at bat.*

"I came to Toronto from Lanigan, Saskatchewan, when I was just a little guy—about three years old. We have family there and I still go back. They even have a street named after me—Bobby Baun Way.

"Saskatchewan is among the 'haves' now. They've got everything there. If it had been like that back then, maybe my dad wouldn't have come east. Father was a mechanic by trade and he moved east a year before my mom came. At first he worked for GM, then for Texaco at Woodbine and Kingston Road. He got his own Texaco station in 1941 beside the Alpine Hotel at Victoria Park and Kingston Road. It was the No. 1 Texaco station in Canada during the war years, pumped more gas than anyone. Mom had a crew of 10 ladies who worked with her sweeping cars out with the little whisk brooms and cleaning windows and pumping gas.

"The trademarks of my game were always preparation and fairness. That came from Lorne Wiseman. He said the only thing that was different in me was that I was very aggressive, but also looking out for the little guy regardless of the circumstances. He said that I just had that drive and desire. He said you never abused people.

"I'm one of the few people who continued to work while I was playing hockey. When I decided I wanted to be a hockey player, I quit school. I worked construction in the summers and it was hard work. I kept 11 block layers going when I was 14 years old! The block layers couldn't believe that I could handle two 12″ blocks, one on each arm, and throw them up in the air to their scaffolds. And then throw the 'mud', the mortar to hold them in place to build the walls. You had to keep these guys loaded up. They were all Italian and they couldn't speak much English. They couldn't believe I could keep them going.

"I really never played hockey as far as dad was concerned. He kept me pretty grounded and humble. He only acknowledged that I was a hockey player the day before he passed away. But he watched every game, just shovelling [candy] into his mouth.

"The influx of new Canadians into Canada, and especially Toronto, is amazing. It started with the Anglo-Saxons. English people came into Canada right after the war. My wife is English. English and Scotch took to hockey just like ducks to water. Italians were exactly the same as soon as they started pouring into Canada in the early '50s. They loved the game just as much. Right now the Asians are fantastic. I'm the honorary chair of a golf tournament for the Canadian Cancer Society tournament. The Maple Leaf alumni field a team for the last day. There's a little Chinese fellow who served as my bodyguard. He knew everything there was to know about me and he wasn't that old. He was still at university but he sure as hell knew what I was about.

"I was always close to the Chinese community and I have a big Chinese following. After we'd return from a road trip, I'd always go directly to Chinatown and have a bite to eat before I came home. We'd be flying at 2 the morning and end up in a little restaurant in Chinatown and watch them play fantan for a while. I'm not a card player but they were such avid and passionate players

Bobby Baun played 14 of his 17 NHL seasons for the Maple Leafs. He is best remembered for scoring the winning goal in Game 6 of the 1964 Stanley Cup Finals while playing on a broken ankle.
Bruce Bennett Studios/Getty Images

"Hennie's [Paul Henderson's] goal was rated 29th as a sporting event in the 20th century and mine was No. 17! I tell Hennie that and he just gets sick every time. It was a piece done by *Sports Illustrated* in 2000—the highlight in all sports, and Hennie's was 29th. So every time I see him I say, 'What number were you?' That's the only time I see him flustered. But my jersey isn't worth a million six."

—Bob Baun, comparing his game-winning goal scored on a broken leg in Game 6 of the 1964 Stanley Cup Finals to Paul Henderson's goal in Game 8 of the 1972 Summit Series

and that's how I met a lot of the old families. Toronto really was a special city to play in. I just met [Leafs general manager] Brian Burke for the first time and I asked how he was enjoying Toronto and of course it hasn't been very enjoyable for him so far. I told him it's one of the toughest cities that he's trying to crack right now and it takes a special person to do that. It just can't be done overnight. It's either going to grow on him and he'll make it or he'll move on, away from those pressures.

"The hockey players face the same pressure. Unless you have your family and friends around you in that environment, it's pretty hard—especially for a kid coming from Sweden or Germany or Russia or whatever— when everyone wants to know how you wipe your backside. Toronto is not an easy place to play. It's a showcase. Every visiting team plays above their ability level because they're playing in front of friends and family. They don't want to screw up.

"Toronto has demanding fans. They certainly know the game as well as anybody, but ultimately they're no different from all the armchair coaches. They all think they know the answers but no one does. You've gotta be on the inside track 24 hours a day.

"The worst thing you can do is listen to all the TV and radio sports shows. It's like getting two accountants disagree on which way the country should be going. Or watching Congress and the Senate in the US and getting the Democrats and Republicans to agree on *anything*. That's one of the problems in this world—everyone is so open to criticism. And if you don't have thick skin, you're just toast. If you take everything to heart with critics, there's just no way to survive.

"Montreal was a fun place to play. Here's one of the neat little stories. In every game, starting with my first three or four years in the league in '59 or '60, Senator Molson used to come into the dressing room and welcome me to Montreal and then turn around and walk out again! I was the only one he'd talk to. And Punch used to get really quite upset. He'd say, 'What is he doing here?' And I'd say, 'Oh, he's just welcomed me to Montreal and wished me to have a good came.' This went on for years but it was always so nice. I used to give him a little salute at the start of the game and he always acknowledged that and it was just one of those little quirky things that make the game so great. It went on and it was really quite different. I'd never say a word, just 'Thank you very much,' and he'd turn around and walk out and that was it. Everybody took it matter of factly. Just one of those things.

"The Forum was a great place to play. I loved playing there and I loved the people.

It seemed to me that I had as many good friends and fans there as I did in Toronto. Of course, I had all my big rivalries there—like Dickie Moore. He was always a pain in the ass for me. But I was fortunate to play with him too and we really hit it off when he came to Toronto. Horton, Dickie, and I were inseparable because we were all interested in business and Dickie was a good business person.

"Tim Horton and I worked our whole lives. We didn't just play hockey. We both had jobs that we went to every day pretty well. I was in the car business all of my hockey career except for the first years when I had a construction company. I sold it to a boyhood friend and it's still going.

"When I lost all my money I went into real estate for a short period of time and I made a nest egg back and that would be a whole book in itself—my life in the business world. We had three Tim Hortons donut shops in Toronto and I often thought Tim would be laughing at us if he saw me working in the Tim Hortons donut shop.

"When Toronto played Montreal it was war for the first five minutes and then things got straightened out and it was a wonderful hockey game. Guys like Dickie Moore and our good friend John Ferguson. When his son, John Jr, got the job in Toronto, John Ferguson and I were salmon fishing out in Queen Charlottes. Fergie was my roommate and he was anxious to see if John Jr. got the job so I made a couple of phone calls. I found out he got the job. I made John put my Maple Leafs sweater on and he put his Canadiens sweater on me and we wrote "turncoat" on John's—he didn't know that we took a picture so we sent it back to Montreal. John Ferguson with a Maple Leaf sweater on! John and I had a great time, as much as we disliked one another when we were playing against one another.

"I coached the Toronto Toros of the WHA. When we took the Toros to Sweden, I couldn't believe what these Europeans were getting away with. It was all the spearing and the poking the stick in the back of the legs and butt ends and stuff like that. The head of the Swedish Ice Hockey Federation came to me in Stockholm before the last exhibition and he said, 'I hope you don't let your boys get out of hand tonight.' I looked at him and I said 'Sir, if it was my game and I was playing tonight, I'd start a third world war out here. You guys deserve everything you get tonight. Our guys have been wonderful. They haven't retaliated one bit. It's just a shame what you guys are doing.'

"It's the influence that the Europeans have brought to the NHL. The positives are all great but that's the negative part of the game that they have brought—the retaliation and hitting from behind. They weren't used to a body-check! They thought a body-check was a personal insult, an attack! They thought it was putting them down. Well it wasn't! It was part of our Canadian game. It was like a flying tackle or cross body block in football, but now all those things are taboo."

JIM McKENNY *came to Toronto from the nation's capital. His skills as a defenceman in the junior ranks were so highly touted that comparisons to Bobby Orr were not uncommon.*

"In Ottawa there was nothing to do all winter. If your parents had a lot of money, I guess you could go skiing or something. But for us there was just hockey. We played hockey all day, every day. We played ball hockey at recess after school. There were two covered rinks in Ottawa—the auditorium and the Minto and there was another one out

on the army base out at Rockland. We used to sneak into the auditorium. We'd climb up the garbage door and then wedge it at the top and then you could slide through at the top and we'd go in and skate around in the dark at 5 in the morning.

"We played road hockey all day. [In response to Paul Henderson's claim to being the best road hockey player] I don't think Henderson was that good. I don't think he could play the off-wing in road hockey. And you had to block shots and I never saw him do that. Not unless he made a drastic give-away.

"One road hockey rule we had rule was 'no slices.' You could slapshot, but no slices, where you cut underneath the ball so the ball went straight up so it was almost like a broom-ball swing. And if you shot it you had to chase; if you were on the street and missed the net then you had to go after it. If you scored then the goalie had to get it. Cars would pretty well stop on our street because we had an incident with one of our guys. He got tired of these guys driving over our goalposts so once he hit a car with his stick. The guy stopped and when he got out of the car he hit him right over the head with his stick. We had to lay low for about a month after that.

"Road hockey is how you learn how to stickhandle. If you can stickhandle with a frozen tennis ball, on a street with sand and ice, you can stickhandle anywhere. You really had to have a pretty good touch. Plus our sticks were all worn down so you all had tooth-picks, and you had to keep your sticks down too. I played 1,000 road hockey games and nobody ever lost an eye! Now you have to wear helmets and everything on the rinks. I don't know who made those rules, but it was someone in Birkenstocks.

"In the NHL in those days, when a stick went above the elbow there'd be a fight. If a guy gave you a high stick he'd say sorry. Even if it was Reggie Fleming. He'd say 'Geez, I didn't mean that.'

"I wasn't in great shape when I went to my first [Maple Leafs] training camp. I was about 215 pounds. I was 19 and I was eating all the time. So I got sent to the minor leagues. I played three years in the minors but I didn't care because I got the same money. They sent me to Tulsa first and then at Christmas they sent me to Rochester. They gave me $6,000 to sign and $8,000 and $9,000 my first two years. That was big money back in 1965.

"I was compared to Bobby Orr—but that was in Junior. Good juniors are a dime a dozen. Imlach had his own guys and I didn't fit in there and didn't make it. It didn't look to me like they were having much fun in Toronto anyway. I was having more fun in Rochester. And I liked playing in Rochester. It wasn't just guys like Don Cherry, it was guys like Bronco Horvath, Al Arbour, Dwayne Rupp, Tom McCarthy, and Warren Godfrey. Wonderful guys.

"There's an area in Toronto for every ethnic group—Korean, Russian, Italian. They're all Leafs fans. The fans in Toronto aren't hockey fans, they're Leafs fans. I don't know why they were ever worried about [RIM owner] Jim Balsillie bringing a team to Hamilton because fans would never support them. It's all about the Leafs.

"As a Leafs player you can't go anywhere in the city, especially back in the days when we didn't wear helmets. Everybody knew you instantly. When the team wasn't winning you had to wear a toque down over your face when you went into Mac's Milk. Guys would be asking, 'What's wrong with the team?' and 'Why is this player not playing?'…It was unbelievable. The coverage they get now that Rogers is involved is distorted. You never get

Jim McKenny played in parts of 13 seasons for the Maple Leafs in the 1960s and '70s. In retirement, McKenny became a television sportscaster in Toronto.
Portnoy/Hockey Hall of Fame

149

an objective view on the team! Nobody in the media can say what they really think about the Leafs because if they stonewall you, you can't get any interviews. The result is that fans can't get a good read on the team.

"The difference between Montreal and Toronto when I played was that Montreal had money and Toronto didn't. Harold Ballard and Stafford Smythe had their own private jet and they were pissing away money like crazy in the late '60s. So they ended up selling their whole farm system to Joe Crozier and Imlach. It was three teams of guys, and they bought them for like $100,000 and then turned around two years later when expansion came in and sold those players for over $1.5 million.

"We had no bargaining power. The Montreal Canadiens kept their farm system and they were smart about the guys they traded away—like Billy Inglis and Ralph Backstrom be in position to draft Guy Lafleur! [Montreal GM] Sam Pollack did deals like that for the next 10 years because he had the resources. Toronto didn't. We kept losing all our players to the WHA because Harold couldn't pay them. We lost Henderson, Keon, Jimmy Harrison, Ricky Ley, Brad Selwood, and Bernie Parent.

"They were so embarrassed that they didn't have money. Here they were the most successful franchise in the league and had no money! So when anyone asked them any questions they just told them to piss off.

"As captain, Darryl Sittler was for the players! He, Lanny MacDonald, and Tiger Williams were so good. You didn't have to coach those guys because they coached the team. If you weren't working out there, they'd tell you to get off your ass and get moving. And they were all let go. It was total mismanagement by the Leafs. If you wanted to rebuild you'd bring in young players and have them play behind guys like MacDonald and Sittler and learn how to play—and *then* get rid of Sittler and Lanny.

"I thought it was a godsend for hockey—not for Toronto, but for hockey—to get rid of Lanny because it gave guys on Colorado and Calgary a chance to play with him. There aren't many guys like him. He had so much joy and he loved the game. Every day was fun with him. When he'd be pissed off when he wasn't scoring he'd be even funnier—sort of self-deprecating stuff, getting on himself. He worked so hard—and so did Darryl.

"Punch Imlach was probably one of the most powerful men in Toronto or in Canada. When Punch came around, he was the guy. When he walked into the room with the Prime Minister people would say, 'Geez, Punch Imlach's here.'

"The problem with him is that he didn't come from any money in his life either and he was given a budget to pay the Leafs. And I think the most he ever paid Johnny Bower was $26,000. When Andy Bathgate was traded to the Leafs, he was making $38,000; so he was making $12,000 more than Bower, which was ridiculous. The only reason they won all those Cups was because of Bower and Sawchuk. Mainly Bower. When Jim Gregory took over and found out how much [Bower] was making he was embarrassed. He called Johnny up to the office and said, 'Holy Christ, John, look at what you're making here—$26,000.' And Johnny said, 'Yeah,' and Gregory said, 'What do you think? How much should I pay ya?' Johnny said, '$28,000?' And Gregory said, 'No I gotta give you $80,000.' Johnny had tears in his eyes. That kind of shit went on all the time, but Punch was a hell of a coach. All the guys were terrified of him. He had so much power. They also had such a good team down in Rochester—four or five guys that were interchangeable with four or five with the Leafs. So you knew if you didn't do exactly what Punch wanted, you were gone.

"As a commentator, you were always riding the fence. You couldn't say what you really wanted to say because then when you went down to get an interview no one would talk to you. I always felt really uncomfortable going into the dressing room. I don't know if it's meant to be like that, but I hated doing it. You'd see what was going on but you couldn't really report it or you'd get blackballed. It's even more so in Toronto now.

"Writers like Milt Dunnell, Red Burnett, James Kernahan, and Frank Orr—they were all friends of the players. We used to hang out with those guys after the games. They didn't write about any of the stuff that happened at the bar, but if it happened on the ice it was okay. And they'd tell you, 'I'm going to have to shit on you a little bit tomorrow.' I'd say, 'Go ahead fill your boots. Want a couple of quotes?' The only guy that helped me out at the end of my career to try and get a job was [former *Toronto Sun* sports editor] George Gross. He took me around and introduced me to people and tried to get me a job. He was fantastic."

BRIAN CONACHER *played for the Canadian Olympic team in 1964 and played in the NHL for parts of five seasons, including four with the Maple Leafs. Conacher also had a notable broadcasting career, including serving as the colour man for the 1972 Summit Series. The name Conacher is synonymous with sports royalty in Canada. Lionel Conacher, Brian's father, starred in football, baseball, and hockey in the 1920s and '30s.*

"*As the Puck Turns* [Conacher's 2007 book] is a takeoff of the old soap opera *As the World Turns* in that hockey is Canada's never-ending soap opera. It just goes on and on. It's very prominent in the media, certainly in a city like Toronto. It goes on and on and on and it just plays like a long-running soap opera. The book was written in the context that my experiences didn't make me a main character, but I was a character in it.

"Surprisingly hockey did not permeate our household when I was young. I was born in 1941 and my father's sports career was long over. It had ended in the mid-'30s so I never really knew my father as a sportsman. I knew as young boy that he had done something special in hockey. But he was a parliamentarian and a politician at that time, so I would as a youth hear repeatedly—people come up to me and say, 'I remember when...' and of course I didn't because I hadn't been born. So I'd hear these stories. But there was no encouragement in our household for me to either play sports or certainly play professional sports. Had my father lived I may never have played pro sports because he grew up in a family of 10—five boys and five girls—and they were a very poor family and they played sports to get out of poverty so they wouldn't have to play sports for a living. Education was very important. My mother was a university graduate and it was important that we went to school and a lot of the things that were done were to create opportunities so that you didn't need to rely on just your body to make a living. That was the culture that I grew up in.

"The fact that I eventually became a professional hockey player was almost a secondary thing. My father had long since passed away. I played for Father Bauer because I was an idealist and a young 22-year-old who thought that you could combine education with hockey and still excel at both. Those thoughts at that time were just totally for-

eign. I was one of probably half a dozen players at most who had gone to university—Bill Hay and a few others had gone and been better hockey players than I was. But there weren't many and it certainly wasn't encouraged. Nowadays the US colleges are a huge recruiting ground.

"I absolutely remember listening to Foster Hewitt on my white Crosley radio that sat at my headboard. You'd go to sleep listening to the hockey game. But I can honestly say as a kid I never listened to the games with the context that I was going to be a hockey player. I played hockey but I was never even in an indoor arena until I was 10 or 11. I played outside down in Hog's Hollow in York Mills in an outdoor rink and I played public school hockey, but my dad never really wanted me to be on organized teams even as a 9- and 10-year old. He died when I was 12. His life was full of broken bones and he was in the business and it was a tough business. Something most people don't know is that in 1926 or 1927 my father was one of the first players to help organize the players, not unlike what Ted Lindsay did late in the '50s. My father, in spite of being—not a great hockey player but certainly a good hockey player—was traded around a lot to three or four hockey teams. He won a Stanley Cup one year and then was traded. He just didn't see that as a way of life for his children. He'd worked hard and long and took lots of bruises so that his kids wouldn't have to do that.

"There was an expectation based on what my father had done in sports. I can remember Milt Dunnell in the Chicago series, which was probably the highlight of my short career. In that final game I scored those two goals to get us into the finals and Milt Dannell came over and his attitude was, 'Well, what you did was what you were expected to do.' No, 'great game kid.' It was, 'Why didn't you score the third goal?'"

"Honest to God, I don't know why Toronto fans are so loyal. We lived briefly in the U.S. in New York state for three years and our son grew up watching the New York Yankees. To this day he's a Yankee fan for life, so I don't know what it is that makes a Leafs fan so loyal for better or worse. The reality is they don't do themselves any great service for being so loyal. In some other cities if they played the way the Leafs do at times there wouldn't be enough fans there for two tables of bridge. And it would force them to put on a better product. For some reason they've always accepted mediocrity. They can lose a game and get booed off the ice one night and then they come back and win a game in a shootout against Boston and you'd think they were Stanley Cup champs again.

"One thing irked me and I wrote a couple of things and the *Sun* was the one paper that did respond. I have great regard for Wayne Gretzky and I was in Edmonton for the seven years when he was in his prime. I think unquestionably Wayne Gretzky was the greatest offensive hockey player that there has ever been. Is he the greatest hockey player that's ever been? In the hockey community there's lots that don't think he is. They say either Gordie Howe or Bobby Orr might be the greatest hockey player ever. So when they promoted him—and that's what they did—to become the greatest athlete of the century, that is modern-day marketing to a very younger orientated audience. Because there was no one left to argue his case. For Wayne Gretzky to be named a greater athlete than my father is a joke. There was no one left to argue his case. Milt Dunnell was gone, Allan Lamport, the mayor of Toronto was gone. There was no one there to tell that story."

Brian Conacher skates alongside Montreal's Terry Harper during the 1967 Stanley Cup Finals. Conacher played for Team Canada in the 1964 Olympics and in the NHL for parts of five seasons, including four with the Maple Leafs.

Frank Prazak/Hockey Hall of Fame

HOW HOCKEY EXPLAINS CANADIAN CULTURE

IT DOES GET TIRESOME, those musty Canadians running around the country searching for our identity. They seek it out in the foothills of Alberta and in the fishing villages of Nova Scotia. They pursue it across the Prairies and into the cities of Ontario and Quebec. Poets try to capture this national character in verse and singers in song. Novelists sometimes think they've nailed it but invariably it turns out to be mistaken identity. Academics and intellectuals are the worst because it's in their vested interest to keep looking, even when they have found it. The CBC was formed and funded to figure it out. Who are we? They ask it as if the nation were waking from a coma with a severe case of collective amnesia. It tests the gag reflex, it really does.

We look to our southern neighbours and they seem to know exactly who they are. We, on the other hand, sometimes define ourselves by what we are not; i.e. Americans. We know that our culture, as inundated as it is by theirs, is not their culture.

To the great unwashed, a demographic seldom consulted on cultural matters, there is much less hand-wringing on the subject. Hockey is our identity and our culture. We are a hockey nation.

The very notion infuriates some. When the *Globe and Mail* ran a front-page hockey story a reader responded with a letter to the editor: "I mean, you would have to be a troglodyte to be entertained by a piece of rubber being slapped back and forth by a bunch of overpaid Neanderthals.... Aristotle talks of mimesis. It seems that sports 'writer' after sports 'writer' simply

Wayne Gretzky led the Edmonton Oilers to four Stanley Cup championships in the 1980s before departing to play for the Los Angeles Kings.
Bruce Bennett Studios/Getty Images

mimics the person before him. Whether it be voice or print, you're all the same. You're a dime a dozen and the masses are so stupid as to put sports and its players and its 'writers' on a pedestal that it's now front-page news." The writer goes on to ask, "What is so spectacular about hockey anyway? If you've seen one game, you've seen them all. You'd have to be, well, completely void of brain activity to choose a profession in which you 'write' about Neanderthals slapping a piece of rubber to one another. Good God, what happened to intellectualism?"

This sentiment has some traction across the country. Many see a culture that is wrapped up in sticks and pucks as a subculture at best.

In the United States the use of sports as a national metaphor has a long history, although the sports have changed. "Here in the US," suggested Richard Johnson of the New England Sports Museum, "some would say that football is what we've become but baseball is what we were and what we still hope to be."

Johnson lives in Milton, Massachusetts, and is a self-described Canadaphile. His family often vacationed in Northern Ontario and Quebec. His perspectives on hockey and Canada were formed during those idyllic trips north of the border. He watches *Hockey Night in Canada* like it is some secret portal into the psyche of Canada and Canadians, which of course it is. Johnson has no doubt that hockey is a real part of Canada's cultural identity.

"How many countries are there where a piece of sporting equipment could be the alternate flag?" he asked. "You know how hockey teams have alternate uniforms now? The alternative Canadian flag would be one with simply a hockey puck. It would be cultural accuracy at its best. Soccer in Brazil and hockey in Canada are *it*—the two countries on this planet where sport can almost define the country. I challenge anyone to come up

Richard Johnson is the curator of the New England Sports Museum and lives in Milton, Massachusetts. He frequently vacations in Northern Ontario and Quebec and is an avid fan of *Hockey Night In Canada*.
Courtesy of Richard Johnson

with another country and another sport, even here in the US."

If hockey is our cultural marker, the question is what made it so. Johnson thinks that the answer is to be found in history, geography, and climate.

"You know what I think it is? Very simply this: In a cold, hostile climate, you found community indoors during that two-thirds of the year when you needed to be out of the elements. The gathering place for many communities was the local hockey rink and the sport very much embraced some of the almost ritualistic parts of the old country— either England or Scotland—that the people loved. That was the regiment or the battalion or the military unit or the club and the fact was that a hockey team was a more benign and friendly version of a lodge—an Orangeman's lodge or a Catholic club in Glasgow—someplace where there was community to be found under the roof.

"Not only did hockey put a roof on the hostile climate, it also lit the hot stove of community. It provided that sense of having an ecumenical gathering place—not a church, not a Masonic hall, not a veterans hall—a place where anybody was welcome as long as they had the talent—or the mettle—to take part. That certainly speaks to what I think of any of the Canadian national teams: I always have the sense of the stars giving themselves to the unit—of the team being the most important thing, and stars not just playing lip service to that. I think of someone like Bobby Orr giving the last measure of his career to Canada. Those last little pieces of his knee cartilage were basically placed on the Canadian flag in 1976. I don't think that's ever highlighted enough. When the time came to stand up and be counted, Orr stood up for country more than for preserving what was left of his NHL career."

Johnson sees the best of Canada reflected in our national game, the notion of people working together against the elements. Instead of denying our northern heritage, Canadians allied with it and harnessed it for their purposes. "You guys got that part of the continent where it was harder to build roads, harder to do everything, so what sport spoke to that? Hockey speaks to a certain pragmatism," Johnson said. And what is more Canadian than hockey? We invented it, refined it, and presented it as our endowment to the world. It reflects our nation like few other things ever could. It differentiates us from neighbour America and mother Britain. And yet there is always resistance, always from within our country, to fully embracing this side of ourselves.

The idea of Canadian culture wars summons images of very elite armies indeed. They are facing each other across a well-manicured lawn somewhere in Rosedale. Leading the forces of the Literati, Major Margaret Atwood hurls well-worded verbal grenades across the battlefield at an opposing platoon of singers and artists, led perhaps by a chest-thumping Celine Dion. Canada's various dancers, dramatists, and painters all join in the fray, cavorting and overacting while sporting stylish berets. The victors go home with Canada Council grants and so—in the Canadian way—do the vanquished.

The actual cultural war may be quite different. In 2010 when Prime Minister Stephen Harper dared hint at his government's willingness to help fund a new hockey arena in Quebec City, there was an outcry that echoed through the concert halls and art galleries of the nation. Sports, especially professional sports, do not deserve such public funding, said the outraged intelligentsia. Speaking from their garrets and street corners, struggling artists—are there any other kind?—saw the very suggestion as repugnant, just another sign that Canadian culture is being degraded by a regime of right-wing yahoos. At the heart of their case seems to be a belief that hockey is not culture at all, and especially not hockey-for-pay.

There is a considerable amount of hypocrisy in that narrow view. Canadian taxpayers fork over billions of dollars each year to various cultural sectors: artists, writers, actors, and musicians. These individuals are every bit as professional as the wealthiest NHL hockey star. And this is where the cultural divide occurs. As columnist David Asper wrote in the *National Post*: "If we are to have a legitimate definition of our national culture, it must be based on the totality of who we are and what we do." Warming to the theme, he goes on to ask, "Are we being true to ourselves if we say that Delores Claman's former *Hockey Night in Canada* theme song is 'culture' because it is music ... but the game itself is not?" He argues that the majority of Canadians are being snubbed when governments fail to dis-

Canadian Prime Minister Stephen Harper, left, attends a Canucks game in Vancouver during the 2010–11 season alongside retired Canucks star Trevor Linden. Harper is an avid hockey fan who is researching in preparation for a book on the sport.

AP Images

tribute support based on "the cultural reality of Canada, which must include the so-called low-culture of professional sport."

Former Maple Leaf Brian Conacher thinks that hockey and the fine arts actually have much in common. "The reality is that our government has been ambivalent about both," he said. "They are undersubscribed and undersupported. I'm not against the fact that the government doesn't want to subsidize the building of more NHL hockey rinks. The NHL is interested in only one thing and that is making money. They would do better in the province of Quebec to go and build 10 municipal rinks than to provide monies for an arena for another pro franchise."

In a November 16, 2010, column in the *Globe and Mail,* television critic John Doyle talked about the recent Gemini and Giller awards as examples of "rewarding obscurity, underlining the gulf between the arts elite . . .

and the public." He goes on to say that, "For as long as the minority Conservative government is in power, and while someone such as Rob Ford is elected mayor of Toronto, we need to be aware that there is a culture war going on in Canada. The government fetishizes hockey and Tim Hortons as true, authoritative emanations of the Canadian culture as they see it." In spite of this new reality, he argues that because the more traditional capital "C" cultural groups are well connected and speak with a unified voice, they inevitably hold sway over politicians of all stripes.

This makes the divide between the cultural elite and the rest of us even wider. The fact is there is room within the cultural arena for everyone. To imagine that people who play the game or merely appreciate its beauty are somehow lowbrow is insulting and arrogant, and denying that hockey is a part of our cultural identity is patently ridiculous.

There was a time in this fair land when Gordon Lightfoot was about the only Canadian artist to be heard on the radio. Aside from a few homegrown staples, television was content to cherry-pick the best shows from American networks, producing very few indigenous broadcasts. And then along came CanCom, the Canadian Radio-Television and Telecommunications Commission (CRTC) regulations that require radio and TV stations to air a certain percentage of Canadian content. Although the idea was first panned for limiting consumer choice and being too dictatorial, it has succeeded in jump-starting the careers of countless Canadian artists, many of whom have gone on to international fame. Thanks largely to CanCom and other federal programs (NFB and CBC), we now have a vibrant and varied Canadian presence in TV and radio.

Other crown corporations have subsidized other aspects of our culture, like the National Ballet and the Royal Conservatory of Music. Canadian writers enjoy the benefits of taxpayer support of their craft as well. Overall these efforts to promote and protect Canadian culture worked and have been very successful in enriching our culture and showcasing it to the world.

About the only Canadian cultural entity that didn't require or even seek safeguards and subsidization was hockey. It has benefited from television of course, but it could be argued that television networks have benefited even more from hockey. In the early '50s, Saturday night hockey probably sold more television sets than all other programming combined. Since it began, hockey—both the kind played on ponds and in the NHL—has never had to worry about Canadian content (although ironically if the Montreal Canadiens were a rock band, their current roster might not have enough Canadian content to qualify for radio play).

If it's true that Canadian culture reflects the artistic, literary, and social contributions of our country then hockey is pure, unsubsidized Canadian culture—and not just the pop variety either. The fact is that hockey is integrated into every aspect of Canadian art, from music to comedy to drama. Hockey is like a common language. It's the great Canadian crossroads where our diverse elements intersect.

Not only is hockey, in and of itself, a key element of Canadian culture, it is the inspiration for various other cultural triumphs. It is a national muse every bit as much as the Rockies, prairie wheat fields, the rich diversity of Toronto and Montreal, or Atlantic breakers striking the shores of St. John's or Peggy's Cove. These are certainly things that helped shape us as a people and continue to stir emotions deep within: pride of place, national identity, and unity. But so did hockey. In fact, in that way hockey is doubly blessed; it is a culture unto itself and it is a culture builder—both medium and message. Musicians, dramatists, comedians, and graphic artists have all used hockey as their inspiration because it triggers something different in each of us.

There are those who would argue that hockey is not art but to Canada's great unwashed, the Spin-O-Rama move defined by Danny Gallivan and performed by Serge Savard was every bit as artistic as ballet's equivalent "Fouette en tourant" as performed by Karen Kain. And in case you might question the degree of difficulty, Kain didn't have to look over her shoulder to see if some goon was trying to slash her in the proverbial tutu in midspin.

The beauty of end-to-end rushes down ice by Bobby Hull, Maurice Richard, or Frank Mahovlich were to many Canadians as much a thing of beauty as anything you see onstage at Massey Hall. The artistry of a Wayne Gretzky deke or a subtle Sid Crosby shift is understood and appreciated by countless Canadians who are steeped in the subject and are discriminating critics. Others see a different kind of beauty in a controlled passing game or a tight defensive style. And that is what makes hockey itself so artistically rich and diverse. At its best, it has elements of ballet and grand opera, except that the fat lady sings a bit later in hockey. Each season is an odyssey, each game a battle, until the playoffs bring more epic battle. This isn't meant to be a faceoff between "pas de deux" and "pass the puck." It simply illustrates that hockey too is an art form and those who play it at an elite level are true artists.

Yet when Federal Cabinet Minister John Munro waxed eloquent after Canada's victory over Russia in the 1972 Summit Series, some guardians of Canadian culture were openly disgusted that mere hockey games should be mentioned in the same breath as Canadian and Russian ballerinas. You could feel their haughty contempt as it emanated from Toronto's cultural castle and fell disdainfully on the rabble below. Munro was verbally eviscerated for daring to describe Canadian hockey players as "artists in a very real sense." He was dismissed as "a raging bull with hemorrhoids" by one outraged culture maven for daring to equate Canada's hockey skill with the sublime artistry of Russian ballet. The game of shinny was just not to be discussed in polite company. Meanwhile, the rest of Canada was going crazy with pride, patriotism, and something else, possibly a belief that we had shared with the world a considerable glimpse of our culture—through our national game. The fact is that hockey had become both a mirror to ourselves as Canadians and a window for the world to look in. Surely that qualifies as culture.

In the *Journal of Canadian Studies* (Summer, 1995), Neil Earle suggested, "If

Wayne Gretzky wipes a tear during his 1988 news conference in Edmonton announcing his trade from the Oilers to the Los Angeles Kings. The trade of "The Great One" to an American team is noted as a significant event in Canadian history.

AP Images

hockey is just a game in Canada, then the Rockies are just hills on the prairies. The game, like the mischievous 'puck' itself, has the ability to ricochet and careen unexpectedly in and out of the Canadian experience." Earle went on to say that "Wayne Gretzky's move to the United States in 1988 during the Prime Ministership of Brian Mulroney was a cultural signpost to an era, as was the refusal of Ontario's Eric Lindros to play for the Quebec City Nordiques in the aftermath of the Meech Lake constitutional crisis."

G.M. Trevelyan penned a social history of Britain and ignored any mention of cricket champion W.G. Grace, a man revered throughout England. It's hard to imagine that a degree of elitism and/or antisport snobbery did not enter into his thinking. If Rocket Richard were to be omitted from a cultural history of Quebec, we might well have another Richard Riot on our hands. The same is true of Gretzky and other hockey luminaries.

If culture is partially shaped by history, September 28, 1972, may have been the date on which the importance of the game hit home with all of us. Of course it always had been there, but being Canadians, we didn't realize it until suddenly a light went on for the 12 million Canadians who were watching Game 8 of the Summit Series. The light was red and it shone behind the back of Vlad Tretiak to signal the winning goal scored by Paul Henderson, the newest keeper of the culture we call hockey. The realization struck many for the first time. One writer suggested that it was when, "a lot of Canadians discovered their nationality." So this is who we are. We are Canadians. We excel at many things and at the top of the list is hockey, the game we invented, the game we played as kids, and the game that we still watch on Saturday nights.

The Summit Series with the Soviet Union has often been referred to as our "coming out party" as a nation. It too was a cultural war of sorts. It was about two distinct philosophies, one political system against another. It could scarcely have been more of a cultural clash if the Bolshoi had faced off with the Royal Winnipeg.

Even the culture giants of the day were suddenly struck by the significance of hockey to our country. Novelist Morley Callahan was still basking in the glow of victory when he framed the competition as an epic confrontation. Callahan saw high art and high drama in the passion of the Canadian effort. After Game 8 he said, "What fascinated me was that our pros were really the beloved amateurs emotionally, and Russia, the land of Slavic romanticism...their players behaved with a kind of mechanical exactitude." In the land of Dr. Zhivago, it was the Canadian icemen who emerged as the romantic heroes.

He went on to say that when Russia got a penalty, the players, "sat on the bench impassively," and when a Canadian player was penalized, "He became a romantic figure. He sat there and he was bleeding, all of his emotions were stirred that was lacking in the Soviets, who were there primarily to score propaganda points about the superiority of the Soviet way of life." What he was seeing was not just what he chose to see. It was what all Canadians saw but few were equipped to verbalize. Callahan, with his writer's eye, had picked it up.

Goalie Tony Esposito admitted years after the series that it had been so important to his teammates that "after that series [they] were never the same." If that sounds theatrical, even operatic, it was. After all, wrote Earle, hockey was "nurtured amid the eternal mountains, lakes, and prairie that make up Canada—scenes of lyricism and menace..."

Shakespearean actor William Hutt, in full voice as King Lear at Canada's cultural Mecca in Stratford, Ontario, interrupted the storm scene and informed the audience that Canada had won Game 8. As far as we can determine, no one has ever blown the whistle in the midst of a playoff game to announce a winning performance at Stratford. But that's unfair. Culture is an all-embracing kinship and every part of it complements the others.

Referring to the victory in Moscow, British Columbia Premier Dave Barrett evoked images of Canadians taking Moscow with our cultural army. "The French couldn't do it, the Germans couldn't do it; now Canada has done it and they had better get out of town before it starts snowing."

As much as we hate to admit it, Canada measures itself by the United States. We crave America's approval while ridiculing her tastes. Sometimes the information highway seems like a one-way street running from the US to Canada with no off-ramps. There is no doubt that most Canadians know a hell of a lot more about the US than most Americans know about us. We follow their politics, study their history and government, watch their TV shows, and absorb their social and cultural trends. Meanwhile, many Americans are hard-pressed to find Canada on a map. Literally.

CBC's *This Hour Has 22 Minutes* had a feature called *Talking to Americans* in which host Rick Mercer was able to convince a shocking number of US citizens that our leader was either Prime Minister Jean Poutine (his victim in this case was presidential candidate George W. Bush), President Tim Horton (elected on a rare "double-double;" i.e., support from both houses of Congress), King Svend 1, or King Lucienne Bonhomme. The American gullibility didn't stop there. They seemed genuinely pleased that Canada had recently legalized insulin, VCRs, and the stapler. They were proud that our centre of government, the National Igloo, was an ice replica of their Capital building. They congratulated us on joining North America but chastised us for our practice of sending our elderly out on ice floes. They insisted that we cease the Toronto polar bear hunt and the Saskatchewan seal hunt. They approved of us giving Irish Canadians the vote despite objections from the French Separatist Movement. The truly cringe-worthy assault continued until 9/11 when, in the cause of good taste, Mercer discontinued the segment.

It is sometimes infuriating, occasionally humiliating, always humbling, and often laughable. We are often a kind of reverse–hip pop culture reference and the butt of jokes by late night comedians, perhaps because an inordinate number of the writers on those shows are themselves Canadian. The jokes are seldom nasty; in fact they are usually of the benign nature. It is precisely because

we are seen as being so innocuous, so inoffensive, so boring and bland, so damn *nice* that we are mentioned at all. During the 2010 Winter Olympics, faux (possibly pronounced FOX) right-wing satirist Stephen Colbert variously referred to us as "ice holes," "syrup-suckers," and "Saskatchew-whiners." He described the country as "Europe with toilets." Leno, Letterman, and Conan have all taken shots as have Homer Simpson and the *Family Guy's* Peter Griffin.

Rightly or wrongly, Canadians judge themselves by the way they are perceived abroad, especially in the United States. It's part of our massive inferiority complex. That perception from the underside of the 49th parallel is mixed to say the least. Comic references and Olympic coverage notwithstanding, US media coverage of Canada is sparse. Many Americans hold us personally responsible for that ubiquitous "cold front moving down from the north." Others think that we exhibit disturbing socialist tendencies. We are soft on crime and hard on innocent gun owners. We are good allies but a bit too slow to come aboard. We are a breeding ground for terrorists and lax on border security. Our industries are too heavily subsidized and our drug laws too liberal. We are cold, desolate, sparsely inhabited, politically irrelevant, and brimming with natural resources.

Sometimes warm, sometimes slightly cool, our official relationship with the US is seldom less than civil. "You are our best friends whether we like it or not," said Jean Chretien when President Clinton paid a state visit to Parliament Hill a few years back. With the exception of the Mulroney-Reagan Irish lovefest, many Canadian prime ministers have preferred to maintain an arm's length stance with his US counterpart. US president Kennedy reportedly disliked Diefenbaker and Dief called Kennedy a "boastful son of a bitch." President Johnson had little time or respect for Pearson. Nixon referred to Trudeau as an "asshole" to which Trudeau replied that he'd been "called worse things by better people." Chretien's top aide referred to George W. Bush as "a moron." Publicly of course, it is all rosy. Kennedy proclaimed, "Geography has made us neighbours, history has made us friends, economics has made us partners, and necessity has made us allies." No doubt the truth lies somewhere between the behind-the-scene jibes and the public pabulum.

In terms of historic ties, we have progressed from being hewers of wood and drawers of water to become "America Lite," little brother to Big Brother, the proverbial mouse living next door to an elephant. In the beginning we sent our raw materials south for use by the world's most industrialized country. We're still doing that, of course. We provide the trees from which they make magazines and books which they sell back to us at inflated prices. Nowadays we also provide cheap pills. But over the years and decades, the resources we ship south have gradually become human as well as natural. Hollywood is one US destination that has benefited greatly from the influx of Canadian talent and culture.

Ironically we provided them with America's sweetheart, Mary Pickford, and equally sweet Fay Wray, the innocent young thing that King Kong took out on the town. To counteract all the sweetness, we sent them insulin, Pamela Anderson and, in an act of unnecessary cruelty, Howie Mandel.

Occasionally a hockey player would even take a shot at Hollywood. Howie Young was a handsome, charismatic young defenceman for the Detroit Red Wings. On the ice Young was fearless. Off the ice he was a heavy drinker, more rebellious than a truckload of James Deans. His once promising career went downhill rapidly as the alcohol intake increased. Finally he was shipped to the L.A. Blades of the WHL. With the kind of tough good looks that Hollywood loves, he was soon cast for a minor role in the movie *None But the Brave* with Frank Sinatra.

"Frank liked him so much he didn't have him killed until way later on," said friend and former teammate Jim McKenny. "Howie got a little out of control at the windup party on the yacht in Hawaii and threw Frank overboard. He was all hammered up and he said 'You're not so tough.' He threw Frank in the water and the toupee came off and everything. I guess one of Frank's goons grabbed him and beat the shit out of him. Then they took him out and threw him on the beach. He woke up in the morning with the Hawaiian sun over him and he looked out over the surf and then he looked in his pockets and he had two hundred dollars and he thought he'd died and gone to heaven. He didn't remember a thing about what happened and there he was stuck in Hawaii with two-hundred bucks in his pocket and nothing else—and Howie being Howie thinking, *geez, this is the greatest thing that's ever happened to me.* He ended up being the Marlboro man there for a while." Young died of pancreatic cancer in 1999.

Canadians actually helped to create Hollywood. Pioneers like Pickford, Louis B. Mayer, Mack Sennett, and Jack Warner were instrumental in building the movie infrastructure. Later we offered up directing geniuses such as David Cronenberg to raise hackles and James Cameron to sink the *Titanic.*

We sent Wayne and Schuster south to teach Americans that Shakespeare doesn't have to be boring. We sent Chong to pair up with Cheech and Dumb to join up with

Dumber (or is it the other way around?). We showed them two typical Canadian hosers in Bob and Doug McKenzie. We sent them arch-villain Dr. Evil but added international man of mystery Austin Powers to put him in his place. We sent them John Candy, Martin Short, Rick Moranis, and Eugene Levy.

We exported—some might say deported—Alan Thicke. We sent Ben Cartwright to tame the Old West and Captain Kirk to conquer space. Then we sent Michael J. Fox to transport them back to the future. Canada gave them Lieutenant Frank Drebin (Leslie Neilsen) to maintain law and order, Barry Morse to track down the Fugitive, and Perry Mason to ensure everyone got a fair trial. We sent them Dean Vernon Wormer to give them respect for authority and a solid university education. We sent them Captain Hawkeye Pierce (Donald Sutherland) to win the Korean War. We gave them the Lone Ranger's sidekick, Tonto, and Chief Dan George. We sent them Superman's girlfriend (even the original Superman came not from Krypton, but Canada).

Despite the law preventing people of foreign birth from being President of the United States, we provided them with at least three: Abe Lincoln (Raymond Massey), John F. Kennedy (Glenn Ford), and Richard Nixon (Dan Aykroyd). Not to mention one runner-up (Norm MacDonald as Bob Dole).

As if that weren't enough we sent them our music. We courted them with Paul Anka, Leonard Cohen, Anne Murray, and Gordon Lightfoot. We seduced them with Sara McLaughlin and Michael Buble. We rocked them with Steppenwolf and Neil Young and Robbie Robertson. We schmaltzed them with Celine Dion and Robert Goulet. We showed just how cool we were by sending them hipster Paul Shaffer.

We sent them a suave multilingual host

to ask them tough questions (Alex Trebek), another to ask easy ones (Art Linkletter) and yet another to allow them to make fools of themselves (Monty Hall). To stimulate, inform, and shape public opinion, we sent them Peter Jennings, Keith Morrison, Robert MacNeil, John Roberts, Morley Safer, and "scud stud" Arthur Kent. We sent them economists and philosophers (Marshall McLuhan, Kenneth Galbraith, etc.).

In short, we sent all aspects of Canadian culture to the United States. We sent them all and wished them well as they spread the Canadian story via Hollywood and across the US heartland. We were generous because we thought we were proving ourselves to them. It didn't work. They still didn't know who we were or what we were all about.

Proponents of free trade say that everyone wins. Unions disagree. What did we get in return from the United States? We got McDonald's and Walmart, *Time* and 24 hours of CNN. And Ronnie Hawkins and Oscar Peterson and Errol Garner. We got countless movies and countless TV shows and a flood of magazines and...

To each NHL team, we sent a franchise player. To Detroit we sent Gordie Howe and Ted Lindsay. To New York we sent Andy Bathgate. Boston got Ernie Shore and eventually Bobby Orr. Chicago was given Hull. Each of these players and countless others were instrumental with other Canadians in spreading hockey culture to the United States. Proving that the NAFTA Free Trade agreement is inherently flawed, they sent us Roger Clemens and Vince Carter.

We are constantly looking for that nod of approval from America but it's a losing battle. Despite countless examples of Canadians who have met with success in Hollywood, Nashville, New York, and other centres of America culture, we are largely ignored and seldom taken seriously. When praise comes, it comes grudgingly. We are, however, sometimes unfairly blamed.

The gang from South Park even sang about it in the 1999 movie *South Park: Bigger, Longer and Uncut*. The soundtrack hit *Blame Canada* got an Academy Award nomination. The song featured such inspired lyrics as:

Blame Canada
With all their hockey hullabaloo
And that bitch Anne Murray too.

It was the ultimate in American scapegoating, a fact acknowledged in the last lines:

We must blame them to cause a fuss
Before someone thinks of blaming us!

The impact of all this has been negligible. For those who wish to learn about Canada, its history, its culture, and its people, hockey is the perfect tutor. What does hockey tell our American cousins about us?

During the 2010 Vancouver Olympics, former NBC News anchor Tom Brokaw did a feature on Canada that was guaranteed to make the hairs on the back of your neck stand at attention. It was fair, balanced, generous, and substantive. It was heartwarming and it showed the true relationship between our two countries. That is, after all, the purpose of the Olympics—to bring countries closer together through sport.

The NHL has 30 teams, and ironically 23 of them are located in the United States. What better way to teach Americans about Canada? These are our ambassadors—or perhaps fifth columnists—whose mission is to spread the doctrine of Canada. The commissioner of the NHL is an American. And yet, the sport has not caught on with national audiences outside of those northern US cities close to the Canadian border.

Of course, not all Americans are ill-informed.

Recently arrived from Boston, Bill Lee used to sit in the storied Montreal Forum and observe. Lee is a Southern California native with an impressive baseball lineage. His father played the game at a high level, and his aunt Anabelle Lee was a star in the All American Girls Professional Baseball League.

He sees social and historic relevance in the games played by Americans and Canadians. "Football is territorial," said Lee. "It reflects the way we Americans pushed all the Indians off the plains and from one coast to another. To understand the best of America it's baseball, not football. Football is a game of aggression."

Despite the violence inherent in hockey, the man they called "Spaceman" sees hockey players as noble warriors who give their all on the battlefield but respect the enemy. "Hockey is a vestige of colonialism," he said. "It was created by the military and like football it's a game of aggression, but with a difference. Unlike football, you can't lob bombs from far away because you put those lines up there to prevent it. You have to engage the enemy to score, unless it's an empty-netter. If you miss the goal it's icing and they send you back to your own territory. So there's that symbol.

"I love every hockey player I've ever met—Clark Gillies, Bobby Hull, Dennis Hull, Bobby Orr, Dave Schultz, Frank Mahovlich, Eddie Shack—and it's because they're Canadian. You take the toughness of an Odelin and all the guys from the West, or a pugnacious hard worker like Forbes Kennedy from peaceful Prince Edward Island. How could Forbes Kennedy come from Prince Edward Island? It seems like he would come from Glace Bay or Whitney Pier in Cape Breton—some tough town. Schultz told me about fighting with Clark Gillies. Gillies was a big, strong guy and used to hold his arms down so he couldn't move them so Schultz

"**Americans think it's always frozen up there. They think you don't even have a summer. Americans are so naïve, so stupid. On the Weather Channel the weather stops right on the 49th parallel. That's how dumb Americans are. They think everyone's an Eskimo. They have no concept of geography, especially in the South. I tell them that 90 percent of Canadians live near the border and that they're preparing to attack.**"

—**Bill "Spaceman" Lee**

head-butted him. He got a misconduct. He actually changed the rules in the middle of the game. They will fight tooth and nail during the game and then they will go and drink together, and that is the essence of sport. They don't hold grudges. And that's the difference between the Canadian and the American."

He thinks Canadians' healthy skepticism of politicians was reflected in former Hab Guy Lapointe. "He used to grease up his hands whenever he had to shake a Prime Minister's hand."

Lee was an outspoken supporter of bussing in the '60s in Boston and has always supported the underdog. He makes annual trips to Cuba to distribute equipment and goodwill to young Cuban ballplayers. He thinks that Canada is that "kinder and gentler nation" that George H.W. Bush once promised Americans. He even sees our French-English conflict in an optimistic light. "Quebec sovereignty was expressed in their love of Les Canadiens," Lee said. "The greatest animated film made in Canada was *The Hockey Sweater*. It describes the whole idea of being the outcast. My take on that is that in Quebec, the Quebecois is in the majority—therefore the minority rights supersede his rights at that place. In the entire scope of Canada the Francophone is in the minority so his rights supersede that of the majority. That's the way harmony is expressed in

Canada. Through hockey you as a country seem to embrace that concept more. You're more tolerant.

"That's what I see. I love crossing into Canada. Whenever I cross the border into Canada I have a burden off my chest. I feel relaxed. It's weird. And whenever I'm in Canada and have to go back to the US, I feel big pangs of anxiety."

"It's these little vignettes of friendship and the desire to take care of everybody that you have in your country that we don't have in our country. Here in America they use that term 'Canadian socialism' in a negative way. Our conservatives in America have really long pockets and really short arms but your conservatives seem to have shorter pockets and longer arms. It extends to everything. In the old days you played hockey on a pond where down here we have to play in rinks because our ponds don't freeze over enough. It could be because you have a colder environment you have to be kinder to one other. The difference between Canada's foreign policy and ours is that you have Physicians Sans Frontier (Physicians Without Borders) and we have Homeland Security—which really means *raise the fences*."

Lee sees disturbing elements of American football creeping into the game of hockey. "In the old days hockey was very personal," he said. "You knew who was out there. There's

Bill Lee pitched for the Montreal Expos from 1979–82. During that time the eccentric left-hander came to enjoy hockey and recognize the sport's place in Canadian culture.

Focus on Sport/
Getty Images

no difference now because of the helmets and visors. You knew who Derek Sanderson was and you knew that if someone took a shot at Bobby Orr he was going to come to his defence because no one messed with Bobby. Everyone looked after everyone then. Now it's so impersonal when you have a scrum you don't know who's fighting who. In the old days it was an honourable sport and you kept your head up a lot more and there were fewer concussions because you had less equipment. If you want to reduce violence in hockey make the rinks a little bigger, make the shifts a little longer, and take off the equipment. Now you're going to be playing hockey the old-fashioned way."

Hockey Night in Canada's Ron MacLean has interviewed countless hockey players who perform on both sides of the border. He remembers Wayne Gretzky's take on the relative importance of the game in the two countries. "Gretzky always said that the differences he experienced when he went south is that the US is a little more conflicted—they have their football, their baseball, their NASCAR, while we just seem to have the one sport," said MacLean. "Figure skaters might take issue with that but the fact remains that even though lacrosse and football and baseball and soccer have all had rich histories here, hockey seems to be the one that just epitomized what we thought was great about ourselves. We admired our own pluck, pure and simple. That seemed to be representative of what it takes to live in a place where the winter is as harsh as it is. It was a fun, creative game. It sparked amazement, it was speedy—lots of things that we, if we were going to tag ourselves, we'd sort of tag ourselves hockey, that's all."

Richard Johnson lives in Greater Boston. Boston is steeped in patriotism, history, and tradition. Heroic statues and historic sites are around every corner. The city is a veritable museum of Americana. Boston is also

a Mecca of education and a complex mix of progressive and conservative thought. It has the blue-collar element and the university element living side by side.

As curator of the Boston Sports Museum, Johnson has intimate knowledge of the rich sports culture in the city. It's a city that features the Boston Celtics (17 NBA titles), the Boston Bruins, and the New England Patriots as well as the Boston Red Sox. It has been home to some of the greatest professional athletes in American history: Bill Russell, Larry Bird, Bobby Orr, Tom Brady, Babe Ruth, and Ted Williams to name just a few. The author of several books on baseball, soccer, and other sports, Johnson is a dedicated Montreal Canadiens supporter despite living in the capital of Bruins Nation. Johnson sees hockey as Canada's calling card and its defining symbol.

What about baseball, you might well ask? What about Jacques Barzun's oft-quoted emporium about America and the national pastime? Born in France and educated in the United States, Barzun spoke from personal experience when he said: "Whoever wishes to know the heart and mind of America had better learn baseball, the rules and realities of the game…"

There is little question that this statement was accurate when first spoken. Barzun was 12 when he came to America in 1919 to attend prep school before going on to study at Columbia University. Baseball was a burgeoning force at that time, as was America. Babe Ruth was reinventing the game with his home run power and New York's American League franchise was emerging as the greatest dynasty the game has seen. The game was changing from one of finesse and strategy to one of power.

The supremacy of baseball as the national pastime went unchallenged for many years.

Football had pricked but had not yet penetrated the nation's consciousness and basketball was in its infancy. That situation changed in the intervening years until today many would argue that it is football, or even basketball, that best defines America. All three sports hold a claim on Americans for different reasons. The book *How Football Explains America* argues that the gridiron sport is what America is all about. Author Sal Paolantonio points out that football has evolved with the country and has been created according to American principles. He asserts: "It's corporate. It's democratic. It's American." That may well be. The game has obvious military elements interspersed with committee meetings, and depends heavily on a single individual to mastermind things, a trickle-down approach to success. Oh yes, it also has as its ultimate goal land acquisition by force.

In truth, there is no longer a single American sport that defines the country, rather it is a combination of sports that speaks to various aspects of the American character. Football reflects a militaristic past and a strategic view of the world. Paolantonio's book traces many connections between his country, its military traditions, and the gridiron. Many people would argue that baseball is and always has been the national pastime of the United States. The game was the first to bear the Made in America tag and has reflected and occasionally led the country's social evolution. Jackie Robinson opened the doors for many blacks outside of baseball and offered hope for countless more. Basketball is the city game—the game of inner-city blacks and farm kids from Indiana. It is fast-paced, high-scoring, and hip and appeals to younger audiences and minorities. Some might argue that NASCAR with its corporate logos adorning each car, is actually the sport most representative of America, but that would assume that it is a sport at all.

The fact is that American sports are now regionalized. The South loves its college and pro football and even NASCAR is a major force. The northern inner cities gravitate to basketball. Baseball has supporters throughout the nation. If there is a game that reflects present-day America—a nation that is polarized at best—it is pro football.

Johnson gives Canadians credit for preserving the one game that symbolizes the country. "Hockey is community," he said. "And what you have more of in hockey is that the squadron is more important than the general. The cult of football in this country is the cult of Bear Bryant and Lombardi."

"People *still* talk about the Trail Smoke Eaters winning the World Championship. Canadians think of the *jersey* of the teams that have won. You think of the *uniform* before you think of the individual stars. Even with someone like the Rocket, the CH meant more than just what he did. Credit Toronto and Montreal with this: they haven't changed the uniform. Changing those uniforms would be like changing the national flag. There would be a furor."

In Canada, there is no debate, nor is there regionalization—at least where hockey is concerned. Hockey is our pastime, our passion, and our passport. Along with the Mounties and the cold weather, it is the one thing that all Americans know about our country.

When Canada won the 2010 Olympic gold medal in hockey, Canadians celebrated from coast to coast. They celebrated because they were once again the best in the world and had reconfirmed Canada's reputation as The Hockey Nation. But there was another reason that Canadians celebrated, a reason why Canada's win was especially satisfying. We

"**Because of immigration there are more people in Canada that are fans of hockey that have never been players. They wouldn't even know how to skate. They are from countries where hockey isn't part of the culture—nonhockey countries in Asia or the Caribbean.... It's more a spectator thing at first and then as second and third generations come along, they become active participants. Eventually every kid plays hockey. It's a rite of passage.**"

—Morris Mott, history professor and retired NHL player

had won against the United States, "our best friends whether we like it or not."

In Canada, one sport somehow satisfies the entire Canadian demographic. Hockey is the one-size-fits-all solution to all your sporting needs. This does not suggest that Canadians are a monolithic lot.... It's just that everyone seems to find what they want in one sport. Hockey expands and contracts to meet the requirements in a very diverse and far-flung country. Some see the beauty and grace of movement, the skating skills, and finesse of the old Flying Frenchmen. Others see toughness and resolve—a blue collar work ethic that rewards those who give 100 percent all the time. Still others like the violence, perhaps as a way of working off their own aggression by proxy. In short, hockey seems to possess—in one sport—the aspects that America needs at least three to attain: the power of football, the poetry of baseball, and the pace and passion of basketball.

The NHL has 30 teams, and ironically 23 of them are located in the US. Four are in the American South where NASCAR and college football are much more popular than the Canadian game. Of course, the further north you go in the US, the bigger the hockey factor is. Under Gary Bettman's leadership, the NHL has done its best to proselytize the sport in unlikely outposts in Florida, California,

Texas, and Arizona. Often it's like driving a square peg into a round hole. The commissioner of the NHL is an American. And yet, the sport has not caught on with national audiences outside of those northern US cities close to the Canadian border.

Aside from being the longtime executive director of *Hockey Night in Canada*, Ralph Mellanby directed the Miracle on Ice in Lake Placid, named by *Sports Illustrated* as the No. 1 sports event in US history. The irony is clear: the sport that has fewer viewers in the United States than the Pro Bowling Tour produced its proudest sports moment.

Hockey can be tacky at times, even ugly. The game is sometimes vulnerable to a kind of violence and intimidation that provokes comparisons to pro wrestling or roller derby. Youth hockey can be hijacked by obnoxious parents and professional hockey by greed and shortsightedness. Any kind of cultural expression is vulnerable to trends and missteps. Consider those as glitches, the hockey equivalent of "dogs playing poker" art.

Canada is a country of immigrants and every year we welcome people from countries that know nothing about our national game. This change in the ethnic makeup is most obvious in major cities like Toronto and Vancouver. Morris Mott, a professor of history at Brandon University, thinks that this influx will have an impact on the game. "Because of immigration there are more people in Canada that are fans of hockey that have never been players," he said. "They wouldn't even know how to skate. They are from countries where hockey isn't part of the culture—nonhockey countries in Asia or the Caribbean. They're content to be fans. It's more a spectator thing at first and then as second and third generations come along, they become active participants. Eventually every kid plays hockey. It's a rite of passage."

That's our culture. It meets all the prerequisites. It is forged by geography and shaped by history. When Wayne Gretzky moved from Edmonton to Los Angeles in 1988 it probably prompted more talk of cultural loss than a hundred actors and a thousand singers taking up residence below the 49th parallel. His move was seen as the loss of a cultural icon. A piece of ourselves had been stolen away by the Americans.

Hockey becomes so pervasive and invasive that everyone recognizes it in all its manifestations: drama, art, literature, and comedy. Who can forget *The Royal Canadian Air Farce's* Big Bobby Clobber, a just ever-so-slightly brain-damaged Toronto Maple Leafs star played brilliantly by David Broadfoot? Here's a sample:

"Well, it's a great game at the Gardens tonight, with the final score Toronto Maple Leafs 15, Penticton Pigeons 12. And I have one of the three stars here with me tonight... Big Bobby Clobber. Hi, Big Bobby."

"Hi, Big Jim."

"Bobby—you scored 42 goals last season. Do you think you'll have a better year this season?"

"Well, on that, Big Jim, I gotta say so far this season I got, uh, two goals, so I figger if I get another... uh... 20... uhhh... another 40 goals... and then add them to the two that I already got, that's going to give me forty and two..."

"42!"

"Right on, Big Jim. Which is what I got last season. Then, of course, if the season isn't ended yet, like we still got one extra game to go and I get another goal in there, well then, that could give me another one. Of course, I'm only guessing on that, because, like, we don't know how the season's going to go, but I believe that with that extra effort out there on the ice, and the kind of spirit the team is showin' out there, with that extra goal we could end up havin' a better season this season than the season I had before this one, which wasn't as good a season as this one could be yet with the other goal that we're talkin' about in the future. So, uh, I have to answer your question with a qualified... I dunno."

"Bobby... a lot of hockey players get injured in the head every year."

"Whazzat?"

"Do you think hockey players should be made to wear helmets at all times?"

"No way. Only durin' the game."

"Bobby... you have an incredible number of teams that you have to play these days. How do you find the game schedule working out?"

"It's ridiculous, Big Jim. Ridiculous. You're playing 363 days outta the year. So how many days does that leave off? Figure it out for yourself. You got one day for a bit of skate sharpening... and one day to catch up with the wife. He shoots... he scores... and then we're back on the road again. Some of the younger guys go back with dull skates.... Dull skates!"

Big Bobby was someone that every Canadian who ever watched a postgame interview could recognize; this wasn't a Toronto actor turning in some inauthentic imitation of a streetwise New York detective. Nor was it a watered-down sitcom about some family who could just as easily have been in Boston as Brampton. This was Canadian, pure and very simple.

171

12

HOW HOCKEY EXPLAINS MODERN CANADIAN DENTISTRY

Hockey and teeth don't mix well. They never have. Just ask Bobby Clarke or Bobby Hull or countless other Hall of Famers. Hockey is one of the few occupations where a toothless smile will actually *help* in the job interview. Aside from being a badge of honour, missing molars and absent incisors are a tangible sign that a player is tough, rugged, and willing to give it all for the team.

Thankfully, dental issues do not generally extend to hockey fandom. Mere fans can still smile broadly, without embarrassment, after their team scores. Or can they?

The on-ice rivalry between the Montreal Canadiens and the Toronto Maple Leafs can sometimes appear tame compared to the feud between fans of hockey's two most storied franchises. Richard Galpin, of Coldbrook, Nova Scotia, is a diehard Habs fan. Dr. Robert MacGregor, a dentist from nearby Kentville, is a Toronto Maple Leafs fan. This is a cautionary tale of tooth and consequences.

Behind his surgical mask, Dr. MacGregor concealed a devilish grin as his friend Galpin settled into the dental chair. The rivalry between them is intense and had recently escalated from verbal sparring to practical jokes, with Galpin consistently getting the upper hand. When friends gathered every Saturday night to watch *Hockey Night in Canada*, Galpin would place Montreal signs all around MacGregor's house. On two occasions, he affixed Montreal Canadiens license plates to MacGregor's vehicles without his knowledge. The dentist's patience was wearing thin. "The final straw

Bobby Hull holds up the puck he shot to score his 50th goal of the 1961–62 season, tying the NHL regular-season record. Hull lost his front teeth to an opponent's hands early in his Hall of Fame career.

AP Images

172

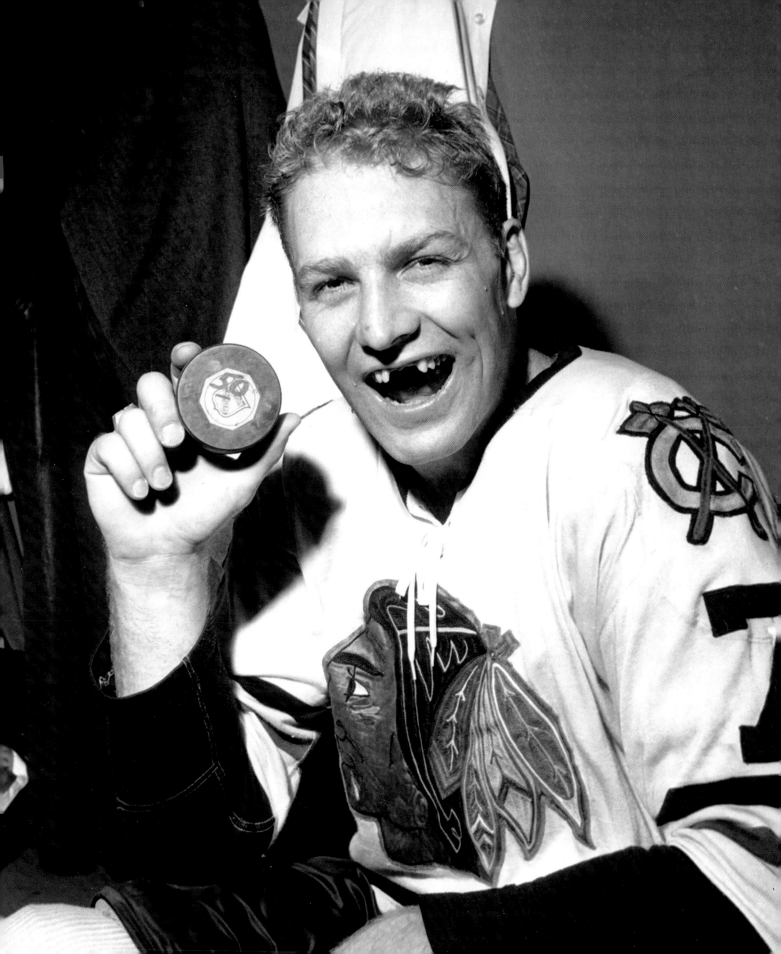

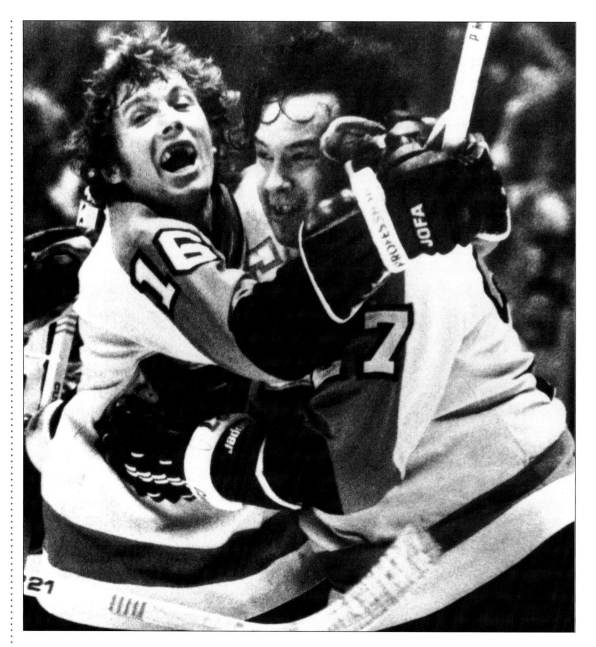

Bobby Clarke, left, hugs teammate Reggie Leach seconds after Leach scored an overtime goal to defeat the Boston Bruins in a 1976 playoff game. Clarke is remembered by fans as much for his captivating, toothless smile as he is for the three Hart trophies he collected as the NHL's MVP.

AP Images

was when he somehow managed to put a Canadiens plate on my brand new car before it left the showroom," he said.

As luck would have it, Galpin also happened to be a patient of Dr. MacGregor's, so when he chipped a tooth he naturally came to MacGregor's office to have it repaired. As MacGregor was finishing the restoration, he had a sudden flash of inspiration. He thought

how great it would be to have something appropriate with which to adorn his tormentor's teeth—an enamel emblem to answer the pranks played on him. Alas, there was no such item at hand and the opportunity passed.

But as things sometimes happen in the world of sport, McGregor was handed an unexpected second chance. A few days later, while standing in line at a grocery checkout, he spied a package of Maple Leafs decals in various sizes. Taking it as a sign that the hockey gods were smiling on him, he bought the decals, took them to his office, and placed them in the Galpin file. Then he waited.

Just a few months later the tooth fairy once again delivered Galpin into his Dr. MacGregor's hands. Galpin had called the office to report yet another chipped tooth. Since his friend's workplace was an hour away in Halifax, MacGregor, who is vice president of the Canadian Dental Association, suggested a Friday-night appointment, followed by dinner with their wives at a local pub. Galpin readily agreed.

When Galpin arrived for his appointment, there was no one around except MacGregor and his wife Noreen, who served as his assistant. The two exchanged their usual hockey jibes before finally getting down to the business at hand. It took MacGregor about 30 minutes to repair the chipped tooth, and then the real work began. With Richard still numb from the local anaesthetic, and with a rubber dam in place, Rob peeled off two blue Maple Leaf decals and very meticulously placed them on his two front teeth. He then applied several coats of clear resin to seal them on, all completed under the pretext of repairing the chipped tooth. Since most reputable schools of dentistry do not offer instruction in the procedure, it took a while to get it just right. Galpin hardly helped his own cause. "I told him that a large monkey could do the job quicker," he recalled. Unable to contain her laughter, Noreen was forced to leave the room on several occasions. She used the opportunity to remove any mirrors from the reception area.

With the job finally done, Galpin slurred a thank you and the three drove to the local pub where Galpin's wife Leslie and a dozen friends had gathered.

It was happy hour and soon everyone was in a weekend frame of mind. Conscious of his frozen mouth, Galpin was unusually quiet. Finally, on a prearranged cue, a co-conspirator asked Richard what was wrong with his front teeth. He mumbled that he had just had a filling. She insisted that there was something stuck to his teeth and passed him her compact mirror. Baring his Leafs teeth for all to see, he stared in complete horror at his reflection. His friends collapsed in fits of laughter and within minutes the entire pub was in an uproar as patrons gathered 'round to view the phenomenon.

"I looked at Rob and he was grinning like a dog eating thistles," recalled Galpin. "I tried to scrape it off with my fork but they said it had been surgically cemented there."

Despite his friend's desperate pleas, Dr. MacGregor was in no hurry to remove the decals. "He said that he was quite busy but might be able to fit me in when he returned from a scheduled business trip to Calgary," said Galpin. "I can't repeat what I said. Then he casually mentioned that he had eight yards of concrete that had to be moved to his backyard, so on Saturday I spent six hours at hard labour. At least I didn't have much reason to smile." On Sunday night, MacGregor finally relented and the decals were removed.

"The time for tooth and reconciliation is past," vowed Galpin. "It's time for tooth and consequences."

Richard Galpin, a diehard Montreal Canadiens fan from Nova Scotia, shows off the Toronto Maple Leafs decals on his teeth, received courtesy of his friend and dentist Dr. Robert MacGregor.

Courtesy of Richard Galpin

13

HOW HOCKEY EXPLAINS WESTERN ALIENATION

WESTERN CANADIANS HAVE complained long and loud about their treatment at the hands of Ottawa and Eastern Canada (it should be duly noted that to most Westerners, Eastern Canada means Ontario and Quebec; the Atlantic Provinces are a different kettle of fish). Whether the subject is wheat, oil, Tar Sands, proportional representation, or just plain respect, the perception seems to be that the West is getting the short end of the Confederation stick.

Eastern villainy is often embodied in the figure of a shrugging Pierre Trudeau asking desperate Prairie farmers, "Why should I sell your wheat?" Sitting on their reserves of energy in the form of oil and natural gas, their visceral response was a hearty "Let the eastern bastards freeze in the dark." Such sentiments still resonate with many living left of the Ontario-Manitoba border, despite the fact that the current Prime Minister is one of their own. Calls for western independence have been temporarily muted however, if not silenced forever. It hardly matters because independence is a trait that every westerner has in abundance. They are indeed a special breed and their hockey players reflect the fact.

It's entirely fitting that his hometown of Flin Flon, Manitoba, is named for a fictional character in a dime novel, because Bobby Clarke's story reads a lot like pulp fiction. Clarke is a naive small-town western hero who not only overcame childhood illness but also became tough as nails in the process.

After proving himself on the rinks of his home province, he goes to the big city and becomes the fuzzy-cheeked leader of a gang of Philadelphia street

Two of Saskatchewan's better-known products, Gordie Howe and Johnny Bower, meet with *Hockey Night in Canada's* Frank Selke Jr. during the 1963 Stanley Cup Finals. Bower's Toronto Maple Leafs defeated Howe's Detroit Red Wings in five games.

Imperial Oil—Turofsky/ Hockey Hall of Fame

177

Originally from tiny Flin Flon, Manitoba, Bobby Clarke overcame diabetes and led the Philadelphia Flyers to two Stanley Cups. The Hall of Famer was awarded the Hart Trophy three times in a career that spanned 15 NHL seasons, all with the Flyers.

Bruce Bennett Studios/Getty Images

toughs known as the Broad Street Bullies. He leads these ruffians and malcontents to two Stanley Cups. Along the way he double-handedly saves his country from a humiliating defeat at the hands of a foreign power.

Bobby Clarke did for the toothless grin what Clark Kent did for glasses and Popeye for spinach. More evocative of a choir boy than an action hero, the absent incisors nonetheless symbolized not only his dedication to winning but a toughness well out of proportion to his very mortal 5′10″, 176-pound frame.

Clarke adheres to an old-fashioned honour system that has fallen out of favour, replaced by political correctness and conformity. Throughout his NHL career, his tactics were often just on the edge of the rules. To some he remains a villain. Many saw his Game 6 slash of Valeri Kharlamov as a blemish on an otherwise glorious 1972 Summit Series. But there is a nobility about Clarke that may be hard to spot at first. He is a hero with a definite edge and a take-no-prisoners attitude, but he is also the most loyal of men, refusing to turn his back on old friends who have fallen out of favour. How deep is Clarke's loyalty? He refuses to attend Summit Series reunions with his Team Canada mates because his friend Alan Eagleson is not invited.

"I started playing hockey when I was two or three years old on the outdoor ice," Clarke said. "We had no television. We were way up north and the winters were six or seven months long so every kid played hockey, and in the summer we played street hockey. Hockey was the main, consistent ingredient of our growing up. Television may have changed that for some but I was 14 by the time we got TV. When it was 30 degrees outdoors, playing hockey, some of the kids kind of faded away and got into TV. I never did. I just wanted to play hockey.

"We watched hockey a little bit but not that much because when we finally got television, the games were a week late. I listened to it on the radio, but even then not so much because I went to the junior games and they always played on Saturday night in Flin Flon. Everybody in Flin Flon loved Gordie Howe. My hero was Teddy Hampson, the captain of the Flin Flon Bombers who won the Memorial Cup in 1957. That was as far as my vision ever took me. That's what I wanted to do—play for the Bombers.

"I don't have any idea why I wanted to get on the ice at 5 in the morning before school because the outdoor ice had just been flooded, and why I would stay out after dark playing. Of course it was dark in Flin Flon *all* the time anyway. I'd stay there and stay there until my mom would get really mad at me. It was cold. I have no idea why this sport had such a grasp on me.

"My dad had a pretty good outdoor rink set up for us a couple winters. It was okay when I was four or five but once I could skate it was too small. Flin Flon was a mining town of about 10,000 people. You knew everybody in your neighbourhood. Everybody was friends, all the kids up and down the street. We had an indoor rink uptown and we played Saturday hockey there. As we got older we started playing on school nights but mostly on outdoor ice. We only played about 15 games until I was 12 or 13 years old.

"My father worked in the mines. Most of my friends were sons of miners. Some stayed in Flin Flon and some still work in the mines or have retired. It was a good job, but that was a generation when our parents were really pushing school. After they finished high school, a lot of the kids went down to Winnipeg and went to university and made successful careers.

"My dad wasn't happy when I told him I was going to quit school and play for the Bombers. I was 17 at the time. He said, 'You're too old for me to stop but I hope you know what you're doing.' It was never part of what we talked about—my playing hockey. He enjoyed watching it but his whole philosophy was that a man works. When the time comes you're going to have to work and get a job and support your family and do the right things in life. It so happened that my job became hockey but had I not made it in hockey I would have been doing something else. It was preached into me, the whole 'you work' piece.

"I think the geography of the West makes you tougher. When I played junior our closest opponent was 400 miles away. That was Brandon and we travelled by bus. We couldn't go to school because when we went on the road it was for two weeks at a time. You made a choice very young in your life if you were going to choose hockey over school, and a lot of us did.

"We always thought that we played a tougher style out west. There was an attitude. Coming from Flin Flon we even thought the guys from Winnipeg were suckies, big city boys, spoiled. So we were going to beat the shit out of them. When it came to the Easterners— it was all the West against the East. They were all spoiled. By East I mean Ontario—that's as far east as we thought. The Memorial Cup was always the West against the East and the West was always tougher—we could always outfight them. Even if we weren't tougher we always thought we were. You didn't see kids from the West showing up in matching jackets and matching hockey bags and stuff.

"Flin Flon is one of those very few places that for whoever lived there it's a uniting factor. Whether it's the name itself, or the nature of the town, or a combination of both, if you lived in Flin Flon you're from Flin Flon and you hold that wherever you go. I've found it wherever I've travelled and I've travelled a lot. If someone's from Flin Flon, they get a hold of you and it's 'let's go for a beer, let's go talk about it.' You never lose that clutch to Flin Flon.

"I knew nothing about Philadelphia before I went there. I didn't know where it was. I don't even know how to describe the feeling when I got there. It was incredibly scary because it was so big. We didn't have contact with very many black people. In Flin Flon there were none, one or two maybe. All of a sudden you're in a city with a million cars, four million people all different nationalities and colours and hockey was really the only thing that I had to grasp on to. That and the players that were there of course. At first I just kept to myself and didn't venture far. I did stuff with teammates that had been there a few years before me. They all looked out for me because I was only a kid. They made it as easy for me as they could and I wasn't going to go anywhere that I would get lost.

"The Flyers did ask their doctor if he thought I could play in the NHL with diabetes, and I got to know the doctor late of course and he said, 'Of course. If he follows the rules that diabetics have to follow there was no reason he can't.' I never felt any resentment and stuff. I never looked at it. I didn't need that to motivate me to play hockey. I wasn't angry at anybody. I just wanted to get on the ice and show that I could play. No special diets. I learned awful quick. At that time you couldn't test your own blood sugar, so it was more backward than it is today but still pretty good. You took insulin and you balanced it with the food. I didn't have any choice and it worked for me—that's what I had to do if I wanted to play hockey.

"Because I'd seen Teddy Hampson do it as a kid, I always ran in the summer. I don't

know it if it was good for you or whatever, but Teddy did it so I did it. That's where I picked it up. So when I went to '72 training camp, I was in better shape than most of my teammates but I don't think I was in good shape, not by any standards of the Soviets—or today's standards.

"I think if you went back far enough Flin Flon might challenge Winnipeg for the most NHL players from Manitoba. We go back to Sid Abel, and Jimmie Skinner played up there. Orland Kurtenbach, Eddie Hansen."

Another Flin Flon native who made it all the way to the Hockey Hall of Fame is Eric Nesterenko. Bobby Clarke doesn't talk much about the beauty of the game or the fact that it can be brutalizing. Nesterenko does. In 1971, legendary Chicago journalist Studs Terkel interviewed a broad cross-section of people about their jobs. The results appeared in a classic little book called *Working*. The long time Blackhawks forward was one of those people and his contribution should be required reading in high schools across our country.

Nesterenko was an NHL survivor, a junior scoring ace who lasted 20 years in the big leagues by transforming himself into a checker and hitter. He was a good player, scoring 250 goals in 1,219 regular-season games, including one 20-goal season in the old six-team NHL. His skills and durability eventually took him all the way to the Hockey Hall of Fame, and yet Nesterenko instinctively knew that the profession he had chosen was in many ways a false one. In his interview, he shows a vulnerability that most players in the macho world of hockey would never admit to.

Even though his family moved to the Toronto area when he was 11 years of age, Nesterenko kept the rough Western edge throughout his hockey career. He became a hockey oddity, playing in the NHL while studying at the University of Toronto. In

Working, he seems to lack the ego and confidence that would be required to rise to the top in the cutthroat world of the National Hockey League.

"I have doubts about what I do. I'm not that sure of myself. It doesn't seem clear to me at times. I'm a man playing at a boy's game. Is this a valid reason for making money? Then I turn around and think of a job. I've tried to be a stockbroker, [but] I'm not good at persuading people to buy things they don't want to buy. I'm just not interested in the power of money. I found that out. That's the way one keeps score—the amount of money you earned.... I've worked construction and I liked that best of all.... I was interested in seeing how a big building goes up—and working with my hands.... A stockbroker has more status, [but] the real status is what my peers think of me and what I think of myself."

And yet, despite his apparent inner turmoil, few players have managed to convey the sheer joy of playing hockey the way Nesterenko did.

"You can wheel and dive and turn," he said, "you can lay yourself into impossible angles you never could walking or running. You lay yourself at a 45-degree angle, your elbows virtually touching the ice as you're in a turn. Incredible!"

Eric Nesterenko hailed from Flin Flon, Manitoba, and scored 250 NHL goals during a career that spanned the 1950s, '60s, and early '70s. The Hall of Famer was known for his physical game and effectiveness on power play and penalty-killing units.

Frank Prazak/Hockey Hall of Fame

It is hard to imagine Nesterenko, a man known to possess two of the sharpest elbows in the league, thinking about the game in those terms. He played like an ugly duckling but there was a graceful swan inside at all times. Most of us will never know the feeling of playing the game at the highest levels but thanks to Nesterenko we can at least experience it vicariously.

"I'm leaning into a turn. You pick up the centrifugal forces and you lay in it. For a few seconds, like a gyroscope, they support you. I'm in full flight and my head is turned. I'm concentrating on something and I'm grinning. That's the way I like to picture myself. I'm something else there. I'm on another level of existence, just being in pure motion. Going wherever I want to go, whenever I want to go. That's nice, you know."

Nowhere is the chasm between NHL past and present wider than in the area of money. In the era of multimillion dollar rookie contracts and players speaking through agents and other soulless mouthpieces, Nesterenko's introspection is remarkable.

"There's an irony that one gets paid for playing, that play should bring in money," Nesterenko said. "When you sell play, that makes it hard for pure, recreational play, for play as an art, to exist. It's corrupted, it's made harder, perhaps it's brutalized, but it's still there. Once you learn how to play and

Toronto's Dave "Tiger" Williams (22) tussles and Boston's Terry O'Reilly look for the puck during a 1978 game in Boston.

Focus on Sport/Getty Images

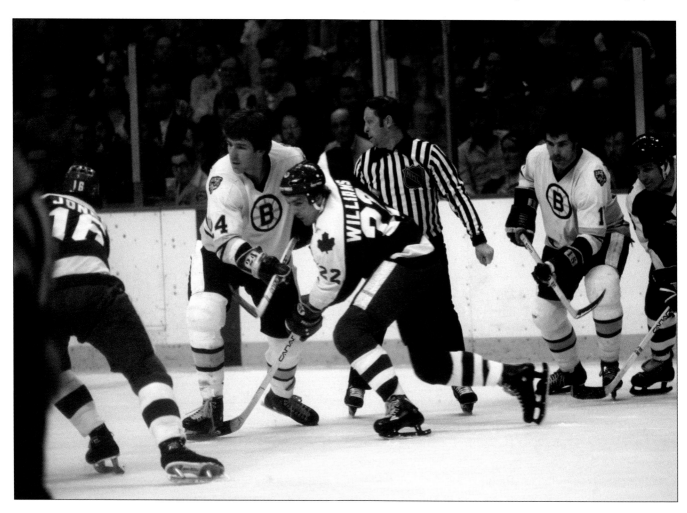

are accepted in the group, there is a rapport. All you are as an athlete is honed and made sharper. You learn to survive in a very tough world. It has its own rewards.

"I think it's a reflection of the North American way of life. This is one of the ways you are somebody: you beat somebody. You're better than they are. Somebody has to be less than you in order for you to be somebody. I don't know if that's right anymore."

As for the risks inherent in the game, Nesterenko offers personal insights into the lonely, impersonal world of hockey injuries. "There is always the spectre of being hurt," he said. "A good player just comes into his prime, cracks a skull, breaks a leg, he's finished. If you get hit, you get hit—with impersonal force. The guy'll hit you as hard as he can. If you get hurt, the other players switch off. Nobody's sympathetic. When you get hurt they don't look at you, even players on your own team. The curtain comes down—cause it could have been me. One is afraid of being hurt himself. You don't want to think too much about it. I saw my teammate lying—I knew him pretty well—they put 40 stitches in his face. I saw him lying on the table and the doctors working on him. I said, 'Better him than me.' We conditioned ourselves to think like that. I think it's a defence mechanism, and it's brutalizing."

Nesterenko played his last game some years before Dave "Tiger" Williams first suited up for the Toronto Maple Leafs. They were both rugged players, but Tiger took it to a whole other level. Williams is another rugged son of the Prairies. He came east to play for the team he had cheered for all his life.

Williams holds the dubious distinction of being the most penalized player in NHL history, having been sentenced to 3,966 regular-season minutes, a grand total of 4,421 if you include playoff infractions. That amounts to more than three full days in the hoosegow.

There is little doubt that Tiger saw himself more as a sheriff than an outlaw, despite his record of incarceration. As the toughest guy in the NHL, he was a marked man. Every team he faced had a pretender looking to enhance his own reputation by hunting Tiger. Dave Schultz, Terry O'Reilly, Dave Semenko. He faced them all and more often than not came out on top.

Unlike other NHL "enforcers," Williams was far from one-dimensional. As a member of the Swift Current Broncos he had 44- and 52-goal seasons before riding into Toronto. In the NHL he continued to be a legitimate offensive threat, scoring 241 goals, including four seasons with 20 or more and one 35-goal outburst as a member of the Vancouver Canucks of 1980–81. And after scoring his goals, he often underlined his western cred by mounting his hockey stick and riding it down the ice, much to the displeasure of opposition goalies.

One thing that hockey statistics can't show is heart, and this Tiger had the heart of a lion. Even today he often wears it on his sleeve. Like most western lawmen he shoots from the hip. He admires loyalty and respects authority. He has an aw-shucks attitude when he talks about himself and an unabashed admiration for the quiet heroes of the game. He's one of those guys who would bite your nose off in a barroom brawl and when it was all over slap you on the back and buy you a beer. He talks glowingly about the Leafs, Don Cherry, Harold Ballard, and the Canadian military but when it comes to pinkos, Easterners, bankers, and BS, it's a different story.

"I grew up with five brothers on the Souris River in our first home in Weyburn, Saskatchewan. That's where we started and it just kind of never stopped. We never had TV, so I used to go to a guy's house on Saturday nights and watch *Hockey Night in Canada*, and of course Foster was around then. He was still around when I started with the Leafs too. I was always a Toronto fan. Most people out in our part of the woods were either for Montreal or Toronto. The only other team guys cheered for—and there were a lot of them—was Saskatoon. They would be Gordie Howe fans because that's where Gordie was from. But in my neck of the woods, a lot of guys were Leafs fans and I was always a Leafs fan when I was a kid."

"Out west our particular brand of hockey is kind of like our lifestyle. I mean the city kids or the down-east kids—even if they were farm kids—they were still different. They weren't 100 miles from town and so it was just a different cup of tea. When you started playing junior you played in places like Flin Flon where they instilled that toughness in you as the opposition. I mean you go into Flin Flon and you had two games to play: you had to beat the fans and you had to beat the team. They always had great teams and the building was always full. And it doesn't matter when you're a young player if the building has 2,000 screaming fans or if it had 10,000. At the end of the day it's always the same noise.

"The Western League was always—and we still are—fighting with the BS of down east. We *are* different and we *want* to be different. When I was a kid—and even now—we had lots of kids in our league who when they were 17 or 18 years old not only did they go away to play hockey but they'd go on the oil rigs and they'd do a man's job at a young man's age. The 'down-easties' don't get that opportunity and I don't think they'd come out west anyway because it's a lifestyle. It's a different ballgame.

"Johnny Bower is typical of the tough western attitude. Johnny is one of the nicest men I've ever met in my life. A real gem. Johnny was Toronto's western scout or the junior scout at that time. The head guy they had out here was

a guy named Torchy Schell, who looked after the games played in Saskatchewan—Regina, Saskatoon, Swift Current, Brandon, and so on. Torchy actually drove me to training camp my first year in Toronto and was a great mentor for me. Torchy was a 35-year-old RCMP officer who became a scout. That was typical around the Leafs and it was because of Connie Smythe. There were lots of people with badges who were involved with the team—whether they were military people or RCMP or OPP. In the West it was the RCMP. They were always around our team and it was kind of a tradition with Mr. Smythe that that was something that we should all strive to be for and support and all that. Whether in that case or whatever, it's still that way around the Leafs organization."

Tiger noted that the cultural divide between Canada's east and west extends far beyond the rink. "You get up one day and you can't fight city hall," he said. "You're not going to go and get a $20 million loan from your bank in Saskatchewan, you're going to have to go talk to some guy in Toronto. That's just the way it works. You don't like it. I still don't like it. I think it's bullshit but that's the way our system works. It's beyond me why if I'm running the Vancouver office or the British Columbia region or the Alberta region why I have to call some little faggot in Toronto to get the okay on a measly $20 million loan. That's the way it is even today and it annoys me. It annoys me that we'll have people in Toronto and in Montreal, not so much the Maritimes but in that Ontario-Quebec area where the massive populations are.... They still want to drive their cars and they still want to flick the switch and have their power come on. They still want to eat their bread, they still want to have their steak. Well that—sure some of it comes from there, but nothing compared to what comes out of the west.

"I always find it very amusing when the

Russians and Czechs used to come and they used to make comments, 'Well, he's a little bit out of his environment playing in Toronto or Montreal. He comes from Moscow.' Yeah? Well take a kid from Smithers, British Columbia, and throw him in downtown Montreal and see how far he's out of his environment. So to me that doesn't hold water. There will be a time when one of those kids who won't be white will be the leading scorers in the National Hockey League. There's no doubt in my mind that that will happen and there's been some kids that have been awful close. Whether they let the media wear them down, or they didn't have as much passion for the game as they really thought, because you can have all the talent in the world but if you don't have the passion to go with it, and the commitment to yourself to be the best you can be every day, it's tough playing in the best league in the world.

"That's what drives me nuts about hockey. Who gives a shit if the guy's from some reserve in northern Alberta or if he's a Muslim?! Who gives a shit? He's a hockey player! That's all that matters. And he's either a Canadian hockey player or an American hockey player or a Russian hockey player. That's all that should be on the table."

Williams takes pride in his role in hockey. He was not a goon and quickly separates himself from a brand of one-dimensional players that he has little respect for.

"I scored more goals in one season than all those so-called enforcers will in their whole career," he said. "So it was totally different. In my case I just played longer for a guy that played on the extreme physical side of the game. I just played longer than anyone else.

"On a team I don't care what part you play. When you're on a team your job is to do what you do best and what you do better than the rest of your teammates. And if you do it better than them, perform that duty! No matter what it is. It's the old King Clancy line—he said to me my first year—'I just want to tell you something, kid. I've seen it a thousand times. You come in the league as a crusher, you get up one morning thinking you're a rusher, and the next day you're an usher! Remember what got you in the league.' I never ever forgot that and that's what you've got to do. You have to do what you're good at. Some guys [in baseball] are DHs and some guys in the NFL run one play in the whole game, and if he runs it right he gets to do it again. That's the way it is...everybody in Pittsburgh wants to play on Crosby's line. Well, guess what? You can't! So find what you're good at and be better than anybody on your team and try to be the best guy in the whole league."

One easterner that Tiger has deep respect for is a guy who went west to earn his fame and fortune in the heart of Alberta.

"Wayne Gretzky is probably the most important guy in hockey, maybe forever. He changed the way people looked at the game. He changed everything. He's a good person. He loves the game. He's got passion for the game. The two greatest guys in the modern age—in the last 30 or 40 years—have been Bobby Orr and Wayne Gretzky. Bar none. They set the bar for the odd guy and maybe a guy like Crosby will equal it or maybe he'll go beyond the bar, but there ain't going to be many. Gretzky is one of the greatest athletes in the world and he's a Canadian and he played our game. I mean the game of hockey couldn't ask for better than that. He's the Michael Jordan and Babe Ruth of hockey. Gretzky is known around the world in countries that don't even know anything about hockey. That speaks for itself.

"He's a great person. I'd walk through a mile of broken glass to help him. He's a great

Canadian. I can't say enough about Gretzky because everyone talked about him so much in the '80s and '90s and I guess we got tired of it—well, you know what? How can you ever get tired of the best? That's the difference between Canadians and Americans. Americans, they'll blow smoke up your ass about anybody. They're still talking about Babe Ruth and Hank Aaron and Mickey Mantle and I don't think anybody should mention a word about anybody. He's unbelievable this guy. I'm glad he did what he did because if he hadn't made that trade to L.A., you might not see all the expansion in the US. Now whether you like it or not is irrelevant. The fact is, he set the table. Never mind the people on the hockey teams he played for in Edmonton, L.A., and New York—the money they made. He made the whole league money—he made all the players money."

Howie Meeker has theories about the unique aspects of western Canadian hockey: "For 50 years, western Canadian hockey is like what the Saskatchewan Roughriders have been to Saskatchewan: pride. Hard work. 'We can beat those bastards from the East or from Vancouver or from Ontario. We're better than they are. We're tougher than they are. We're harder than they are and we're as good as they are.' Half of our Leaf teams came from the West. In those days it was tough going for westerners to get ahead, tough to make a living on the farm, tough to get an education. Same with northern Ontario, where you either worked in the goddamn mine underground to keep from freezing or you're on the breadline. The majority of the hockey players grew up in a tough environment, and all of a sudden this door opens. *I might be able to go down to Toronto and get $1,500 or $2,000 a winter playing hockey. And that's what I'm going to do if I have to kill.* It was a way out of poverty for many."

○   ○   ○   ○

Dr. Morris Mott is currently a professor at the University of Brandon.

"Where I'm from out here on the prairie it's the sport of the winter, along with curling," Mott said. "The two tend to go together out here. They're in the same building most of the time and the younger people play hockey and the older people curl. In the cities that's not so common. You have separate facilities so it's a different kind of arrangement. In western Canada—along with northern Ontario and northern Quebec—the weather has a lot to do with it. It's the one sport you know you're going to get a chance to play.

"There's one thing that people don't often realize—and this goes back to when I was a kid. I knew when I played junior hockey, there were very few people who played hockey out of British Columbia or certain parts of it. Maybe the interior a little bit, but coastal British Columbia was not hockey country. There was a professional team there but no participant level. Artificial ice has made a big difference to the nationalization of the sport. It's milder in the east.

"Everybody plays hockey now, whereas at one time in the past there were large geographic areas in Canada that didn't have much hockey—southwestern Ontario, Vancouver Island, the lower mainland of British Columbia—those are large population areas by Canadian standards.

"Here you can get outdoor ice by late November, but we always had indoor rinks out here on the prairie. With the wind and the snow you would never…I mean you can play hockey outside, but it isn't very pleasant. The sport was played in these little unheated but covered rinks. Sometimes they were colder than outside, but they were at least sheltered.

They were memorial rinks for World War II. A lot of towns had them in the mid-'50s. Many don't have rinks anymore.

"Nowadays every kid plays hockey. Whether in Chilliwack, British Columbia, or wherever. And I think that had something to do with the popularity of the sport among people who were born in Canada.

"Westerners at the elite hockey levels tend to regard themselves as tougher. I'm not sure it's true. No matter where you go there are tough guys and not-so-tough guys. I do think there are harsher environmental conditions. You have to be mentally tougher because it's very hard work. You have to be committed to it at a very young age. [At the time of the interview], the Brandon Wheat Kings [had] been on the road for two full weeks—on a bus. They went to Prince George to begin with—that was 1,800 kilometers!

"Don Cherry would say it builds character and there is probably something in that. You are forced to decide whether you like it or not. You've got to make a decision whether you are going to stick to this or go back home and go to school. Of course, a lot of them do well in school, surprisingly. If you're going to do well in school you really have to be good at budgeting your time. You've got to concentrate on it when you have time. This is all at the Junior Tier 1 level. There's a commitment that is demanded at an early age."

Western Canadian hockey has a quality that distinguishes it from other areas of the country. Like the vast prairie landscape. It's just a little more rugged, a little tougher, and requires a bit more intestinal fortitude to navigate. Self-deprecating, noble, battle-scarred Johnny Bower epitomizes the no-excuses, salt-of-the-earth nature of the west and of the western game. You had to be equal parts inventor and pioneer just to play the game. Bower grew up in the Saskatchewan of the

Dirty '30s when the Depression and drought combined to turn the once and future breadbasket of Canada into an economic and agricultural wasteland.

The Regina Riots reflected the fact that two-thirds of rural families were dependent on welfare. In these times, self-sufficiency was not just a virtue, it was a necessity. People sought out whatever kind of simple diversions they could find to get them through the long harsh winters. Johnny Kiszkan, who

Morris Mott played 199 NHL games over three seasons with the Seals in the 1970s. Mott earned his Ph.D. in history from Queen's University in Kingston and is now a history professor at Brandon University in Manitoba.
Portnoy/Hockey Hall of Fame

later would change his name to Bower to make it easier for those eastern hockey writers to spell his name correctly, was a product of this place and this time.

"I was born in Prince Albert, Saskatchewan," Bower said. "We didn't have hockey sticks at that time. It was 35 below zero. My dad and I went across the river and found a tree there. It was curved like a hockey stick and he shaped it down and boy was that thing ever heavy! It helped a great deal when I turned pro because I kept my stick down on the ice. That thing was a solid oak. There's no way that would ever break.

"We used to play with the kids there and we used to shoot at each other. There's a lady next door and she threw a baby crib mattress out. So this other kid there was a pretty smart guy—he cut that right in half and he made a goal pad, one for the left foot and one for the right foot. We used that and we didn't have tape, we used big tire tubes as elastic to keep them together again so they wouldn't fall off.

"After school, farmers would come in with loads of wood and we'd be following the horses for maybe about a block. All of a sudden they'd drop a load off and it didn't take long to freeze and we'd use those for pucks because we couldn't afford real ones. We called them road apples.

"We were dressed up real well. It was 45 below zero. Boy, you'd come in and cheeks and your ears and all that would turn white, eh? And you're froze, and you had to go back out and get a handful of ice and put it on both of your ears. But we had some nice heavy jackets and we had scarves and everything but it's so bulky when you're out there chasing the puck—or road apple—and we'd take it off and the first thing you know all our cheeks were frozen again. Our hands were cold, our feet were cold. Oh boy.

"At one time the city of Prince Albert owned the schoolyards and they came up with a great idea and put up a fence. One side was for skating and one side was for shinny hockey. They divided it and we used to go to the school and play there. We played on the rivers as well. Wherever there was ice. And of course there was ice in Prince Albert. Even the highways were just like ice.

"Christmas time they would come around with their horses and all dolled up with their bells and there was a package from the city of maybe apples and oranges and candy. There was only maybe about 15,000 to 20,000 people there in Depression time and it was just great to live there. The fresh air was great and you could breathe heavy as can be. You'd very seldom get cold because you'd get used to it.

"We couldn't afford skates. I got a pair of skates from a chap who used to play intermediate hockey and I had a small foot and he had a pair of size 12 and he gave them to me to try to and learn how to skate a little bit. I filled the toes up with paper. I was maybe 10 or 11. So I filled them up and tried to [skate] on edge and I broke my ankle a few times. But that's where you learn your stuff. My dad was pretty strict at times. He said, 'Come and do your homework and then go out and play.' Sometimes between school and home we'd be fooling around a little bit—and it would take us a half hour and he would get a little mad at us and say, 'Hey, you shoulda been here doing your homework and I told you before so you have to get your education…' and he was right.

"I wanted to be Frankie Brimsek because he was called Mr. Shutout. I never made it though, not like Frankie did, but that was my ambition. My father never played the game at all. He lost two fingers when he worked for Burns and Company on the machines, and he never did. He was just a hardworking slave man, you know. Every day he'd go to work and that was it. It was a job for him to feed his kids.

"We had Scotsmen, we had Indians, we had Ukrainians, we had Polish guys, Jewish people who ran fur stores—we had a mixture of everybody really. But we all got along really well. And that was a great thing. My dad told me, 'You'll go a long way if you keep your nose clean and smile. It doesn't cost you nothing for it to smile my boy.' I used to do that a lot I guess—and I'm still smiling.

"I played against Gordie Howe in juniors. He played for Saskatoon and they used to come into Prince Albert. We were mostly farming kids and they had a powerhouse and I used to see Gordie Howe and I'd say, 'Uh, oh, I'm gonna get bombed.' But anyway, he'd score about five or six goals on me like there was nothing to it. But it wasn't fair because Saskatoon had about 60,000 people at that time and they had a better choice in picking up players. Prince Albert, we only had 15,000 or 20,000 and it was rough to play against them, but we put on a good show. The fans used to come into the old barn there—the old Mint Arena—and we just had a great time in there. It was cold but everybody would just cuddle up in there and cheer when we scored a goal. I got to know Gordie really well after that. I kept him in the league—in the juniors and later in the pros.

"It's the weather and the ice that we have and the determination if you want to go out and play. The weather has changed over the past years but we had nothing else to do other than hockey. We did our homework, we went out, and we played hockey. You went to a show once in a while if you were lucky enough to have 10 cents.

"When war broke out, all my buddies went to Vernon, British Columbia, for training and we were there for a couple of years. And then all of a sudden they started to recruit players overseas. I was about 15 and they found out I lied about my age. I finally snuck in there but they found out later and they held me back. And then when I was 17 they were recruiting and I finally went overseas but I didn't see any action. Oh no, I didn't see action. Thank God for that because I think most of the guys who went to Dieppe didn't come back. We had about four or five real good hockey players.

"I was only there for a short time—about a year. And then the war ended and I came back to Prince Albert. I didn't go over to Dieppe because I got sick and they took five of us guys off the list and I was one of them. I had arthritis—caught arthritis in my hands and they swole up all the time and I had trouble with them and I took a convalescence. I went down and took treatments but they couldn't do anything and so they discharged me. And I went back to Prince Albert. Actually they wanted me to go to Regina and be an orderly and I said, 'I am not going back there to see these soldiers coming back with broken legs and no legs. So I went right straight back and got my job back, coming back on the railroad and then a couple of scouts came in from Saskatoon that were scouts for the New York Rangers. We had an exhibition game and I had a pretty good game there. They asked me—Hub Wilson was one of the scouts there in Saskatoon—if I'd be interested in leaving my job and going to play hockey in Cleveland. Well, my father didn't like that too much! He felt that I should continue on in my schooling and he was right in a way because I only went up to grade 11.

"So there was a big opportunity right there for me and I talked to a lot of teammates at that time who said, 'Don't be silly Bower, go. This is what you want. Go ahead.

You'll be okay. This is best. You'll get a good education by talking to other people here and there and reading books in your travels.' They were right too. They helped me out a great deal—most of my teammates. As the years went by my father forgot about it, but when he went and got older he used to sit home and when I lost my mother and he'd sit and listen to Foster Hewitt on the radio and later he'd call and say, 'There's a tough hockey player you've got there in Toronto.' I said, 'Who's that?' He said, 'Eddie Shack. I don't like him, he's too rough. He's always fighting.' I said, 'Hey, Eddie's okay.'"

How Hockey Explains Our Darker Side

The city of Vancouver made us all proud during the 2010 Winter Olympics. The support shown to all Canadian athletes and especially the men's and women's Team Canada hockey squads was nothing less than inspiring. The Olympics showcased the beauty and culture of the city and the province of British Columbia. Enthusiastic crowds exploded the myth of the laid-back citizens of Lotus Land.

The 2011 Stanley Cup final was a classic match-up of two teams with very different styles, reflective of two very distinct cities. The Boston Bruins had a blue-collar, lunch pail work ethic and a chip on their shoulder. The Vancouver Canucks were a skilled team with two of the best players in the NHL and the goalie who had led Canada to a gold medal at the Olympics.

Both teams reached the finals with hard-fought victories over archrivals. For the Bruins, the challenge was to get past the high-flying Tampa Bay Lightning, which they did in seven games. The Canucks' perennial roadblock was the Chicago Blackhawks, a team that had made their playoff lives miserable. This time they prevailed against the Hawks and many Canucks fans though the team had exorcized its demons.

Most Canadians were cheering for Vancouver to finally bring the Stanly Cup back to Canada after an absence of 18 years. Meanwhile, Bruins fans wanted to revisit the euphoria of 1972 when Bobby Orr flew across the front of the goal, arms already raised in celebration of his Cup-winning goal.

After six games in which the home team won each time, Game 7 on Vancouver ice was the decider. After weathering an early offensive barrage from the home team, the Bruins scored the first goal, which seemed to deflate the Canucks. The Bruins added three more, including an empty netter to win 4–0. The Canucks, especially much criticized goalie Roberto Luongo, were gracious in defeat, carefully extending congratulation to each and every Bruin. It was a nice show of class after a brutal and sometimes spiteful series.

Thus did the Stanley Cup champion Boston Bruins and runner-up Vancouver Canucks both emerge bloodied and bruised from the gruelling Game 7 final. But it was the city of Vancouver that ended up with a giant black eye. The Bruins' 4–0 victory brought the Cup back to Boston for the first time since 1972. While the Bruins' players and their families were still celebrating on the ice and the dejected Canucks were licking their wounds, the game took a backseat to rioting in the streets outside. Fuelled by alcohol, howling mobs attacked cars, store front windows, and anything else in their path. The aftermath of an entertaining if uneven series made news across the country and around the world. The final toll was 140 injured, one critically, and extensive damage to 50 businesses, including Hudson's Bay, London Drugs, Bank of Montreal, Sears, and Chapters. Upwards of $2 million in damage was done.

"What happened after the final game in Vancouver has been well documented," Ron Ellis said. "Having 100,000 fans watching the game on large screens in the downtown core speaks to the importance of hockey in Canada. However, this was quickly negated by the riot that was seen around the world.

"Vancouver the city will recover, Vancouver the team might not."

Put aside all the plaudits and platitudes about the unifying properties of our national game. This was ugly. How many participants in the ugliness were actual hockey fans and how many simply used the opportunity to loot and pillage may never be known exactly. Vancouver's police chief placed the blame at the feet of "anarchists and criminals." Suffice it to say there was enough blame to go around, criminal elements and hockey hooligans combined to disgrace the city and the country, not to mention the sport. The NHL brain trust would be wrong to ignore the league's role. In a sport that often seems to condone or at least ignore on-ice violence, it's not entirely surprising that this mindset would spread to the streets beyond the arena. In fact, there were countless instances in the seventh game that went unpunished because the refs had made the decision to "just let them play." Even for the mindless troglodytes who roamed the streets, the message was not all that subtle.

The media across the globe quickly picked up the story. CNN called Vancouver "loser city." After listing a litany of troubles in the world's usual hotspots, the *Globe and Mail* segued to the ludicrous hockey riot with a clause all the more powerful for its reserve. "…meanwhile in Canada—somebody lost an ice hockey match to the Americans."

Vancouver mayor Gregor Robertson called the riots "extremely disappointing." Bloggers to the Huffington Post had stronger words. "Absolutely disgusting," a poster named Canuck Lefty concluded. "In other countries, people take to the streets in riots to protest oppressive regimes and fight for freedom. In Canada, where not even enough people could drag their butts as far as the polling station to vote, the people take to the streets in violent rioting over a fricking hockey game. Bread and circuses."

It would be comforting to report that this was an isolated incident, that hockey-related violence is usually confined to the rink. It would be nice, but it wouldn't be true. You had to look no further back than 1994 on these same Vancouver streets to prove that the event was far from unique. The excuse that time was another Game 7 loss, this one to the New York Rangers. The rampage continued throughout the night and well into the next morning. Aside from more than 200 reported injuries, many serious, over $1 million in property damage resulted. This despite the presence of 540 police officers.

In 2006, the Edmonton rioters set fires and looted shops on Whyte Avenue to "celebrate" the Oilers winning the Western Conference title. In 2010, on Ste. Catherine Street in Montreal, a large disturbance took place after the Canadiens defeated the Pittsburgh Penguins in round two of playoffs. So it isn't losing that triggers such behaviour, it's something far darker, something that Canadians aren't known for and don't wish to see in themselves.

A day after the event, Huffington Post poster Christopher Koulouris asked, "Can a game of hockey really set off so much animosity, or is there some other underlying feeling that isn't getting played out in the Canadian psyche?"

It's a question well worth pondering.

14

HOW HOCKEY EXPLAINS CANADA TO THE WORLD

HOCKEY NIGHT IN THE HIMALAYAS was a pretty hilarious premise when Canadian comedy kings Wayne and Shuster presented the television skit a few eons ago. "The score is 30 to nothing!" complains the coach at the bottom of the slope. "Have no fear," replies the referee, "we switch ends at the end of the period." The same episode featured *Hockey Night in Turkey, Hockey Night in Siam, Hockey Night in Borneo*, and *Hockey Night in the Congo.* The routine finished with a comedic look at a game between the Montreal Canadiens and the Saudi Arabian Oilers.

While playing on a mountainside is still unlikely several decades later, the late comedy team would no doubt be surprised to know that although some of the countries' names have changed, they are no longer so far-fetched as hockey destinations. Turkey has a national team that is a member of the IIHF and is ranked 35th in the world. It is coached by a Canadian. As for Siam, now Thailand, they are also members in good standing of the IIHF and have competed against such powerhouses as Hong Kong, Macau, Mongolia, Malaysia, Bahrain, India, Singapore, Chinese Taipei, and the United Arab Emirates.

The point is that hockey is no longer just a Canadian game, nor is it only played in the frigid north. And it's no longer a joke to see pucks flying in some unusual places. Not when *Hockey Night in Kandahar* is a reality.

The Kandahar military base in Afghanistan has been home for thousands of Canadian soldiers and military personnel. The high-security NATO compound was all that stood between our troops and the Taliban. On this night in February 2010 repeated cries of "Attack!" split the air but were directed

Master Cpl. Mike Lehman guards the Stanley Cup as it arrives at the Canadian military base in Kandahar, Afghanistan, in May 2007. A group of former NHL players including Bob Probert, Dave "Tiger" Williams, Ron Tugnutt, Réjean Houle, and Yvon Lambert participated in the visit.

AP Images

193

at Canadian hockey players armed only with hockey sticks. The enemy was the United States of America, and the enemy was cocky. "How hard can it be?" asked US Brigadier General Ben Hodges before the ball hockey game between his American squad and the Canucks. "I mean you chase a ball around and hit it with a stick." After the Canadians had scored the last of their 16 goals en route to a rout of the shell-shocked Yanks, he knew how hard it can be.

American forward Lt. Jeremy Patelzick, more accustomed to football passes than the hockey kind, felt that his team lacked the basic training that the Canadians get at an early age. "We knew it was going to be a really tough game for us, because that's what these guys do all their lives," he said. "They get sticks and pucks when they're kids. We don't." He added, "They didn't score 20 goals so that's good." It had been promoted as *Hockey Night in Kandahar* and for the 500 or so spectators it was as if a little piece of Canada had been airlifted to southern Afghanistan.

There are upwards of 15 ball hockey teams at Kandahar Airfield. In 2007, the Canadians had hosted some pretty impressive alumni of Team Canada. Names like Tiger Williams, Rejean Houle, Mark Napier, and Bob Probert. It's a safe bet that the few Afghans in the crowd were more than a little perplexed at the sight of Tiger Williams, 56 years old but still mean and lean, exchanging punches with Canadian soldier Michael Loder. Some of them connected. Most were never meant to.

Bobby Clarke once epitomized everything that the international hockey community envied and despised about Canadian hockey. The Russians loved his heart, even after the famous slash that he inflicted on their top star Kharlomov. Clarke thinks that the world sees Canada as a place where the game of hockey embodies the character of its people. "I think that hockey defines the Canadian personality: hard work, toughness, honesty, working together, and lots of stubbornness," he said. "It's the most visual part of our culture. Everywhere in the world we're recognized as hockey players. They don't know that we grow wheat and raise cattle and do mining and have electricity and all that stuff but they all know that we play hockey."

Former *Hockey Night in Canada* executive director Ralph Mellanby has followed Canadian hockey teams all over the world to deliver broadcasts back to Canadians. He claims that hockey has had a significant impact on the international perception of Canada and Canadians.

"We are the most beloved country in the world and it's got a lot to do with hockey," he said. "I remember going to Japan to work and in Tokyo when the TV guys knew you were from Canada it was 'Oh, Canadian, hockey, hockey, hockey.' We are so identified with the game. Thanks to great politicians like Lester Pearson we are only a threat on the ice. Everywhere I've gone, even in the old Soviet Union, we are a loved people. We are considered to be everybody's friend."

There are those who would challenge Mellanby on the depth of affection that hockey has engendered, especially in the early days of international play.

Alan Eagleson found out firsthand how people viewed the Canadians. "There is no doubt that we were not welcome at the World Championships," he said. "First of all because of our rough tough hockey, and secondly because we wrecked every hotel we ever stayed in!"

It took an intervention by a respected clergyman to restore Canada's hockey reputation abroad. There was a time when the face of Canadian hockey was Father David Bauer. No longer would the Canadians be viewed as marauders. Bauer singlehandedly changed that

Former NHL star Troy Crowder shows off his stickhandling skills during a pickup game of ball hockey with Canadian solders at Kandahar Airfield in Afghanistan in March 2011.

AP Images

image and restored dignity to the program.

"Father Bauer changed the entire image of our National Team abroad," claimed Eagleson. "Players had to have a shirt and tie and be well-mannered. If you have a few beers, that's one thing. But no drunken louts permitted. Father Bauer did a great job for this country."

Paul MacLean, who went on to a stellar NHL career, recalls being a disciple of Father Bauer. Raised in Antigonish, Nova Scotia, MacLean is proud to be the only player on the 1980 Canadian Olympic team from east of Montreal. The coaches for the squad were Lorne Davis, Clare Drake, and Tom Watt but there was no question about who ultimately ran the show. Father Bauer held the title of managing director, but he was also the conscience of the team, as MacLean soon discovered.

"We were based in Calgary, but we travelled the whole world with that team. Father Bauer cautioned us not to swear and to be fine young men—and not to be incorrigible. Apparently previous Canadian teams hadn't always followed that example. He had a certain way that he liked to play too. He thought the game was supposed to be played in a gentlemanly way. We were not to get carried away or dirty, like typical Canadian hockey can sometimes be. He frowned on fisticuffs."

One incident in a game against the Czechs stands out for MacLean. "The Czechs can be dirty," he said. "I played in the Rude Pravo Tournament in 1979 and the Czechs were a little dirty at times. I got involved in a situation and was being tugged from the backside and I turned around and hauled off with a haymaker. Actually what happened was that I was being checked over by the Czech bench and my stick ended up going over the bench so they're all grabbing the stick and they wouldn't let the stick go. So I got to take away the stick

195

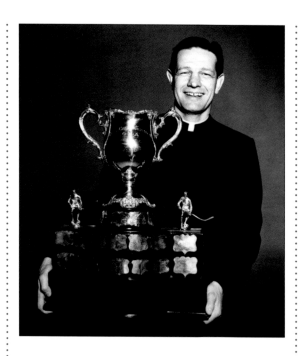

Father David Bauer poses with the Memorial Cup won by his St. Michael's Majors in 1961. A pioneering figure in amateur hockey, Father Bauer started the Canadian National Team in the early 1960s and coached Team Canada in the 1964 Olympics.

Imperial Oi—Turofsky/ Hockey Hall of Fame

and I turned around and I lose the handle on it and my hand comes off and hits the guy right in the face. The only trouble is the guy I hit was Victor Dombrowski, the referee in the game! So he made a big display of kicking me out of the game and giving me a five-minute penalty which the Stastny brothers proceeded to turn into a 7–2 thumping of the Canadian Olympic team. That accorded me an all-night visit with Father Bauer and the coaching staff with me trying to explain myself. I was in an inquisition! He was giving it to me pretty good, asking me all these questions about the incident. You can't do that at the Olympic Games. It's undisciplined and those kinds of things and why we can't have you on the team. I'm arguing like crazy—begging for my life. I promised to be good. And if you look at the penalty minutes in the 1980 Olympic Games, I didn't take any. So I kept my word."

The move from sinners to saints didn't earn Canada a gold, silver, or bronze medal in 1980 (this was the year of the US Miracle on Ice), but it did restore respect for the integrity of the Canadian program. It also taught

some important hockey lessons. MacLean gives Bauer credit for taking his game to another level and advancing his hockey aspirations. "That year probably made a difference between me playing in the NHL or not. Without it I may have remained a minor league pro at best. That year the ice time and the quality of workouts and practice time were key. I learned the intelligence part of the game. The IQ part of it was really enhanced in that year."

"Under Father Bauer, Canadian teams had become great ambassadors for Canada and the sad part—and this is on the present day situation—is what has happened," Alan Eagleson said. "The CAHA since it took over Hockey Canada has just disintegrated the entire international hockey program that we stimulated. We had a National Team and kept it going right up until the CAHA got back involved and now run Hockey Canada. It was a great experience for players and gave hundreds and hundreds and hundreds of players an opportunity to play for their country. And that doesn't happen now unless you're an elite player. A player like Morris Mott would never have made Team Canada in today's circumstances."

Before being named head coach of the Ottawa Senators in June 2011, Paul MacLean spent six seasons as an assistant coach for the Detroit Red Wings. MacLean feels that hockey has become a hybrid of the European and North American games. The Red Wings' roster reads like a United Nations roll call. "We have our share of nations on the Red Wings," MacLean said before accepting the Ottawa job. "I think we're represented by almost all of the nations that play it seriously anyway. When I played it was mostly Canadians. About 85 percent of the league was Canadian. I would agree with the Canadian part of it—heart and desire, etc. The Canadians bring a skill level but they also

How Hockey Explains the Strength of the Loonie

After an absence of 16 years, Winnipeg is once again an NHL city. The announcement regarding the move of the Atlanta Thrashers to the Manitoba city in time for the 2011–12 season was greeted with unbridled joy throughout the province. Impromptu celebrations led to the famous intersection of Portage and Main being closed to traffic as fans waved Canadian flags, drank champagne, and sang Stompin' Tom's "The Hockey Song". Mayor Sam Katz helped lead a conga line of delirious fans.

Manitoba Premier Greg Selinger expressed the feelings of long-suffering hockey fans. "NHL, welcome home," he said. "It's great to have you back here, it's great to have you back here where you belong. We missed you and we're going to make it work forever now that you're back."

In 1996, after 17 years of hosting NHL hockey, the city lost their beloved Winnipeg Jets to Phoenix, where they are known as the Coyotes. The price tag for the franchise was in the $170 million range, $60 million of that being a 'relocation' fee. The franchise left the city due to economic issues including a strong US dollar. With a vibrant provincial economy and a surging loonie, the time was right to bring hockey back. The NHL salary cap and a new arena helped to seal the deal.

"It is clear that times have changed for Winnipeg as an NHL market. And this is a wonderful time to add a club to Canada," said NHL commissioner Gary Bettman. Referring to the departure of the Jets, Bettman struck a conciliatory, almost apologetic tone. "So to be able to come back to, if you will, right a wrong, that's always an extraordinary thing. It's nice to be back in Winnipeg after all these years."

bring physicality. The US players are similar but they play a little bit more of a skating game. It's a speed game. The Swedes are very technical. They're always very systematic and technical. The Finns are very hardworking and defensive. The Russian game is very highly skilled. The Czech game is possession: regroup and regroup and regroup."

Even Mellanby concedes the point but insists that the reputation that we once carried has largely dissipated. "It's true, the Europeans initially thought we were a bunch of thugs on the ice, but everything evolves," he said. "Now we are so welcoming. Having so many Europeans in the NHL has changed things. Now there's none of that stuff. There's no more Iron Curtain. As a Canadian going around the world to live and work with my Olympic experience you are very proud. You wear a Canadian jacket with a leaf on it. You wear a hat that says, 'I'm Canadian.' That's

what you do because they love us. We are not the United States. We are no threat to anyone in the world. Hockey is our identification, and while we play tough and rugged, they know we play pretty fair. We don't cheat."

Hockey Night in Haiti

Lieutenant Commander Jeffrey Hutt likes to call it *Hockey Night in Haiti.* Hutt served aboard HMCS *Athabaskan* during its relief mission to Haiti in January 2010.

Dubbed Operation HESTIA, it was Canada's response to the devastating earthquake that destroyed the infrastructure of the island nation. HMCS *Athabaskan* was operating 30 miles southwest of Port au Prince, providing support to the city of Leogane. Working closely with the Canadians were officers and crew from US Navy vessels.

With the common goal of providing humanitarian aid and disaster relief, bonds

Canadian military personnel load disaster relief supplies onboard HMCS *Athabaskan* in January 2011 before the ship departed on a humanitarian mission to Haiti after Haiti was devastated by a major earthquake. On February 28, 2011, 60 sailors from the *Athabaskan* accepted an invitation to board the American ship USS *Bataan* to watch the Olympic gold-medal hockey game between the United States and Canada. Canada defeated the Americans in overtime.

AP Images

were quickly formed between the two Task Groups. The Canadian Replenishment ship HMCS *Preserver* was unavailable for the operation due to an extended refit, so the *Athabaskan* relied on assistance from the US for some of the "sustainment" aspects of the mission, particularly fuelling at sea.

"As the mission developed, we moved from a priority of saving lives to a priority of easing suffering," said Lt. Commander Hutt, "and so began a concentrated effort to rebuild as many orphanages as we could while the nongovernment organizations began to stand up."

With this shift in focus, shipboard life began to return to normal, with sailors seeking to fill a few hours a day with some form of recreation. "Since Canada was hosting the Olympics in Vancouver, the priority to restore the satellite TV feed grew increasingly more important," said Hutt. "Unfortunately we had left the footprint of our satellite provider

somewhere in the Windward Passage.

"Finally, we had some luck with TV, but with the system purchased at a sustainment stop in Jamaica, our best Olympic coverage came from MSNBC. Although it was predominantly US coverage, it was better than nothing."

As the gold-medal game drew closer, sailors began talking more and more about the possibility of hockey gold in Vancouver. Despite the heat and devastation all around them, hockey once again began to dominate the conversations of sailors both onboard ship and on the sweltering construction sites scattered around Leogane.

Finally the gold-medal game was set—Canada and the U.S. "I thought it was ironic that our two nations were working so closely together in support of Haitians, but would soon face off in a fight of global hockey supremacy," said Hutt. Unsure if they would even get the coverage on TV, they had a tested plan to stream the game online to each of the three messes onboard the ship. Although the signal was of extremely poor quality, the game was too big to miss.

Notwithstanding the priority of hockey, it was a distant second to the selection and maintenance of the mission at hand. Aim is a critical principal of both warfare and humanitarian relief, so with no other scheduling options available, a refuelling at sea was booked with an American tanker at the exact same time as the game. This evolution would not require everyone onboard, but would mean many of the crew would miss a large portion of the game.

Just when it looked like the gold-medal contest between the Americans and Canadians would be missed, the US Navy sailed to the rescue. Recalls Hutt: "The day before the game, I received an email from the US Rear Admiral's logistic coordinator, inviting as many sailors from *Athabaskan* as we could spare to join them in USS *Bataan* [the US flagship] to watch the game. The party was called Operation American Gold." The US officers even rescheduled the refuelling to facilitate this hands-across-the-waters partnership. In no time at all, more than 60 eager Canadian sailors had signed up to join their American counterparts in a break from the demands of work ashore. They would finally see the Team Canada team in action on *Hockey Night in Haiti*.

As sailors gathered on the flight deck of *Athabaskan* awaiting transportation by boat to USS *Bataan*, there was the same hockey excitement that was present in every part of Canada. The food and hospitality aboard USS *Bataan* was outstanding. When Sydney Crosby scored the winning goal, the Canadians celebrated with their only some-what-deflated American counterparts.

"It was fitting that the hardworking Canadian sailors had an opportunity to see the most memorable portion of the Vancouver Olympics, and to do so in such unique circumstances will surely be a sailor's story for the ages," said Hutt.

Hockey Night in Sheffield, England

Dennis Vial was an enforcer for the Ottawa Senators for five seasons. After the conclusion of his NHL career, he joined the Sheffield Steelers of Great Britain's Ice Hockey Super League (ISL) during the 1999–2000 season.

"I was just married and had a newborn baby so we thought we'd give it a try," Vial said. "If we didn't like it we'd just head back home. They had some really nice facilities there. The interest stems back to World War II when the Canadians were there and playing hockey and building rinks. The season had started and it was midseason by the time I played my first game for Sheffield. I actually enjoyed it. This is England so the fans loved their football, and their hooligans! When there were fights they loved it. They got all psyched up. They loved the toughness on the ice.

"I went back the next year and the hockey was a lot better than I had anticipated. We had a lot of Canadians on the team and I really enjoyed the atmosphere. We were playing against Manchester one night and an incident that resulted in a bench-clearing brawl had occurred in the previous game so there was a lot of hype about this rematch. It was a capacity crowd—10,000 people. Totally sold out. They came because they thought there would be another brawl. But a great thing happened—it turned out to be a great hockey game. There were four fights but there were many fans who had never seen the game of hockey before and this was their introduction to it. It was a learning experience for those fans."

SELECTED BIBLIOGRAPHY

Beliveau, Jean. *My Life in Hockey*. Vancouver: Greystone Books, 2005

Cole, Stephen. *The Best of Hockey Night in Canada*. Toronto: McArthur and Company, 2003

Eagleson, Alan. *Power Play*. Toronto: McClelland and Stewart, 1991

Foer, Franklin. *How Soccer Explains the World*. New York: HarperCollins, 2004

Grescoe, Taras. *Sacre Blues*. Toronto: Macfarlane Walter and Ross, 2001

Ludwig, Jack. *Hockey Night in Moscow*. Toronto: McClelland and Stewart, 1972

McKinley, Michael. *Putting a Roof On Winter*. Vancouver: Greystone Books, 2002

McKinley, Michael. *Hockey: A People's History*. Toronto: McClelland and Stewart, 2006

Mellanby, Ralph. *Walking with Legends*. Bolton, ON: Fenn Publishing, 2007

Paolantonio, Sal. *How Football Explains America*. Chicago: Triumph Books, 2008

Sirois, Bob. *Discrimination in the NHL*. Montreal: Baraka Books, 2010

Smythe, Conn. *Conn Smythe: If You Can't Beat 'Em in the Alley*. Toronto: McClelland and Stewart, 1981

Vaughan, Garth. *The Puck Starts Here*. Fredericton, NB: Goose Lane Editions, 1996

Young, Scott. *The Boys of Saturday Night*. Toronto: McClelland and Stewart, 1991